DIRECTORY OF

BRITISH TRAMWAYS

VOLUME ONE

SOUTHERN ENGLAND AND
THE CHANNEL ISLANDS

DIRECTORY OF BRITISH TRAMWAYS

VOLUME ONE

SOUTHERN ENGLAND AND
THE CHANNEL ISLANDS

KEITH TURNER

TEMPUS

For Margaret, without whose help, encouragement and forbearance this book would never have been completed.

First published 2007

Tempus Publishing Limited
The Mill, Brimscombe Port,
Stroud, Gloucestershire, GL5 2QG
www.tempus-publishing.com

British Library Cataloguing in Publication Data.
A catalogue record for this book is available from the British Library.

ISBN 978 0 7524 3901 3

Typesetting and origination by Tempus Publishing Limited
Printed in Great Britain

Contents

Preface

As a writer and transport historian I have felt for many years the need for a comprehensive one-volume reference work on the tramways of the British Isles. Not since 1962 in fact, when the fourth edition of Bett & Gilham's *Great British Tramway Networks* appeared, has the tramway enthusiast had easy access to a single, up-to-date basic 'where, what and when' of these lines. So, as much for my own reference purposes as for any other reason, I decided to compile such a work and now that it has been completed I hope it will prove of use to anyone else with an interest in this important aspect of our islands' transport history. Wherever possible I have endeavoured to check and double-check all listed facts and, if any errors have crept in, the responsibility for them is mine alone.

As regards the illustrations, these have been chosen to portray as many aspects of tramway history as possible, not just the tramcars themselves, with many being taken from postcards – whose own heyday coincided neatly with that of the tramways – to reflect the integral part played by trams in the popular life of the period.

K. Turner
Kidderminster, 1996

Preface to the Second Edition

Since the first edition of this work appeared in 1996 – and went quickly out of print – much has changed in the world of British tramways. Four new systems have opened, serving the Birmingham to Wolverhampton corridor (Midland Metro, 1998), Croydon (Tramlink, 2000), Nottingham (Nottingham Express Transit, 2004) and Dublin (Luas, 2004). As regards the older generation of lines still operational, refurbishment programmes of the last decade have resulted in significant changes readily visible to passengers, whilst in the field of tramcar preservation the number of vehicles returned to exhibition – or even operational – condition continues to increase steadily.

As a consequence of the above events, it has been felt that in order to accommodate the resulting new entries, and to be able to expand many of the original entries in the light of subsequent events and additional information generated by on-going historical research, this new edition of the Directory should be published in three volumes. This decision also meant that many more illustrations could be included. The division of the Directory into three parts has been made on a topographical basis, the scope of each volume being as follows:

Volume 1: The counties of England south of the traditional Severn Estuary to The Wash's north-south boundary, plus the Channel Islands.
Volume 2: The broad central region of the British Isles, comprising the counties of the East and West Midlands, the whole of Wales and the whole of Ireland.
Volume 3: The northern counties of England, plus the whole of Scotland and the Isle of Man.

Finally, please note that the **Introduction**, **Chronology** and **Appendices** included here are repeated in each of the other two volumes.

K. Turner
Kidderminster, 2007

Acknowledgements

I should like to thank all those archivists, librarians and their staff throughout the British Isles who have provided valued assistance over the years in helping to compile this directory. Thanks must also go to those organisations and individuals who have kindly supplied material to help illustrate it; special thanks too to Jan and Lil for coming to the rescue in times of crisis, and to those readers of the first edition who have given freely of their own local knowledge to correct, clarify and add to the historical, technical and other details of many systems. Finally, and most importantly, grateful acknowledgement must be paid to all those writers, recorders and historians who have gone before; without their dedicated efforts my task would have been an impossible one.

Introduction

This Directory is intended to cover all the tramways that have operated within the British Isles: that is Great Britain, Ireland and all the off-shore islands including the Isle of Man and the Channel Islands. It should be pointed out here, at the very beginning, that adjectives of locality are used in their geographical, not political or national sense, so that 'British' hereafter refers to the whole of the British Isles, 'Irish' to the whole of Ireland and 'Welsh' to the Principality of Wales plus Monmouthshire. (Since virtually all British tramways were opened, operated and closed before the 1974 local government reorganisation in Great Britain, the names of the old counties have been used throughout for location purposes only – indeed, several of them have since returned.)

The immediate problem facing a compiler of a directory of tramways is one of definition: what exactly is a tramway? In many cases, nomenclature is not a reliable guide – a tramway might well have been titled officially a 'light railway' (e.g. the Kinver Light Railway) while, conversely, a 'tramway' (e.g. the Rye & Camber Tramway) might actually have been a railway.

This confusion over identification arises from a number of historical causes. During the early years of the nineteenth century the terms 'tramway' and 'tramroad' were interchangeable, both denoting a horse-worked railed way (almost always for mineral or other goods traffic only, situated in a rural area and feeding a canal, river or port) crossing or occupying public highways without restriction or much inconvenience to other road users, few as they were. As the use of steam traction spread however, locomotive-worked lines were separated physically from the roads for safety reasons, thus becoming in the process railways as we know them (though the older lines often retained their original names of tramway or tramroad); when tramways proper arrived on the scene in the latter half of the nineteenth century they could not command exclusive rights to the term. The confusion was further complicated by the fact that tramways in Britain were built under several different authorising mechanisms, one of which was the 1896 Light Railways Act.

How then have tramways been defined for the purposes of inclusion here? Three principal criteria have been employed for the main entries. Firstly, any line accorded a main entry (i.e. with key details listed at the start) must, at some time at least, have operated a regular public passenger service. Secondly, any such line must have had a significant part of its route along or beside a public highway without it being fenced-off from other traffic and, consequently, it will have been subject to certain operating restrictions when using mechanical or electric traction in recognition of this fact. Finally, such tramways should be, or have been, discrete entities and worked as such with their own stock despite any physical connections with other systems or even – in some cases – the national railway network.

Obviously, the 'typical' British tramway found in many towns and cities between, say, 1890 and 1940 meets the above criteria without difficulty: a self-contained system operating a passenger service through the streets. Add an overhead power supply and the stock image of the British tramway is complete. There were however a great many lines which did not conform to this picture – and yet still meet the same criteria. 'Public highway', for example, might in a wider context include both open common and seaside pier decking, whilst for some tramways goods traffic was just as, if not more, important than passengers. Nor should it be assumed that being a tramway meant catering for the general public at large: some needed a prior qualification on the part of the passengers, such as their having paid the price of admission to a pier. Two criteria which have purposely not been used are those of gauge and motive power; these are discussed more fully below.

PICKLES
DUDLEY BUXTON
THE POLICEMAN SAID "FOLLOW THE TRAM-LINES."

Tramways - along with virtually every other aspect of social life - provided inspiration for many early postcard cartoonists, as on this example sent in 1913. *(Author's collection)*

Regardless of its official title (or indeed popular name), a line or system conforming to the above definition of a tramway has been given a main entry, whilst any line or system that meets only the last two criteria (i.e. it was a goods-only tramway), whether it be industrial, military, public or private, has been omitted. Any other line or system officially entitled Tramway but which was in practice a railway, light railway or tramroad, has been given a minor entry if it operated a passenger service and omitted entirely if it did not. In addition, railways with strong tramway connections or characteristics have been afforded minor entries, as have parent companies owning tramways operated through a number of subsidiaries.

Cross-references to main or minor entries have been made from place names elements other than the first in a tramway's title (e.g. Upwell *see* Wisbech & Upwell) and to major places served where this might not be evident from the title (e.g. Great Orme Tramway *see* Llandudno: Great Orme Tramway). Cross-references in capital letters refer to entries in the same Volume and those in lower case to other Volumes.

There is one last category of working tramways to be considered, all afforded minor entries here. These, for want of a better name, may be called 'pleasure lines' since one reason for their existence has been to give pleasure rides in much the same way as seaside miniature railways do. Like the miniature railway, the pleasure tramway is a surprisingly ancient animal, the oldest traced being that opened in Shipley Glen in Yorkshire more than a hundred years ago. Although this venerable example was possibly unique for its time, the number of pleasure lines has grown in recent years: firstly with the construction of several permanent working museum lines, secondly with the opening of a number of semi-permanent miniature tramways and, thirdly, with their temporary use at recent Garden Festivals.

Tramcar preservation is as old as tramway modernisation, for when horse traction was displaced by (usually) electricity, several operators were heritage-minded enough to set aside the odd vehicle for museum display. The precedent for doing this had been set by the railway companies, but not until 1951 however was there a precedent for the preservation of a whole line – the narrow-gauge Talyllyn Railway in Wales – but even with this example to encourage enthusiasts, the prospect of running even part of an existing, or restored, tramway proved elusive at the very time the last great wave of system closures was taking place.

The main obstacle in the preservationists' path was the fact that by and large local authorities wanted shot of tramways completely, citing such reasons as that they impeded traffic flow (often true), or that they were holding up road improvement schemes (where there could have been compromises made). Whatever the pros and cons of the tramways *vs* the private motorcar, or even tramways *vs* buses arguments, the fact remains that no local authority was willing to countenance a bunch of amateurs operating trams through its streets – and it was even less likely that national authorities like the Board of Trade would have done so. Thus, by their very nature, most tramways were ruled out immediately as candidates for preservation; all that were left as possible projects were those lines – or portions of those lines – that occupied their own reserved rights of way (i.e. separated from any highway). Two such schemes, both consistently canvassed over many years now, have centred on the former Swansea & Mumbles and Llandudno & Colwyn Bay lines in Wales, but with no success for either as yet.

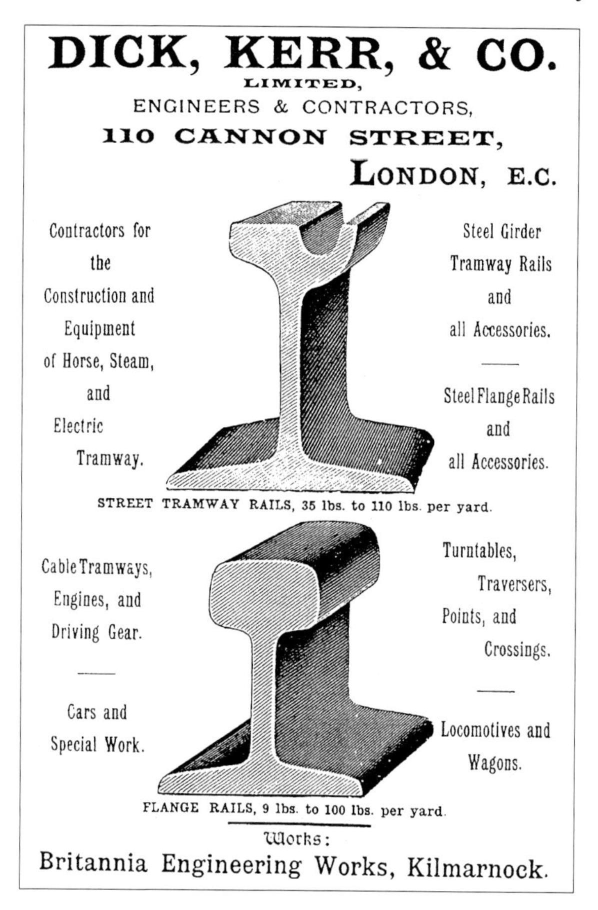

A Dick, Kerr trade advertisement showing clearly the difference between railway and grooved tramway rails.

Inevitably, the number of potential locations (never great to begin with) has decreased as formerly reserved stretches of tramway routes have been swallowed up by road widenings, whilst open-field sections have been built upon. Only one genuine length of tramway route has been restored to operational use – in Manchester's Heaton Park – and then only because of unique circumstances.

Until 1963 tramway preservation, then, meant tramcar or relic preservation (anything from shelters and standards down to tickets and uniform buttons); in that year though a new, purpose-built museum line was opened at Crich in Derbyshire so that preserved cars could be operated in passenger service once more. Since then similar museum lines have opened elsewhere whilst the overall total of preserved cars, working or static (and including imported foreign examples), is now well over the 300 mark. Details of where such cars can be seen have been included in the appropriate entries.

As with their railway counterparts, the difference between a miniature and a narrow-gauge tramway is not primarily one of size – or even gauge – but rather one of proportions. Thus a very narrow-gauge (2ft) line, such as Fairbourne in Wales, could use cars still in proportion to its riders whereas a miniature line such as at Eastbourne, also of 2ft gauge, might employ scaled-down stock in the model engineering tradition that was not in harmony with its full-sized passengers.

Whilst miniature railways are thick on the ground in many parts of the British Isles, miniature tramways are not. There is a simple explanation for this: on a miniature railway usually only the locomotive is a scale model, with the passengers riding in, or on, non-scale carriages. With a tramway, a model tramcar has somehow to accommodate passengers as well. A secondary but still important reason is an economic one: a miniature train driven by one man might easily carry thirty or more fare-paying passengers, whereas a one-man tram is limited to half a dozen or so. For these two reasons miniature tramways have generally been short, portable exhibition lines operated by private individuals or model engineering societies and the like; because of their ephemeral nature these are not included in this work, though the handful of more permanent ones have been.

The Garden Festivals held on various sites during the 1980s and early 1990s were the latest in a long line of Shows, Exhibitions and Expositions dating back to the great-grandaddy of them all, the 1851 Great Exhibition at the Crystal Palace in London. What set them apart from their predecessors however, was that in addition to providing an entertaining day out and a showcase for manufacturers and other exhibitors, their sites were areas of industrial dereliction, chosen deliberately so that the preparatory landscaping and other improvements would result in long-term benefits to their locality.

In all, five Garden Festivals were held: Liverpool (1984), Stoke-on-Trent (1986), Glasgow (1988), Gateshead (1990) and Ebbw Vale (1992). All provided forms of rail transport to move visitors around the site – miniature railways proving especially popular – but of relevance here is that both Glasgow and Gateshead laid full-size working tramways (albeit only temporary ones) for both pleasure and utility.

Although the Garden Festival movement has ended (in the sense that no further ones are planned), the principle of using semi-permanent tramways as crowd-movers (and pullers) has been demonstrated successfully and there can be little doubt that the idea will be repeated someday, somewhere, in a different guise. Indeed, with the number of rescued, renovated, imported and operational tramcars growing yearly, and with a concomitant steady increase in the number of working museum and pleasure lines, either operational or planned – quite apart from the new generation of hi-tech metros – the outlook for the tramway enthusiast/lover/historian/supporter is brighter today than it has been for half a century or more.

In the interests of clarity, information common to main entries has been summarised at the beginning of each under the following headings:

Authority

The legal authority for the construction and operation of the tramway. On a general level, promoting a tramway was very much like promoting a railway: unless the line was to be built on land wholly owned by a consenting individual or body, some form of national or local governmental permission had to be obtained for its construction. The exact form of this authority varied according to the legislative framework in place at the time; to a lesser extent it also varied according to where in the British Isles the line was to be built, and for this reason further details of the different authorities are given in the introduction to each Section within the different Volumes.

Gauge

For tramways laid with railway-type track (i.e. chaired bullhead or spiked flat-bottomed rails on sleepers), the gauge given is the distance between the inner edges of the rails as if it were a railway. For tramways laid with tramway-type (i.e. grooved) rails set flush with the road surface on street sections, the gauge given is the distance between the outer edges of the two grooves (i.e. between the inner edges of the running surfaces).

The range of gauges used by British tramways is a large one, as the (simplified) breakdown below shows:

12¼in. to 15in. – used for miniature tramways.
1ft 8in. to 2ft 6in. – generally regarded as the lower limit for narrow gauge horse and steam tramways.
2ft 9in. – the lower limit for narrow gauge electric tramways.
2ft 11½in. – a gauge which enabled 3ft gauge railway vehicles to run on their (deeper) flanges in the grooves of tramway rails, so allowing through-running to take place.
3ft – Isle of Man 'standard gauge', the most common gauge for steam-worked light railways and tramways in Ireland.
3ft 6in. – the most common narrow gauge for electric tramways in Great Britain.
4ft – a common horse tramway gauge, less common for electric lines.
4ft 7¾in. – a gauge enabling standard gauge railway vehicles to run in the grooves of tramway rails. Widespread in the Portsmouth area and on the Scottish systems alongside the River Clyde.
4ft 8½in. (or its nominal metric equivalent **1.435m**) – standard railway gauge in Great Britain, though if used with grooved rails through-working of railway vehicles could not take place (see above).
5ft 3in. – standard railway gauge in Ireland (and subject to the same restrictions as above).

Other gauges have been employed, usually as one-off examples, in line with this pattern of usage.

Traction

The type(s) of tractive power used on a regular basis to work the system. On British tramways the following have been employed (ignoring unsuccessful experiments with other movers):

Manual – hand-propelled stock, common on pier tramways.
Horse – narrower gauge lines tended to use a single horse pulling a single-deck car; wider gauge lines did likewise, even for light double-deckers on level routes. Where steep gradients and/or heavy double-deck vehicles were involved, two horses were normally used with a third, trace horse being attached at the foot of the stiffest climbs.

Cable – passenger cars attached permanently to a cable in funicular railway fashion, or which could engage/disengage a continuously moving cable, in both cases the cable being housed in a conduit beneath the road surface. A variant was to have the passenger cars not attached to the cable but simply towed as trailers behind tractor vehicles.
Steam – either trailers hauled by special tramway locomotives, or passenger vehicles fitted with their own steam power units.
Internal combustion – as above but with diesel, petrol or similar fuel engines.
Battery electric – as above but with electric motors powered by accumulators.
Gas – passenger stock fitted with gas-fuelled power units.
Petrol-electric – passenger stock fitted with a petrol engine driving a dynamo to power an electric motor.
Overhead electric – passenger stock fitted with electric motors supplied with current from an overhead wire (normally at 500).
Surface-contact electric – as above but with current supplied from roadway studs.
Conduit electric – as above but with current supplied from a roadway conduit.

Where different methods of traction were in use at the same time they are listed in the main entry thus (for example): Horse, steam. Where one method of traction superseded another with no overlapping period of use, they are listed thus (for example): Horse/steam.

Details of other methods of traction used rarely, briefly or experimentally – including sails and clockwork! – are given in the main body of the entries themselves.

Opened/Took over

The date of the first public service. This was often, but not always, the same as that of the official opening ceremony (which occasionally preceded or followed it). Also, especially in the case of the larger systems, only part of the tramway might have been opened at this time. In the case of a significant takeover by another operator, the date given is when services commenced under the new ownership, the actual transfer normally being timed from midnight of the final day under the previous ownership.

Closed/Taken over

In the case of a closure, the date of the tramway's final public service over the last section of the tramway to remain open is given (though stock movements often took place after the date of closure). In the case of large systems, usually only a fraction of the whole remained in use by this time. (It should be kept in mind that final journeys were often run late at night, finishing in the early hours of the day following that cited.)

In the case of a significant takeover, the date given is that on which the new operator began working the system.

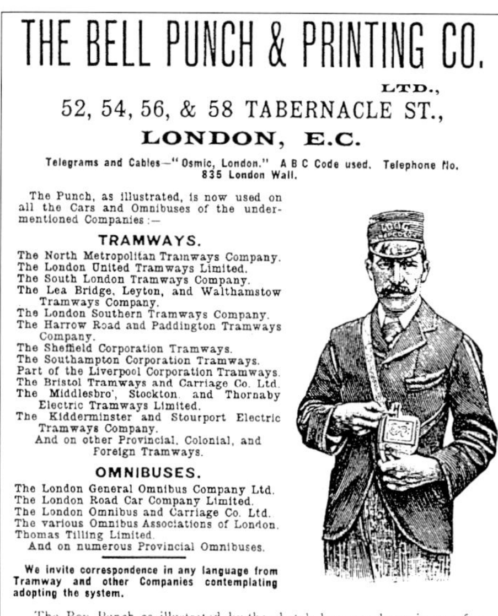

Trade advertisement of the 1890s for Bell Punch, one of the major manufacturers of ticket-issuing equipment, with a list of the systems they supplied.

System

The physical layout of the tramway system's route(s) is codified thus in a roughly-ascending order of complexity (ignoring short spurs to depots, one-way loops in town centres and the like):

Single line – one route from A to B, usually town centre to an outlying district and/or railway station; occasionally from one town to another (an 'interurban').
Split single line – two routes from A to B.
Circle – a single line starting and finishing at the same point.
Branching – a single main line with one or more other lines branching from it.
Cross – two single lines crossing but worked as separate routes.
Radial – a number of routes radiating from a central point (usually a natural focus such as a market square, town hall or railway station).
Radial network – a radial system with one or more linking lines between routes.
Network – a network of crossing and branching routes with no single focus, as found in many large towns and cities.

Combinations of the above are also to be found, e.g. branching circle. All systems should be taken to be predominantly urban in nature (though often extending beyond the original built-up area to serve isolated villages or districts) unless they are described in the notes as rural or interurban.

Length

As far as it can be ascertained, the route mileage of the tramway at its greatest extent, correct to the nearest one-hundreth of a mile (17.5 yards), is based on official returns made by the operator. This may not be the total route mileage worked as, occasionally, a new line might be opened after an earlier section had been abandoned. Modern metro systems, constructed to metric specifications, have their lengths given to the nearest 100m, as recorded in official documentation.

Stock

The total number of vehicles employed on passenger services by the tramway during its lifetime (though not necessarily all in use concurrently) and, where applicable, the number of locomotives used to haul them. Passenger cars are classified as single-deck vehicles (sd) or double-deck vehicles (dd), with numbers given for each traction system listed as being used. Unless noted otherwise, all vehicles can be taken to have four wheels and double-deck horse cars can be assumed to have open tops (i.e. no roof to the upper deck). Also, all cars can be taken as being double-ended (i.e. with a driving position at each end), those horse cars described as 'reversible' having only one driving position but with a body that could be rotated on its underframe at the end of the line so as to then face in the opposite direction. Cars are counted in their original state (e.g. before conversion from single to double-deck form).

Livery

Almost without exception tramcars were painted in what would now be termed a 'two-tone' livery, usually a darker colour such as green, red or blue, and a lighter colour such as white, cream or yellow. There were several aesthetic reasons for the use of this scheme, tried and tested as it had been over the years not only on tramcars but also on horse buses, railway carriages and even stage-coaches. A dark colour around the 'waist line' gave the vehicle a visual sense of reassuring stability whilst a lighter colour around the windows and above them emphasised the visibility afforded to its passengers and the lightness of the car – hence its swiftness – and its spaciousness. Lighter colour panels below the dark band were used to draw attention to the tramway's name, emblazoned on the side. Dark dashes at each end of the car protecting the driver were a legacy of horse tram days, when the colour served to hide the splashings and muddyings they inevitably suffered; running gear would normally be red oxide or black for the same reason, whilst the roof would continue the lightening effect by being a very pale neutral colour such as off-white or grey. Steam tram locomotives tended to be painted with a single dark shade to give an impression of stolid dependability.

The two-tone livery also made the cars highly visible to potential passengers, as did the use of (usually) gold or cream for their often ornate lining, fleet numbers and name of the tramway or operator.

The difficulty in describing long-vanished liveries is that official records have not always survived, forcing the historian to rely on (sometimes contradictory) eye-witness memories. The problem is compounded by the fact that when a new colour was applied it quickly weathered and, if judged unsuitable, was often replaced by a darker shade when the vehicle was repainted (or naturally darkened by the repeated application of varnish). For example, white was frequently used on new horse cars but was quickly replaced by off-white (ivory) in the light of experience. Similarly, pale cream was normally darkened into primrose (or even a deeper yellow). For this reason the descriptions given are sometimes a compromise; e.g. red-brown or cream/yellow. Ignoring minor variations, the descriptions themselves are of the general livery used during a specific period; in the case of a change from one general scheme to another, this might well have taken months if not years to complete, depending on the number of cars involved.

Second-hand vehicles often ran for a while in their old liveries until a new paint job could be arranged whilst during the First World War, for reasons of wartime economy, cars needing a repaint would be given a uniformly grey livery, often retained for several years after the war ended.

Last Car/Train

The closure of a tramway was often a very emotional occasion, with the last public journey marked by speeches, wreaths and crowds trying to board the 'Last Car'. On many such occasions the identity of this tram was recorded for posterity; while on others the line closed without fuss or ceremony, and the identity of the vehicle which made the final trip is not generally known today (although the information might well be residing in private films or papers just waiting to be discovered). Sometimes an 'official' Last Car carrying local dignitaries was run behind the last service vehicle, or even on a later date.

Bibliography

In addition to the above listing of details and the main body of the entry, wherever possible at least one comprehensive history of the line or system in question – which has appeared in book form – is cited in the bibliography at the end of the book. (For minor lines this might well be part of a wider account and their accuracy in all matters is not guaranteed.) Citations are given in the order: Title (Series and number), Author (Publisher, edition if not the first, date of publication), ISBN.

Glossary

In order to save space and avoid tiresome repetitions, several frequently occurring names have been given in entries in an abbreviated form (e.g. those of companies and other organisations). Company titles are given in concise form, e.g. '& Co. Ltd' for 'and

Company Limited'. Other abbreviations used, if not standard forms or cited in full earlier in the same entry, are:

Ashbury – Ashbury Railway Carriage & Iron Co. Ltd, Manchester (later Metropolitan)
Bagnall – W.G. Bagnall & Co. Ltd
BB – Balfour, Beattie & Co. Ltd*
BEC – British Electric Car Co. Ltd, Trafford Park
BET – British Electric Traction Co. Ltd*
BH – Black, Hawthorn & Co. Ltd
Birmingham – Birmingham Railway Carriage & Wagon Co. Ltd, Smethwick
BM – Brown, Marshalls & Co. Ltd, Birmingham (later Metropolitan)
BNCR – Belfast & Northern Counties Railway
BoT – Board of Trade
BP – Beyer, Peacock & Co. Ltd, Manchester
BPs – Bruce Peebles & Co. Ltd, Edinburgh
BR – British Railways (in all its post-1948 guises)
Brill – J.G. Brill Co., Philadelphia
BTH – British Thomson-Houston Co. Ltd, Rugby*
Brush – Brush Electrical Engineering Co. Ltd, Loughborough
Burrell – Charles Burrell & Sons Ltd, Thetford
CIE – Coras Iompair Eireann
CLC – Cheshire Lines Committee
Cravens – Cravens Railway Carriage & Wagon Co. Ltd, Sheffield
DK – Dick, Kerr & Co. Ltd, Preston
EE – English Electric Co. Ltd, Preston (formerly UEC)
ERTCW – Electric Railway & Tramway Carriage Works Ltd, Preston (a DK subsidiary)
Falcon – Falcon Engine & Car Works, Loughborough (a Brush subsidiary)
Fowler – John Fowler & Co. Ltd, Leeds
GCR – Great Central Railway
GER – Great Eastern Railway
Gloucester – Gloucester Railway Carriage & Wagon Co. Ltd
GNR – Great Northern Railway
GNR (I) – Great Northern Railway (Ireland)
GNSR – Great North of Scotland Railway
Green – Thomas Green & Sons Ltd, Leeds
GSR – Great Southern Railways
GSWR – Glasgow & South Western Railway
GWR – Great Western Railway
Hardy – Hardy Rail Motors Ltd, Slough
Hawthorn – Robert W. Hawthorn & Co. Ltd, Gateshead
HC – Hudswell, Clarke & Co. Ltd, Leeds
Hibberd – F.C. Hibberd & Co. Ltd, London
HN – Hurst, Nelson & Co. Ltd, Motherwell
Hughes – Henry Hughes & Co. Ltd, Loughborough (later Falcon)

Kitson – Kitson & Co. Ltd, Leeds
Krauss – Locomotivfabrik Krauss & Cie, Munich
Lancaster – Lancaster Railway Carriage & Wagon Co. Ltd (later Metropolitan)
LBSCR – London, Brighton & South Coast Railway
LCDR – London, Chatham & Dover Railway
LMS – London, Midland & Scottish Railway
LNER – London & North Eastern Railway
LNWR – London & North Western Railway
LSWR – London & South Western Railway
LYR – Lancashire & Yorkshire Railway
Matthew – James Matthew, Bristol
Merryweather – Merryweather & Sons, London
Metro–Cammell – Metropolitan-Cammell Carriage & Wagon Co. Ltd, Birmingham
Metropolitan – Metropolitan Railway Carriage & Wagon Co. Ltd, Birmingham (later Metro-Cammell)
MGWR – Midland Great Western Railway
Midland – Midland Railway Carriage & Wagon Co. Ltd, Shrewsbury
Milnes – Geo F. Milnes & Co. Ltd, Birkenhead
MR – Midland Railway
MV – G.C. Milnes, Voss & Co. Ltd, Birkenhead
MW – Manning, Wardle & Co. Ltd, Leeds
NBR – North British Railway
NCC – Northern Counties Committee
NEC – National Electric Construction Co. Ltd*
NER – North Eastern Railway
Oldbury – Oldbury Railway Carriage & Wagon Co. Ltd (later Metropolitan)
Peckham – Peckham Truck & Engineering Co. Ltd
Pickering – R.Y. Pickering & Co. Ltd, Wishaw
Roberts – Charles Roberts & Co. Ltd, Wakefield
SECR – South Eastern & Chatham Railway
SER – South Eastern Railway
Starbuck – Starbuck Car & Wagon Co. Ltd, Birkenhead (later Milnes)
Stephenson – John Stephenson Co., New York
UEC – United Electric Car Co. Ltd, Preston (formerly ERTCW)
Wickham – D. Wickham & Co. Ltd, Ware
Wilkinson – William Wilkinson & Co. Ltd, Wigan
* see minor entry in all Volumes

Other symbols used are:
[ ] - enclosing unofficial short title
? - preceding information uncertain or lacking
-- - not applicable
c. - about
* - see text/footnote below

Part 1

Tramways of Southern England

Ignoring for the moment anachronistic passenger-carrying tramroads, the history of the tramway in the British Isles is very much the history of the tramway in England. Certainly it was here that the first street tramway was laid (Birkenhead), and here that steam (Wantage), cable (London) and safe electric traction (Blackpool) first came into regular use.

English tramway history is, in turn, a condensed parallel version of the development and growth of Britain's railways. The urban tramway arrived from the USA (where it was aptly known as a 'street railway') in the early 1860s and, just a quarter of a century later, had employed the same four main motive power systems that had been used on railways over a period four times as long: horse, steam, cable and electricity. Of these four, the first held sway during the 1860s and 1870s. It was familiar and acceptable to the travelling public, and a tramcar's journey was smoother than that of a horse bus. It was however not very much quicker, hence the introduction (permitted by the 1879 Act for the Use of Mechanical Power on Tramways) of steam traction using specially designed tank locomotives with side-skirts to enclose the motion, safety guards to prevent anyone being run over, and a driving cab at each end to allow the driver a clear view of the road ahead. In addition, the BoT required them to burn coke rather than coal to reduce smoke pollution, and to be equipped with condensing apparatus for their waste steam. Because of their power advantage over horses, these steam locomotives could pull much larger trailers – sometimes several – up steeper gradients, which meant that many existing horse systems went over to the new form of traction, notably in the major industrial towns and regions, and new, hilly routes opened. Self-contained tramcars fitted with seats and a steam power unit were also experimented with, generally unsuccessfully.

The adoption of steam traction gave birth to the fixed tram stop; for their greater momentum meant that, unlike horse cars, steam trams could not halt for prospective passengers wherever hailed in the street – a legacy later passed on to electric tramway and motor bus operators. However, steam trams were not very popular with the general public, being regarded as dirty and noisy, and when reliable electric traction was developed in the 1880s the use of steam was quickly abandoned, with virtually all those lines employing it being converted by the early years of the twentieth century. (See Appendix 6 for those special cases using no other form of traction.)

During the steam tram era cable traction was also employed – though on far fewer lines – to cope with gradients that locomotives could not manage. Its use met with mixed fortunes: those climbs which could be tackled by electric trams were soon converted to enable routes to become part of an integrated system (as in Birmingham and London), whilst those too steep for conversion (in England, only Matlock) kept faithful to it until closure. (See Appendix 7 for a list of all British cable tramways.)

Undoubtedly, the most successful of the traction systems was electricity. First used (on any scale) in the British Isles in 1883 on Volk's Electric Railway in Brighton and the Giant's Causeway Tramway in Ireland, it was adopted two years later at Blackpool and from then on almost all new tramways employed it, and existing ones that did not were almost all either closed or converted by the outbreak of the First World War. (See Appendix 5 for a list of those horse lines never converted.)

Before 1870 tramway construction was normally authorised either by local authority permission or by a Private Act of Parliament. The former applied when the streets involved were under local authority control and the latter when compulsory purchase of land was required. In return for this power, an Act imposed certain conditions on the company formed to build and operate the tramway, notably the amount of capital that could be raised, time limits for the start and finish of construction, the gauge and type of traction to be used, and so on. Obtaining a Private Act was an expensive business – and it was not guaranteed to succeed in the face of opposition from powerful landowners, railway companies, local authorities and the like – and in 1870 the Tramways Act was passed to make life easier for would-be promoters. Under its provisions an application could be made to the BoT for a Provisional Order which, if sanctioned after a local enquiry, was then confirmed, along with any others outstanding, in a Tramways Confirmation Act.

One important provision of the 1870 Act was to have profound consequences, affecting virtually all those lines built under such Orders: twenty-one years (and at regular intervals thereafter) after the confirmation of an Order, any local authority with a tramway within its boundaries could normally purchase the whole undertaking at just its physical asset value. (Where a tramway crossed municipal boundaries two or more authorities could act jointly in the matter.) This many authorities chose to do – especially if the end of the twenty-one year period coincided with the possibility of introducing electric traction – often to the intense annoyance of the operating companies, resulting in much legal squabbling and eventual independent arbitration to determine the price. (Originally local authorities were not allowed to operate tramways, although they could build them and lease them to private companies. This prohibition was later dropped.)

Another option was made available from 1896 onwards with the passing of the Light Railways Act in that year. Although intended to facilitate the construction of light railways – often as adjuncts to the national network – in much the same way as the Tramways Act had done for tramways, several private and municipal tramway promoters made use of its provisions, obtaining Light Railway Orders to authorise their undertakings. (One advantage of doing so for private companies was that no later municipal buy-out was threatened.)

The first great wave of tramway closures came in the 1920s and 1930s when many tracks and vehicles reached the end of their useful life – often accelerated by lack of proper maintenance during the First World War – at a time when motor buses were claiming a rapidly-increasing share of the public transport market. The situation was not helped by the fact that the bus operators, both private and municipal, were often the tramway operators themselves. Some respite was afforded by the transport demands of the Second World War, but after that the closures came thick and fast with Sheffield, in 1960, the last to go – the last that is except Blackpool which, until 1970 when the Seaton line opened, was England's sole tramway operator. The Devon line was a special case however, and it was not until the opening of the Manchester Metrolink twenty-two years later that the resurgence of the tramway in the streets of England began. With a steady trickle of others following, the next decade or so will see the tramway's continuing fightback, with expanding hi-tech light rail systems designed to free our city streets from the slow and dirty motor cars threatening to choke them to death in exactly the same way as horse-drawn traffic once did.

Aldershot & Farnborough Tramways

Authority: Aldershot and Farnborough Tramways Order 1878
Gauge: 4ft 8½in.
Traction: Horse
Opened: *
Closed: 1906
System: Single line
Length: 2.69 miles
Stock: 6 sd?
Livery: Originally ?, then white, and red & white*
Last Car: ?

The first tramway proposal for Aldershot was made by George Francis Train, of Birkenhead and LONDON fame, whose Aldershot Street Rail Co. Ltd (incorporated 4 December 1861) proposed a line linking the town with Farnborough, though nothing ever came of the scheme. Other similar proposals followed, the successful one being an 1878 promotion for a single-track line south through the town from close to Farnborough's LSWR station, then along Farnborough Road to the Queens Hotel where it turned east along Lynchford Road and past the military establishment known as North Camp (a few miles north of Aldershot itself) to a terminus by the SER's Aldershot North Camp station.

Ambitious extensions to this system were proposed (with subsequent Orders being obtained) but never constructed, the sole line built opening on an unknown date sometime between its BoT inspection on 15 August 1881 and 30 June 1883, when passenger receipts for the previous twelve months were recorded. The tramway was owned by the Aldershot & Farnborough Tramways Co. (itself owned by the Aldershot & Farnborough Tramways Co. Ltd) and worked with a pair of two-horse single-deckers, complete with 1st and 2nd class compartments, shedded at the Farnborough terminus. Here there was a physical connection to the railway via exchange sidings (see accompanying map), though quite why is uncertain unless steam working was envisaged, permitting railway wagons to be run through to the military camps.

It appears that the line closed just a year or two after it was opened, only to reopen soon after with two toastracks painted white and two single-deck saloons painted red and white.

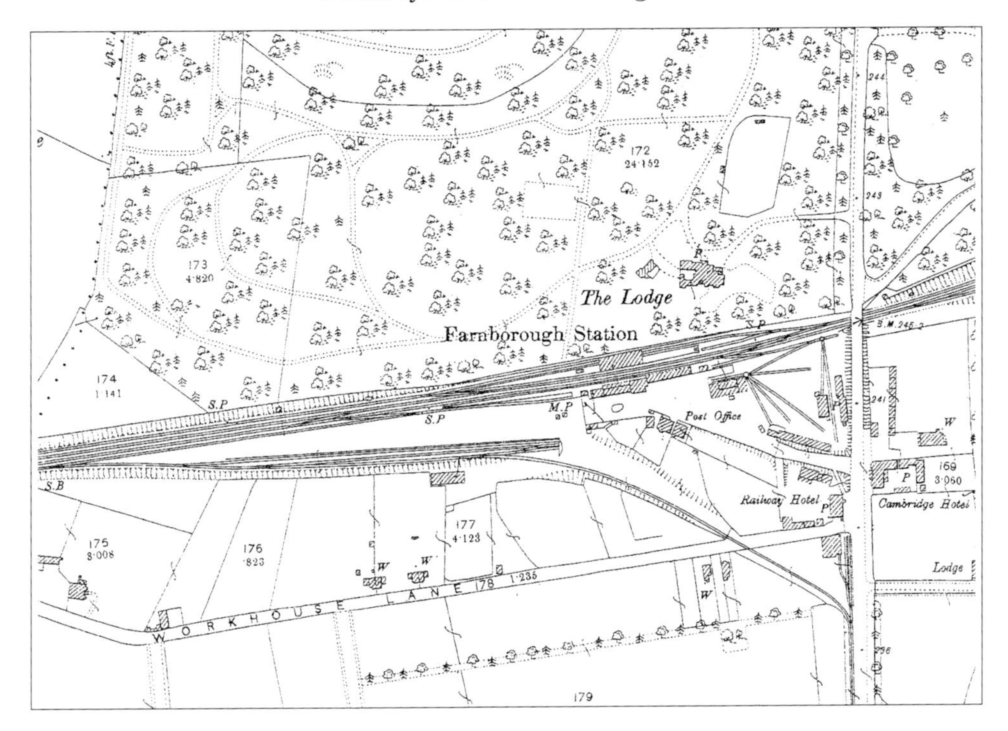

The Aldershot & Farnborough terminal and depot by Farnborough station, on the 1896 Ordnance Survey 25" to 1 mile map. Note the exchange sidings and connection to the railway line.

(These were possibly all new cars, as one report says that the original pair were sold to local gypsies following the early closure.)

The tramway was finally abandoned in 1906, by which time only one trip a day was being run (and this only as far as the Fir Tree Hotel short of North Camp station). This was not quite the end of the story though, for an 1897 company, Power & Traction Ltd, obtained the Aldershot and Farnborough Light Railways Order of 1902 to build a 3ft 6in. gauge electric system to serve the area but, although some 300 yards of track were laid in Farnborough Road near the station, the scheme, like virtually all the P&T's many tramway and light railway promotions, never came to fruition.

Alexandra Park Electric Railway *see* London: Alexandra Park Electric Railway

Appledore *see* Bideford, Westward Ho! & Appledore

Balfour, Beatty & Co. Ltd

This firm was established in 1909 by A.H. Beatty of the tramway contractors J.G. White & Co. Ltd, and George Balfour, a director of several tramway companies. It eventually owned, operated, or had a substantial interest in, a number of tramway and/or electricity supply companies including the systems of Carlisle, CHELTENHAM, DARTFORD, Ilkeston, Leamington & Warwick, LUTON, Mansfield and Nottinghamshire & Derbyshire in England, Llandudno & Colwyn Bay and Llanelly in Wales, and Dunfermline, Falkirk and Wemyss in Scotland.

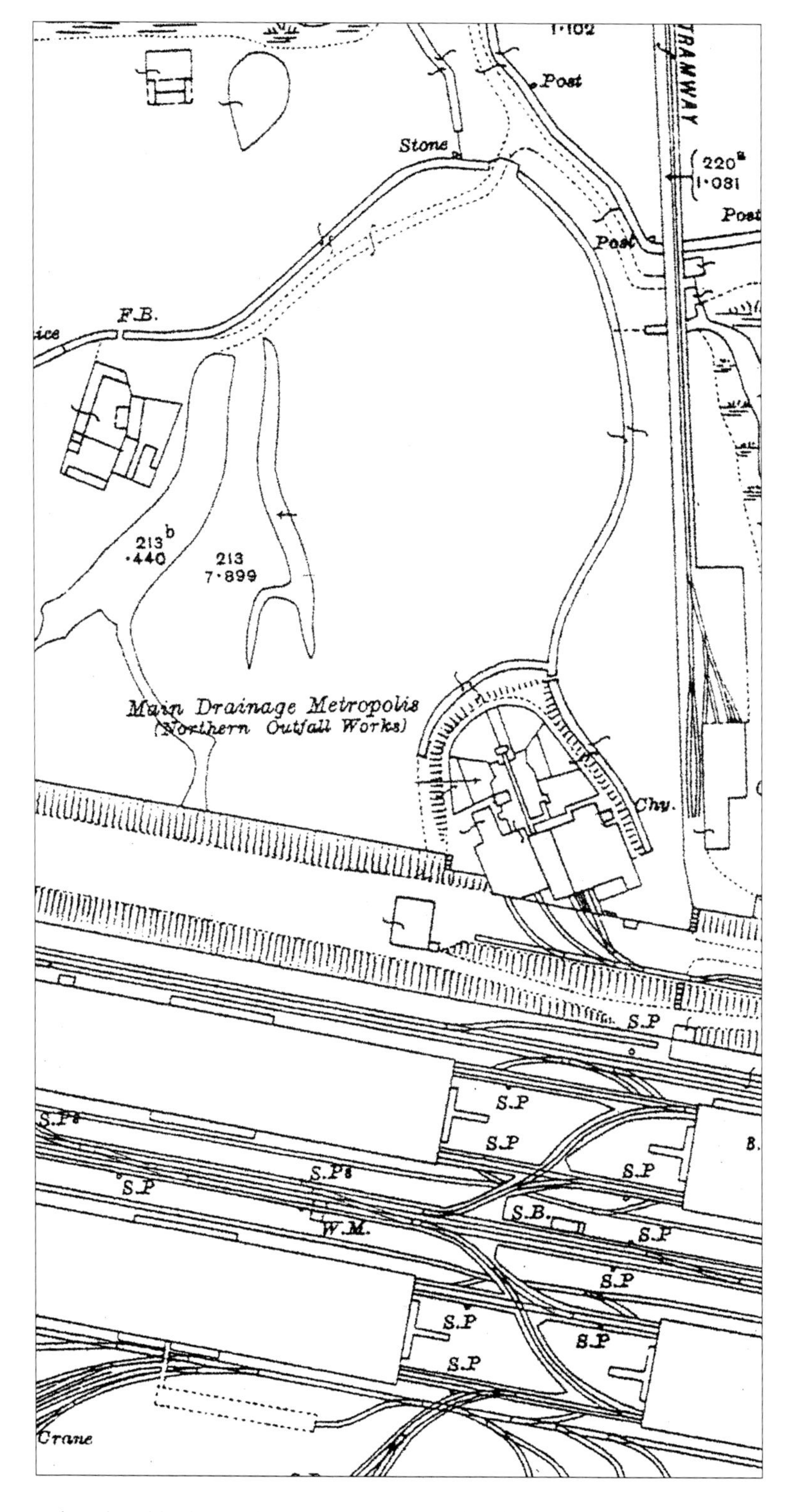

Even shorter than the Aldershot & Farnborough line was the Barking system, though it operated a more intensive service with more (electric) cars. This was the depot, sited just north of the giant Beckton Gas Works, as shown on the 1916 Ordnance Survey 25" to 1 mile map.

Barking Town Urban District Council Light Railways

Authority: Barking and Beckton Light Railways Order 1899
Gauge: 4ft 8½in.
Traction: Overhead electric
Opened: 1 December 1903
Closed: 16 February 1929*
System: Branching
Length: 1.6 miles*
Stock: 10 dd
Livery: Crimson lake & cream to 1906, brown & cream to 1907, then holly green & ivory
Last Car: ?

The first portion of this tiny, single-track municipal tramway on the eastern edge of Greater London, in Essex, had its southern terminus by Beckton Gasworks (and the depot) close to the River Thames. From here it ran northwards beside Jenkins Lane across the marshes and over Barking Creek, thence into the town centre via Gascoigne Street to terminate at the corner of Axe Street (1¼ miles). Delays in completing the bascule bridge over the creek meant that only the southern portion of the line was worked for the first few days, services throughout commencing on 5 December. The initial car fleet was made up of Brush open-toppers 1-7, of which Nos 1-3 and 7 were soon fitted with top covers.

On 6 June 1905 the Council opened an isolated ¼-mile section of single-track from its boundary with Ilford at Loxford Bridge (where it connected with ILFORD UDC TRAMWAYS) south-east along Fanshaw Road to Longbridge Road near Barking station; this was worked by Ilford cars. A similar arrangement was made with EAST HAM to the west when, on 17 November 1905, a double-track line was opened eastwards from that system's terminus in London Road south down the Broadway then north-east (as a single track) along East Street to the station. In this case the line was worked by both East Ham and WEST HAM cars; these two sections, leased to the other municipal authorities, brought Barking's route ownership to a grand total of 2.83 miles. The three lines were not connected until early 1907 when a double-track link was laid from Axe Street into the Broadway to meet the line from East Ham, and a double-tracked road bridge opened at the station (to replace a level crossing) to enable a link to be made with the Ilford line in Longbridge Road (the working of which was taken over by Barking from 1 October 1907).

Top-covered Brush cars Nos 8 and 9 were bought in 1911, and a year later (along with Nos 1-3 and 7) they were fitted with conduit ploughs in anticipation of through-working over LONDON COUNTY COUNCIL lines; at the same time car No. 10 – similar to Nos 8 and 9 – was bought with this equipment already installed. Through-running, via Ilford, to Aldgate began on 20 December 1912 but lasted only until 31 May 1914, it proving a loss-maker for the Council. No. 10 was then sold to Ilford, to be joined there in 1915 by No. 8 whilst No. 9 went to East Ham. In 1926 Nos 4 and 5 were withdrawn as worn-out and three years later, on 16 February 1929, the Beckton-Broadway section was abandoned in favour of buses, and the last cars scrapped. In 1931 track renewals meant that the two leased sections of line became separated with the removal of the Broadway/East Street junction, and two years later both became part of LONDON TRANSPORT routes.

[43 & 44 VICT.] *Tramways Orders Confirmation (No. 1) Act*, 1880. [Ch. clxxii.]

CHAPTER clxxii.

An Act for confirming certain Provisional Orders made by the Board of Trade under the Tramways Act, 1870, relating to Bath Tramways, Birkdale and Southport Tramways, Bristol Tramways (Extensions), Cambridge Street Tramways (Extension), Cardiff District and Penarth Harbour Tramways, Croydon Street Tramways (Extensions), Darlington Tramways, Dudley, Sedgley, and Wolverhampton Tramways, Ipswich Tramways (Extensions), Llanelly Tramways, Merthyr Tramways, Peterborough Tramways, Staffordshire Tramways (Additional Powers), Stockton-on-Tees and District Tramways, Sunderland Tramways (Use of Mechanical Power), Withington Local Board Tramways, and Wolverhampton Tramways (Use of Mechanical Power). [26th August 1880.]

A.D. 1880.

WHEREAS under the authority of the Tramways Act, 1870, the Board of Trade have made the several Provisional Orders set out in the Schedule to this Act annexed:

33 & 34 Vict. c. 78.

And whereas a Provisional Order made by the Board of Trade under the authority of the Tramways Act, 1870, is not of any validity or force whatever until the confirmation thereof by Act of Parliament:

33 & 34 Vict. c. 78.

And whereas it is expedient that the several Provisional Orders made by the Board of Trade under the authority of the said Act, and set out in the Schedule to this Act annexed, be confirmed by Act of Parliament:

Be it therefore enacted by the Queen's most Excellent Majesty, by and with the advice and consent of the Lords Spiritual and Temporal, and Commons, in this present Parliament assembled, and by the authority of the same, as follows:

Short title.

1. This Act may be cited as the Tramways Orders Confirmation (No. 1) Act, 1880.

[*Local.–172.*] A 1

After the passing of the Tramways Act in 1870, many systems were subsequently authorised by Tramway Orders, with several often gathered into a single Confirmation Act. This is the title page of one such of 1880, which includes the Order relating to the Bath Tramways.

Bath Tramways
Authority: Bath Tramways Order 1880
Gauge: 4ft
Traction: Horse
Opened: 24 December 1880
Closed: 25 July 1902
System: Single line
Length: 1.71 miles
Stock: 14 sd
Livery: Blue & yellow?
Last Car: ?

This short line, from the GWR's Bath station to Grosvenor College on the London Road, was worked in later years by the Bath Road Car & Tramway Co. Ltd, operator of several horse bus routes in the city. It is thought that only the northern half of the principally single-track line opened in 1880, with the extension to the station following later. It was originally owned by the Bath Tramways Co. Ltd (incorporated July 1880), who ran it with six (later seven) Starbuck cars before selling out in 1884 to the Patent Cable Tramways Corporation who – despite their name – continued with horse traction (and seven new single-deckers). This concern experienced financial difficulties too and four years later sold out to DK who, in turn, sold the line in 1889 to the BRCT, who ran it successfully until 1902 when it was purchased by Bath Corporation for the arbitrated price of £5,210 to make way for electrification (see below). The depot was in London Road, almost opposite Dover Street.

Bath Electric Tramways
Authority: Bath and District Light Railways Order 1901
Gauge: 4ft 8½in.
Traction: Overhead electric
Opened: 2 January 1904
Closed: 6 May 1939
System: Radial
Length: 14.78 miles
Stock: 6 sd, 34 dd
Livery: Bright blue & primrose yellow/cream
Last Car: No. 22

Work on building Bath's new tramway system began in November 1902, with routes from the city centre north-east to Bathford, south to Combe Down, south-west to Oldfield Park, west to Twerton and Newton St Loe, and north-west to Weston being opened between 2 January 1904 and 5 August of the following year. The operator was the Bath Electric Tramways Ltd (registered 9 July 1902), on whose behalf the Corporation had purchased the old horse line. (See above.)

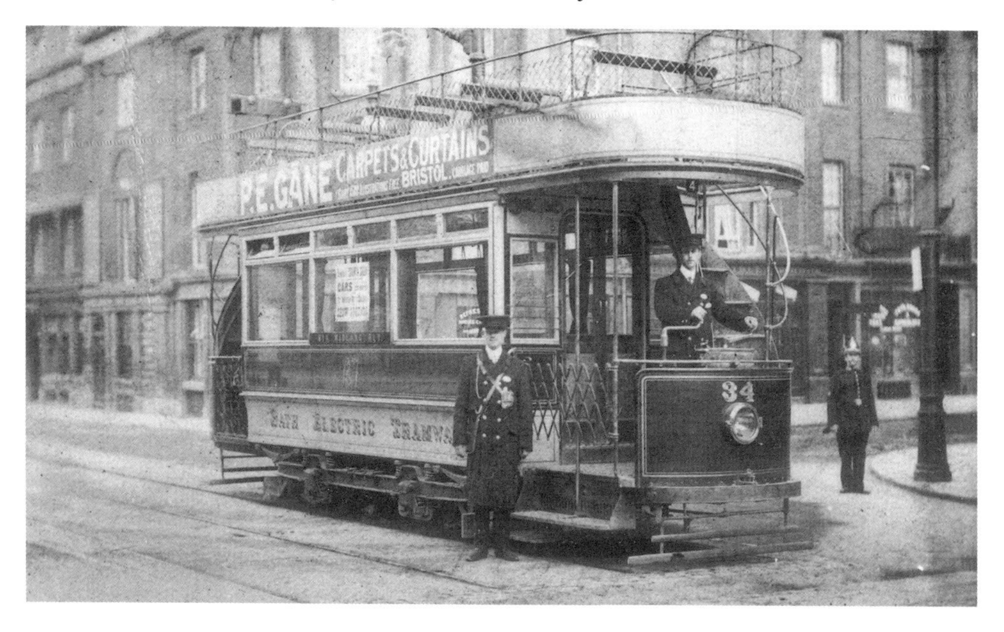

The crew of Bath Electric Tramways No. 34 of 1904 pose for the camera in the city centre (before the terminal loop by the Guildhall was completed), while a policeman keeps a watchful eye on proceedings. *(Author's collection)*

No further lines or extensions to the mainly single-track system were constructed, although the idea of linking with the BRISTOL network was mooted regularly, the two systems being only half a dozen miles apart at their closest points but very much reflecting the differences between the two cities. Bath's system was smaller, more compact and was forced to cope with narrow streets, sharp corners and steep gradients. (The latter were particularly in evidence on the Combe Down line, much used by day-trippers, which climbed to over 500ft above sea level.) The two systems did achieve one link though, in December 1936 when the Bath company was taken over (or rather swallowed) by the Bristol Tramways & Carriage Co. Ltd. By this time the writing was on the wall: both concerns were already operating motor buses and on 3 November 1938 the Newton St Loe route closed. The Twerton line went on 22 April 1939 and the remainder of the system on 6 May of the same year.

After the closure the rolling-stock (Milnes open-top cars 1-26 of 1903 and 27-34 of 1904, plus single-deck combination cars 50-53 of 1903 and 54 and 55 of 1904) was scrapped without any being bought by other systems. All in all it was an almost indecently swift end to the city's tramways.

Bexley Urban District Council Tramways

Authority: Bexley Tramways Act 1901
Gauge: 4ft 8½in.
Traction: Overhead electric
Opened: 3 October 1903
Closed: 23 November 1935

System: Branching
Length: 5.1 miles
Stock: 39 dd
Livery: Maroon & cream to 1917, then chocolate & cream
Last Car: ?

[1 EDW. 7.] *Bexley Tramways Act*, 1901. [Ch. ciii.]

CHAPTER ciii.

An Act to empower the Urban District Council of Bexley to construct and work Tramways and for other purposes. A.D. 1901.

[26th July 1901.]

WHEREAS the parish of Bexley in the county of Kent is an urban district (in this Act referred to as "the district") under the jurisdiction of the Bexley Urban District Council (in this Act called "the Council") and the Council are the local authority of the district within the meaning of the Tramways Act 1870:

And whereas the construction of tramways to form a continuous communication between the district and the metropolis and between the district and the urban district of Erith would be of great public and local advantage and it is expedient that the Council should be authorised to lay down construct and maintain the same:

And whereas it is expedient that the Council should be empowered to run carriages on any tramways for the time being belonging or leased to them or over which they may have running powers and to take charges for the use of such carriages:

And whereas it is expedient to authorise the Council to acquire lands for a generating station:

And whereas by the Bexley Electric Lighting Order 1899 confirmed by the Electric Lighting Orders Confirmation (No. 4) Act 1899 the Council were empowered to produce and supply electric energy within the district for public and private purposes and it is expedient to make further provision with regard to the supply of electric energy by the Council:

And whereas it is expedient that further borrowing powers be conferred on the Council for the purposes of this Act:

And whereas the purposes of this Act cannot be effected without the authority of Parliament:

[*Price* 2*s*. 3*d*.] A 1

Even after the Tramways Act of 1870 a number of tramway promoters still followed the old procedure of obtaining authority in the form of a dedicated Act of Parliament. This is the title page of the 1901 Act for the Bexley municipal system.

In spite of its name this system never served the north-west Kent town of old Bexley, but rather the district to its north. It was promoted by Bexley UDC and ran from a terminus by the end of the WOOLWICH & SOUTH EAST LONDON horse line in Plumstead (see LONDON) in a generally south-easterly direction out across the county boundary and thence to the Market Place in Bexleyheath, beyond which was sited the depot just before the terminus at Gravel Hill. A second route, northwards from the Market Place through Crayford and along the Erith Road to Northumberland Heath provided (from 1905) a connection with the ERITH system. Both routes were single tracks.

Twelve open-top ERTCW cars were bought to work the system, these being followed in 1904 by four more (Nos 13-16) to cope with the heavier than expected traffic.

In 1906 DARTFORD's new tramway from the east opened to Gravel Hill, and from 27 August that system's cars ran through the few hundred yards to the Market Place. The next connection came in 1908 when LONDON COUNTY COUNCIL, having re-gauged and electrified the Woolwich horse line, connected with the Bexley line at Plumstead. A deal was then struck whereby in return for handing over the 8.69 chains of track actually in London, Bexley UDC was given the right to run cars through to Woolwich.

As at Erith and Dartford, the First World War brought increased traffic to the line in the shape of munitions workers. Consequently, in 1915 the Council hired seventeen ERTCW enclosed double-deckers from the LCC, purchasing them outright between 1918 and 1920 when they were renumbered 17-33. During that period another six similar cars were hired but not bought. (These were theoretically 34-39 in the fleet list but it is not known how many, if any, were actually renumbered.)

Following the disastrous Dartford fire of 1917, both systems were operated as one, with Bexley supplying the cars. From 1 April 1921, after BB's lease of the Dartford system expired, they were formally run by a Joint Committee of the two local authorities until 1 July 1933 when both were taken over by the new LONDON TRANSPORT organisation. Thereafter, some cars of the old fleet were withdrawn and ex-LCC cars brought in during the short period before the whole Woolwich-Bexleyheath-Dartford route closed two years later, its trams replaced by trolleybuses – a mere two weeks after Erith had suffered a similar fate.

Bideford, Westward Ho! & Appledore Railway

Although otherwise an English light railway in the conventional sense, the first ¼ mile of this 5½-mile standard gauge line ran through the streets of the Devon town of Bideford, which meant that the railway's three Hunslet tank engines had to be fitted with side-skirts (and later cowcatchers). Another tramway connection was that following the line's authorisation in 1896 the Company was acquired by the BET before the first section opened on 24 April 1901. When completed in 1908 the railway ran westwards from Bideford Quay, on the river Torridge, to the north Devon coast some 2 miles away, then turned north-east to reach the other two places of its title.

Presumably the BET had second thoughts about its purchase of the line as, unlike most of the group's other acquisitions, it was never electrified and, even if the locomotives had not been requisitioned by the Government in 1917 for war service in France, it is doubtful that the railway could have lasted much longer in the face of growing bus competition. The last train ran on 28 March that year.

Bisley Common Tramway *see* Wimbledon Common Tramway

Bournemouth Corporation Tramways

Authority: Bournemouth Corporation Tramways Act 1901
Gauge: 3ft 6in.
Traction: Overhead electric, conduit electric
Opened: 23 July 1902
Closed: 8 April 1936
System: Radial network
Length: 16.11 miles
Stock: 1 sd, 131 dd
Livery: Dark maroon/chocolate & primrose/cream
Last Car: No. 115

Although the idea of tramways in the town was opposed originally by Bournemouth Corporation (which resulted in the POOLE & DISTRICT line from the west terminating at the common boundary), it relented at the beginning of the twentieth century and sought powers to construct its own system – and take over the Poole line.

The first route opened ran from the Landsdowne in the town centre eastwards along Christchurch Road to Warwick Road, Pokesdown. By 17 October 1905, when this line was extended via Seabourne Road, Belle Vue Road and over the boundary on Stour Road into Christchurch, the system within the town was complete. Mainly single-track, it stretched as far east as Christchurch, then travelled north up Wimbourne Road to Moordown, and west to Poole. (This last route, opened on 18 December 1902, stopped short of the Poole terminus, with no physical connection made until April 1905.) Between

The Square in Bournemouth, the hub of the town's tramway network. *(Author's collection)*

the Christchurch and Moordown routes lay a series of interlinking lines and, by dint of careful planning, the system managed to serve (from east to west) the railway stations of Christchurch, Pokesdown, Boscombe, Bournemouth Central, Bournemouth West, Branksome and Poole. As at certain other, more genteel seaside resorts, the Corporation wished to avoid the presence of overhead wires in at least some locations. Consequently the central portion of the network, from the Landsdowne westwards along Old Christchurch Road, through the Square and on to St Michael's church, Poole Hill, was laid with a conduit supply. This lasted until 13 May 1911, when an overhead was put into use.

The only other line added was a Lower Parkstone route in Poole, opened on 3 August 1906 along Castle Hill and Bournemouth Road, which left and rejoined the Upper Parkstone line.

Services began with bogie cars Nos 2-20 and four-wheelers 21-48 from Milnes (like all Bournemouth's double-deckers, open-toppers). These were joined in 1904 by similar bogie cars 49-54 and a year later by former Poole cars 1-17, which were renumbered 55-70 and 82 respectively. To house all these vehicles the Poole depot on Ashley Road was joined by depots at Moordown, Pokesdown, and Southcote Road in the town centre, this last incorporating the municipal power station as well as the main tramway depot and works.

In 1907 eleven Brush bogie cars were bought (Nos 71-81), the last Bournemouth cars to be equipped for dual current collection. UEC bogie cars 83-92 arrived seven years later and in 1921 and 1926 similar type cars 93-112 and 113-132 were purchased, this time from Brush again, to complete the fleet.

The tramway's only single-decker was No. 1, a luxurious Milnes bogie saloon reserved originally for official inspections, wedding parties and the like. It was nicknamed the 'Picnic Car' on account of its wicker armchairs, though these were replaced in 1920 when it was put into normal passenger service during peak periods.

In the years immediately after the First World War much of the system was double-tracked, but by the late 1920s the end was in sight. The first abandonment came on 5 January 1929 when the Lower Parkstone route was closed, to be replaced by Hants & Dorset Motor Services buses. In 1933 the Corporation began trolleybus operations and two years later the Hants & Dorset purchased the remaining Poole route for £75,000 in order to close it – which, on 7 June 1935, it proceeded to do. After this the trams in Bournemouth lasted less than a year, to be replaced by the Corporation's trolleybuses. After the closure Nos 85, 95, 103, 108, 112, 114-116, 121 and 128 were sold to the Llandudno & Colwyn Bay Electric Railway, together with No. 55 which had been converted in 1921 to a rail-grinder. Surprisingly, more than a dozen car bodies from the fleet have survived to become restoration projects around the country, and one complete tram – No. 85 – is now back on its home ground once more, preserved in the Museum of Electricity, Christchurch whilst No.106 of 1921 operates in a rebuilt form at SEATON.

Brighton Corporation Tramways

Authority: Brighton Corporation Act 1900
Gauge: 3ft 6in.
Traction: Overhead electric
Opened: 25 November 1901

Closed: 31 August 1939
System: Network
Length: 9.48 miles
Stock: 165 dd
Livery: Various shades of maroon/chocolate & primrose/cream
Last Car: No. 41

This compact system began operations with Milnes open-toppers 1-25, quickly joined by similar cars Nos 26-30, running from Victoria Gardens inland along the Lewes Road, past the depot at the junction with Bear Road, and on to Preston Barracks. Other routes – a mixture of double and single tracks – were added up to 27 July 1904, going west to the LBSCR's Brighton station via North Road and Queens Road, north-west to Tivoli Gardens via New England Road and Dyke Road, north up Beaconsfield Road and back via Preston Drove and Ditchling Road, east along Elm Grove to the racecourse and back from there down Queen's Park Road to the Rock Gardens, and lastly south to Old Steine Gardens near the seafront, which became the starting point for all routes. (The Corporation refused to allow a route along the seafront itself for fear of spoiling its appearance.)

In 1903 ten more Milnes cars were bought (Nos 31-40), followed over the next two years by another ten open-toppers (Nos 41-50), this time from UEC. Thereafter the Corporation built new (often replacement) cars in batches at the Lewes Road depot and works, having gained the necessary experience by completely rebuilding the original cars from 1908 onwards. In 1914 open-toppers Nos 51-53 were produced, followed by a rebuilt No. 10, which had been damaged in an accident, three years later. (During the First World War some, if not all, of the UEC cars had their motors removed temporarily and were used as trailers on services to the town's munition works.) Immediately after the war, in 1919, replacement cars 1, 7, 17, and 26 and new cars 54 and 55 were put into service. Cars built thereafter were:

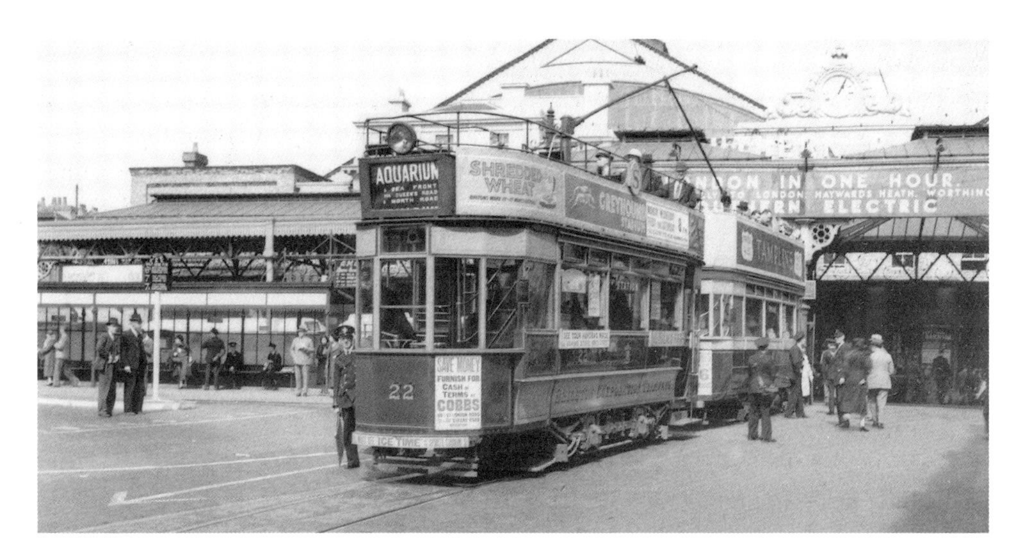

Two of Brighton Corporation's fleet of double-deckers at the Central station terminus. *(Author's collection)*

1920: 9, 11, 14, 56
1921: 15, 20, 23, 24, 27, 30, 41, 42, 57, 58
1922: 46, 49, 50, 59-63
1923: 2, 36, 43, 44, 47, 48
1924: 4, 8, 16, 18, 19, 21, 25, 28
1925: 3, 5, 6, 12, 29, 33, 38, 39
1926: 31, 32, 34, 35, 37, 40
1927: 13, 22, 45
1928: 10, 64-67
1929: 68-70
1930: 71-75
1931: 76-80
1932: 1, 7, 17, 26
1933: 9, 11, 41, 55, 57, 58
1934: 14, 15, 20, 42, 50, 54, 56, 59, 60, 63
1935: 2, 24, 27, 30, 46, 48
1936: 21, 23, 25, 43, 49, 74
1937: 51-53

The system closed just before the Second World War. The trams were replaced by buses and trolleybuses from 26 April 1939 when the Dyke Road line was abandoned, the last service being along Lewes Road to the depot.

Brighton & Rottingdean Seashore Electric Tramroad

Authority: Brighton and Rottingdean Seashore Electric Tramroad Act 1893
Gauge: 2ft 8½in. & 18ft*
Traction: Overhead electric
Opened: 30 November 1896
Closed: January 1901
System: Single line
Length: 2.93 miles
Stock: 1 dd
Livery: Varnished wood & white
Last Car: *Pioneer*

Without doubt this line was the most weird and wonderful tramway in the British Isles – if not the whole world. It was the glorious brainchild of Magnus Volk, who wished to extend his pioneering electric railway along the seafront at Brighton (opened 1883) to the neighbouring village of Rottingdean. He aimed to do this without recourse to an expensive viaduct along the intervening cliff face and his solution was to lay a double line of flat-bottomed rails, fastened to concrete blocks, along the shore (between the high and low water marks) from the Banjo Groyne in Brighton – the then terminus of the Volk's Electric Railway – to a 300ft-long pier built at Rottingdean. A midway loading stage was provided at Ovingdean Gap.

Postcard of the Brighton & Rottingdean Seashore Electric Tramroad's unique car, outside the Brighton terminus. *(Author's collection)*

The track gauge was 2ft 8½in., the same as the VER, with the lines laid 18ft apart as measured between the two outermost rails, this distance being the true 'gauge' of the line as the tramway's one car ran on both tracks at once in the manner of giant dockside cranes. Aptly named *Pioneer*, though popularly known as 'Daddy Longlegs', the car was built by Gloucester and looked like nothing so much as a pier head crossed with a ferry. It weighed 50 tons fully laden, carried up to 150 passengers and was furnished with a 46ft by 22ft promenade deck surrounding a central saloon. It stood on four steel legs 24ft high, each of which stood in an encased four-wheeled bogie. Current from an overhead wire fed two 25hp deck-mounted motors powering two of the bogies via shafting in two of the hollow legs. (The other two carried brake rodding.) The car was required by the BoT to carry lifebelts and a lifeboat – surely the only tramcar ever to do so!

The line got off to a poor start, for in the first week of December 1896 severe storms inflicted a great deal of damage. The car capsized and the tramway did not reopen until 20 July of the following year. The car though proved slow and underpowered – running through 15ft of water at high tide reduced it to a crawl – and the track was given to silting over; by 1900 only short out-and-back trips were being operated from the Brighton end of the line, and even these were terminated the following year by Brighton Corporation's removal of part of the track to make way for new sea defences. The rest of the line (and *Pioneer*) were not scrapped until 1910, with some of the concrete sleeper blocks remaining *in situ* right up to the present day.

A closer view of the BRST's *Pioneer* at the Brighton terminus, this time at low tide, the occasion being the ceremonial opening of the line two days before public services began. The Mayor of Brighton is at the controls of the car, in the 'bows' to the left. *(Author's collection)*

The Rottingdean pier terminus of the BRSET, some time before its 1909 demolition, with the line of tracks just visible on the left, heading towards the similar intermediate structure at Ovingdean Gap in the far distance. *(Author's collection)*

Brighton & Shoreham Tramways

Authority: Brighton District Tramways Act 1882
Gauge: 3ft 6in.
Traction: Steam, horse
Opened: 3 July 1884
Closed: 6 June 1913
System: Single line
Length: 4.64 miles
Stock: 4 locos*, 4 dd steam; 6 sd, 10 dd horse
Livery: Locos dark brown & cream, trailers lighter brown & cream steam; yellow & cream to 1898, then BET dark lake & cream horse
Last Car: No. 10

Opened by the Brighton District Tramways Co., this seaside line was unusual in that it began with steam traction but ended up using horses. Despite its title, it had no tracks in Brighton at all, running as it did westwards as a single track from Westbourne Gardens, Aldrington, on the boundary with Hove just west of Brighton. From there it continued along New Church Road through Aldrington to Portslade, where it turned south on Station Road before proceeding west along Wellington Road, Fishergate Terrace and Albion Street to Southwick and Kingston-upon-Sea. It then journeyed along Lower Brighton Road and Ham Road to Shoreham-by-Sea and the LBSCR station. Here it swung south into Brunswick Road then immediately west into Western road, then north into Shoreham Road to terminate by the Swiss Gardens. The depot was in Albion Street between the tramway and Southwick station.

The tramway's first items of rolling-stock were Wilkinson tram locomotives Nos 1 and 2 hauling Falcon bogie double-deck trailers Nos 1 and 2, fitted with roof canopies; these were joined early in 1885 by a similar pair of trailers (presumably numbered 3 and 4) and an 0-4-2 Fowler loco. Numbered 3, this engine was soon returned to the manufacturer, presumably as it was considered unsuitable. Six single-deck horse cars, then two double-deckers, were then supplied by Oldbury (and probably numbered 1-8 in their own sequence).

In 1887 a second loco. No. 3 arrived: this was an Aveling & Porter 0-4-0 geared locomotive – the Rochester firm's first – designed for street tramway use but it proved unsuccessful in trials and was returned to the manufacturers. That same year the Company went into receivership – one of its problems was that it closely paralleled the LBSCR's railway line – but continued to operate the tramway. At the same time the Electric Traction Syndicate leased horse car No. 3 and converted it to battery power for several months of trials (along with a battery loco). Also in 1887, at the end of the summer season the 0.49-mile Ham Road-Shoreham Road section was closed and single-decker No. 4 sold to the Pontypridd & Rhondda Valley Tramway.

Early in 1892 the Company was wound up, the line having already been sold to the Leicester Tramways Co. Ltd, who had set up the Brighton & Shoreham Tramways Co. on 30 October 1889 expressly to operate it. Official returns for 1890 record the line as being worked by four cars – presumably survivors 1-3 and 5 from the tramway's

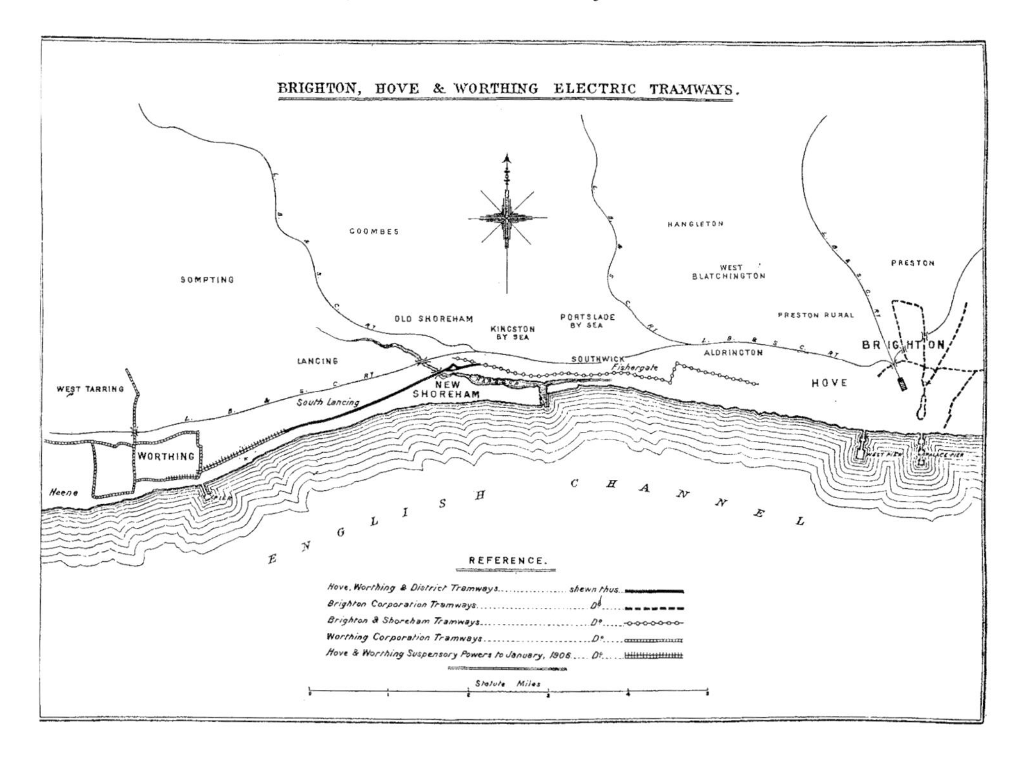

Map of existing and proposed tramways in the Brighton area, from the 1904 *Manual of Electrical Undertakings*.

earlier incarnation, for in 1891 five double-deck horse cars, Nos 4 and 6-9, were bought from Oldbury. Two years later the steam locos and trailers were sold to Wigan District Tramways, the line thereafter operating solely as a horse tramway. (Further stock changes are unclear: official returns show the number of cars in use fluctuating between four and eleven thereafter.) In 1898 the Company was in turn bought by the BET who wished to electrify the line (and extend it westwards to Worthing), but although the necessary Act of Parliament was obtained in 1903 – the Hove Worthing and District Tramways Act – and a company was registered for the purpose, nothing came of the proposal. Before the end of the decade motor bus competition had reduced the tramway to a one-car operation using one of the double-deckers cut down to single-deck form. In 1912 the eastern end of the line in New Church Road was abandoned, with the remainder following a year later.

Brill Tramway

Never a tramway, this line began life as a private, standard gauge light-railway. It was built by the local landowner, the Duke of Buckingham, to link the Buckinghamshire village of Brill with Quainton Road station on the Aylesbury & Buckingham Railway (opened 1868) some 6 miles away. Originally known as the Wootton Tramway, the railway opened in stages during 1871-2, with horse haulage for both passengers and goods until January 1872 when the first of two chain-driven Aveling & Porter steam engines were purchased (later to be joined by a Bagnall tank).

On 1 April 1894 the line was taken over by the Oxford & Aylesbury Tramroad Co.; it was rebuilt to a heavier standard and more powerful locomotives introduced. From 1 December 1899 it was worked by the Metropolitan Railway as its Brill branch and slowly modernised. It closed on 1 December 1935, by which time the Metropolitan had become part of the London Passenger Transport Board.

Bristol Tramways

Authority: Bristol Corporation Tramways Order 1872
Gauge: 4ft 8½in.
Traction: Horse, steam, overhead electric
Opened: 9 August 1875
Closed: 11 April 1941
System: Radial network
Length: 31.16 miles
Stock: 8 locos*, 109 dd horse & steam; 238 dd electric*
Livery: Dark blue & white
Last Car: *

The Bristol tramway network grew out of a single horse route on the northern side of the city, running for a little over 1½ miles from the King David Inn in Perry Road out along Queens Road and Whiteladies Road to the district of Redland, where it terminated at the bottom of Blackboy Hill by St John's church. Owned by Bristol Corporation, the tramway was worked on a lease by the Bristol Tramways Co. Ltd. On 4 December 1874 the line was extended right into the city centre via Colston Street with a new terminus in St Augustine's Parade (to become known later, as the system grew, as the Tramways Centre). Initial services were worked by Nos 1-6, Starbuck double-deckers.

Over the ensuing quarter of a century a succession of routes were opened to create a radial network of 9.31 miles. This stretched out to Eastville and St George (1876) and Kingswood (1892) in the east, Totterdown (1879) and Bedminster (1880) in the south, Hotwells (1880) to the west and Horfield to the north. This last route, opened on 18 November 1880, was worked originally by seven hired Hughes steam tramway locomotives (Nos 1-7), pulling adapted horse cars with primitive roofs, on account of its steep gradients. Apparently the locos were not a success and were returned to the manufacturers at the end of their twelve-month contract. An eighth loco, built by Fox, Walker & Co. of Bristol and used on the Redland-Eastville route, fared no better. (All these routes were owned by the Company, as was the original Redland route from 1882 onwards when it was purchased for £8,000 from the Corporation.)

On 1 October 1887 the Company amalgamated with the Bristol Carriage Co. Ltd, a local cab and other vehicles for hire firm, to form the Bristol Tramways & Carriage Co. Ltd (soon to become part of the IMPERIAL TRAMWAYS Group) and, by 1898 when the last links and extensions to the system opened, its car fleet had risen to 109 in total – mostly double-deckers from a number of manufacturers, numbered 1-85, 98-115 and 119-124, housed in a number of depots sited around the system.

By the 1890s the Company was keen to electrify its lines, and on 14 October 1895 the first converted route, from Old Market to Kingswood, opened. The second, from Old

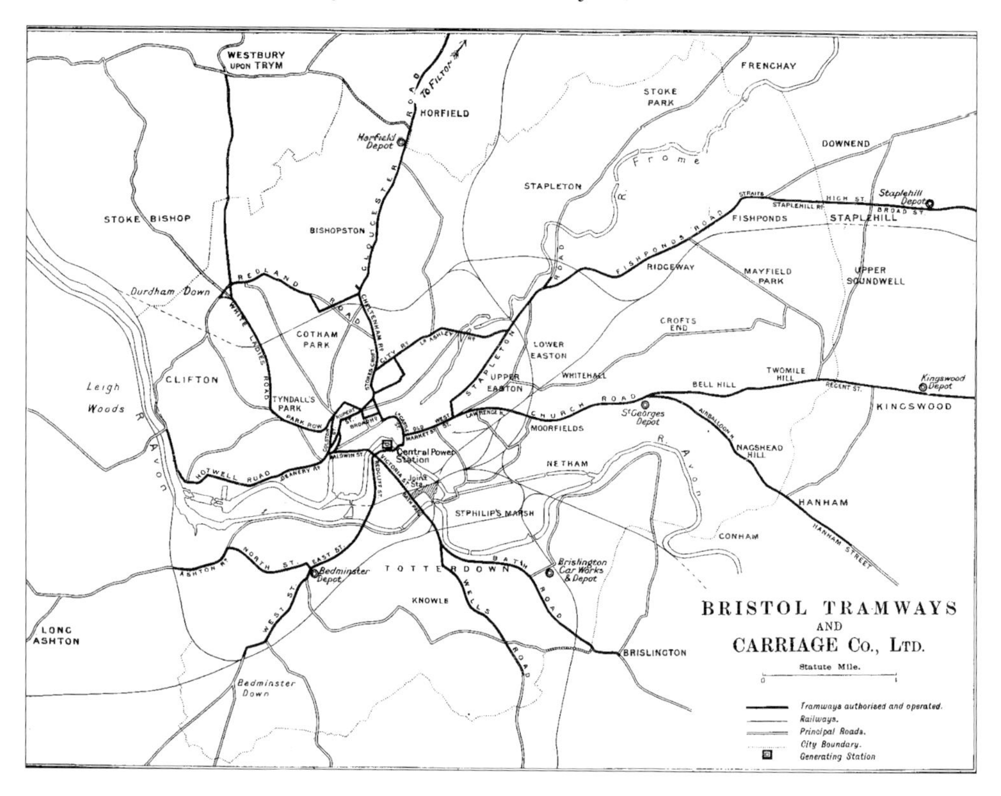

Map of the Bristol tramways system, from the 1920-1 *Manual of Electrical Undertakings.*

Market to Eastville, followed on 1 February 1897 (extended later that year to Fishponds, then Staple Hill) and by 2 December 1900 all the former lines had been converted (and in some cases extended). A new, 1½-mile route to the village of Hanham, running south-east off the Kingswood route at St George, was constructed under an 1898 LRO and known officially as the St George & Hanham Light Railway. Thereafter the only major alterations made to the (nearly all double-track) system were the 1907 extension from Horfield Barracks northwards to Filton and a 1908 extension of the Durdham Downs (Redland) route to Westbury-upon-Trym.

All the electric passenger cars were open-top double-deckers (believed to have been the largest such fleet in the British Isles), numbered in sequence with the horse cars. In chronological order of construction they were:

Nos 86-97:	Milnes of 1895
Nos 116-118:	Milnes of 1895-96
Nos 125-140:	Milnes of 1897
No 141:	Brill of 1897 (used as a directors' car until 1908)
Nos 142-161:	American Car Co. of 1897-98
Nos 162-172:	Milnes of 1900
Nos 173-202:	Midland of 1900-01
Nos 203-232:	Bristol of 1900-01

The Tramway Centre, Bristol, looking towards the Harbour – a popular postcard view during the system's life. *(Author's collection)*

After the withdrawal of the horse cars, the gaps in the sequence were then filled in with Nos 1-85, 98-115 and 119-124 from Milnes in 1900-01. The only other passenger cars to be added to the fleet (Bristol prided itself on keeping its ageing cars in excellent condition) were six constructed by the Company in 1920 and numbered 233-237 and 86 (this last car replacing the earlier one of that number). In addition, several of the horse cars were used as trailers until January 1899. Many of the routes had their own depots, with the main one and the general works being at Bridlington.

The system remained virtually unchanged until the 1930s, when the Corporation decided to exercise its option to buy the tramways, which it did at a cost of £1,125,000, effective from 1 October 1937. The intention was to replace the trams with buses (of which the Company had a large fleet) and, on 8 May 1938, the Hotwells and Westbury routes closed, followed on 3 September by the Staple Hill, Bridlington and Knowle lines.

Further closures followed until by April 1941 only the Kingswood and Hanham routes remained – only to be ignominiously abandoned when a German bomb cut the main power supply, after which all the surviving cars were scrapped.

The Company was one of only two British tramway operators to own a funicular railway (the other being TORQUAY). Comprising four tracks running in a tunnel throughout, this was the Clifton Rocks Railway in the Avon Gorge, opened in 1893 to lift passengers from the riverside (and the tramway's Hotwells line) up to Sion Hill. The Company purchased the railway in 1912 and closed it in 1934 because it was no longer profitable.

One former horse car, from the 1895 batch Nos 101-115 from Milnes, subsequently used as a trailer, was rescued from a Bristol garden in 2000 and is on show, in unrestored condition, at the Bristol Aero Collection at Kemble Airfield near Cirencester.

The entrance to the lower terminus of the Clifton Rocks Railway, a Bristol Tramways & Carriage Co. Ltd interest from 1912 to 1934; the Hotwells tramway route passed conveniently by the door. *(Author's collection)*

TRAMWAY SERVICES IN THE CITY OF BRISTOL

Services marked (*) will be replaced by buses during September, 1938

	Weekdays.		Sundays.	
	First dep. a.m.	Last dep. p.m.	First dep. p.m.	Last dep. p.m.
Tramways C. & Durdham D. (via Zetl'd Rd)				
From Tramways Centre to Durdham Down	6 30	1115	2 20	1015
" Durdham Down to Tramways Centre	7 0	1115	2 30	10 5
" Durdham Down to Zetland Road......	7 0	1140	2 30	1040
Tramways Centre, Horfield and Filton				
From Ashley Down Rd. to Tramways Centre	4 50	1115	2 0	1020
" Tramways Centre to Filton	5 20	1115	2 20	1010
" Filton to Tramways Centre	4 40	11 5	2 10	1010
" Filton to Ashley Down Road	4 40	1140	2 10	1040
" Tramways Centre to Horfield Barracks	5 20	1120	2 20	1025
***Tramways Centre, Eastville & Fishponds**				
From Fishponds to Tramways Centre	4 50	1050	2 0	9 55
" Warwick Road to Tramways Centre...	5 0	11 0	2 0	10 5
" Tramways Centre to Fishponds	5 20	1120	2 30	1025
Tramways Centre and Brislington				
From Brislington to Tramways Centre........	5 25	1120	2 10	1025
" Tramways Centre to Brislington........	5 25	1130	2 15	1030
" Tramways Cen. to Temple Meads Stn.	5 25	1140	2 15	1045
" Temple Meads Stn. to Tramways Cen.	5 10	1130	2 10	1040
Bristol Bridge and Knowle				
From Knowle	5 25	1130	2 20	1030
" Bristol Bridge.................... (Bath St.)	5 45	1140	2 15	1020
***Bristol Bridge and Ashton Road**				
From Ashton Road....................................	5 25	1115	2 10	1030
" Bristol Bridge	5 30	1130	2 15	1035

	Weekdays.		Sundays.	
	First dep. a.m.	Last dep. p.m.	First dep. p.m.	Last dep. p.m.
***Bristol Bridge and Bedminster Down**				
From Bedminster Down	5 10	1115	2 15	1020
" Bristol Bridge	5 30	1130	2 10	1035
Tramways Centre and Kingswood				
From Kingswood to Old Market	5 15	1055	1 55	10 0
" Kingswood to Tramways Centre........	5 25	1035	1 55	9 50
" Tramways Centre to Kingswood........	6 5	1115	2 35	1025
" St. George to Kingswood	5 55	1140	2 0	1050
" Old Market to Kingswood	5 45	1125	2 25	1035
***Zetland Road and Staple Hill**				
From Staple Hill to Old Market	5 0	11 0	1 55	10 5
" Fishponds to Old Market	5 5	11 5	2 5	1015
" Staple Hill to Zetland Road	5 10	1030	2 0	9 30
" Old Market to Staple Hill	5 35	1130	2 25	1035
" Warwick Road to Staple Hill	5 40	1140	2 0	1045
" Zetland Road to Staple Hill..............	5 55	1110	2 40	1015
Hanham, Old Market and Knowle				
From St. George Depot to Old Market	5 0	1115	2 0	1020
" Hanham to Knowle	5 40	1040	2 15	9 40
" Old Market to St. George	5 30	1145	2 15	1045
" Old Market to Hanham.....................	5 30	1120	2 15	1020
" Old Market to Knowle	5 45	11 5	2 15	10 5
" Old Market to Nags Head Hill.........	5 30	1125	2 15	1030
" Knowle to Old Market	5 25	1125	2 35	1025
" Knowle to Hanham	6 20	11 0	2 35	10 0
" Knowle to Nags Head Hill	6 20	11 5	2 35	1010
" Knowle to St. George	6 20	1125	2 35	1025

26

Tram Services

The BTC Co.'s summer 1938 bus timetable included just one page for the dwindling tramway service.

Parry People Mover No. 10 at work on the Bristol Harbour Tramway - a forerunner of things to come at this location? *(Courtesy JPM Parry & Associates Ltd)*

Bristol Harbour Tramway

At the very end of the twentieth century, Bristol saw a tram in public service once again, though only for temporary (but useful) demonstration purposes. The tramway in question utilised a section of former railway quayside track on the north bank of the River Avon, on the long spit of land between the river and the Floating Harbour; the tram was a Parry People Mover built by J.P.M. Parry & Associates of Cradley Heath in the West Midlands. The single track used, some 700m in length, ran from the Lifeboat Museum by the swing bridge linking Wapping Road and Prince Street across the Floating Harbour. From there it continued westwards past Bristol Industrial Museum to Brunel's preserved *SS Great Britain*, the world-famous tourist attraction. The tram had its first trials at the end of November 1997 using PPM prototype No. 10, a wheelchair-accessible, four-wheeled, single-deck vehicle with wrap-around skirts built that same year. (The line was – and is – also used by occasional steam specials.)

Public services began on 28 May 1998, after two months of further trials and driver training, using No. 10 again, with power for the car's flywheel picked up at both terminals. (The PPM design of tramcars and railcars uses stored energy contained in a large flywheel, mounted horizontally beneath the floor, driving the wheels via a variable transmission. In the case of car No. 10 this energy is 'topped-up' by a small electric motor at regular intervals using 70V dc current supplied by fixed trackside feeds.)

The tram was operated by Bristol Electric Railbus Ltd, a concern established by environmental entrepreneur James Skinner (with the car owned by a related leasing company), with four round trips per hour made during the summer operating seasons, until services were suspended at the end of October 2000. At this point more than 50,000 passengers had been carried; No. 10 – renumbered 238 to follow on from the last BRISTOL TRAMWAYS car No. 237 (see above) – found a new home at the Midland Railway Centre at Butterley in Derbyshire. The end came because negotiations between Bristol City Council and Railtrack Property over extending the service a further kilometre to the new 'Create' Environment Centre development at the Cumberland Basin, which had been going on for two years, appeared to be getting nowhere. Always intended as a demonstration line only, largely funded by Skinner as founder and Chairman of BER Ltd, the tramway was intended to publicise the virtues of the clean and energy-efficient PPM system for tramways and light railways of the future. In this particular instance, a longer line here, linking back into the city centre, might yet come about as part of the development of Bristol's tourist industry.

British Electric Traction Co. Ltd

The BET was far and away the biggest private tramway owner in the British Isles. It was formed in 1895 by Emile Garcke and set about, at that timely juncture in tramway history, buying up existing horse and steam lines with a view to extending and electrifying them (usually successfully), thereby creating a number of linked networks in the process (notably in the LONDON area and the Black Country). The Company also had extensive business interests other than tramways, particularly in electricity supply and, later, bus operations.

In the tramway field the Company controlled, at one time or another, the METROPOLITAN ELECTRIC and SOUTH METROPOLITAN systems in and around London. Further assets were the Barnsley, Barrow-in-Furness, Birmingham, Birmingham & Midland, DEVONPORT & DISTRICT, Dudley & Stourbridge, Gateshead, GRAVESEND, Hartlepools, Jarrow, Kidderminster & Stourport, Leamington & Warwick, Middleton, Oldham, Ashton & Hyde, PETERBOROUGH, POOLE, Potteries, SHEERNESS, South Staffordshire, Southport, TAUNTON, Tynemouth, WESTON-SUPER-MARE Wolverhampton District, Worcester and Yorkshire (Woollen District) electric tramways elsewhere in England, not to mention those of Merthyr Tydfil, Swansea, Swansea & Mumbles and Wrexham in Wales, Airdrie, Greenock & Port Glasgow and Rothesay in Scotland, and Cavehill & Whitewell in Ireland.

The lines at BRIGHTON & SHOREHAM, CAMBRIDGE, Rossendale Valley, South Shields and Yarmouth were all at one time controlled by the Company, but never electrified.

British Thomson-Houston Co. Ltd

The BTH, as well as being a major supplier of tramway equipment and the parent company of the British Tramways & General Construction Co. Ltd, owned or controlled the electric tramways systems at CHATHAM and the ISLE OF THANET in England, Paisley and Lanarkshire in Scotland, and Cork in Ireland.

Broadstairs *see* Isle of Thanet
Camber *see* Rye & Camber
Camberwell *see* London, Camberwell & Dulwich

Camborne & Redruth Tramway

Authority: Camborne and Redruth Tramway Order 1900
Gauge: 3ft 6in.
Traction: Overhead electric
Opened: 7 November 1902
Closed: 29 September 1927
System: Single line
Length: 3.45 miles
Stock: 2 sd, 6 dd
Livery: Dark green & cream up to 1920, then dark green
Last Cars: Nos 3 and 4

Cornwall's only tramway, this operation linked the two towns of its title with nearly 3½ miles of mainly single track down the main road (now the A3047) along the spine of the county, linking a succession of hamlets housing the workers employed in this tin-mining region. A further 0.56 miles laid as spur routes to the tin mines and smelting works for the C&R was unusual amongst English street tramways in that it carried freight on a regular, sizeable basis (and unique in that this was mineral traffic). For these workings the owners, the Urban Electric Supply Co. Ltd – owner of the Glossop tramway – employed two small electric locomotives (Nos 1 and 2) and fourteen ore wagons. The goods service began in 1903 and lasted beyond the closure of the rest of the tramway (brought about

ELECTRICAL ENGINEERS & CONTRACTORS,

WHOSE

INCLUSIVE CONTRACTS FOR ELECTRIC TRACTION APPARATUS FOR

The
Central London Railway
(5,100 K.W. in Gens, 22,700 H.P. in Motors),

The
Dublin United Tramways Co.
(4,490 K.W. in Gens, 11,016 H.P. in Motors),

The
Bristol Tramways & Carriage Co.
(2,790 K.W. in Gens, 11,032 H.P. in Motors),

The
London United Tramways Co.
(3,450 K.W. in Gens, 7,000 H.P. in Motors),

ARE AMONGST THE . . .

LARGEST ORDERS for Electric Traction Apparatus ever placed in the United Kingdom. . . .

HEAD OFFICE :

83, Cannon Street, London, E.C.

by the appearance in 1926 of bus competition), continuing until 1934 when the goods trains, which ran only over the central mile or so of the tramway, were replaced by an aerial ropeway.

The tramway's first six passenger cars, built in 1902, were open-top double-deckers Nos 1-4 and single-deck combination cars 5 and 6; these were joined in 1903 by Nos 7 and 8 (two more open-toppers). All the cars – and the two locos – were from Milnes and the depot was at Carn Brea, west of the hamlet of Pool roughly two-thirds of the way along the line from Redruth's West End terminus. The Camborne terminus, at the western end of the line, was in Trelowarren Street, the idea of reaching as far as the town's railway station having been abandoned early on.

Cambridge Street Tramways

Authority: Cambridge Street Tramways Act 1879
Gauge: 4ft
Traction: Horse
Opened: 28 October 1880

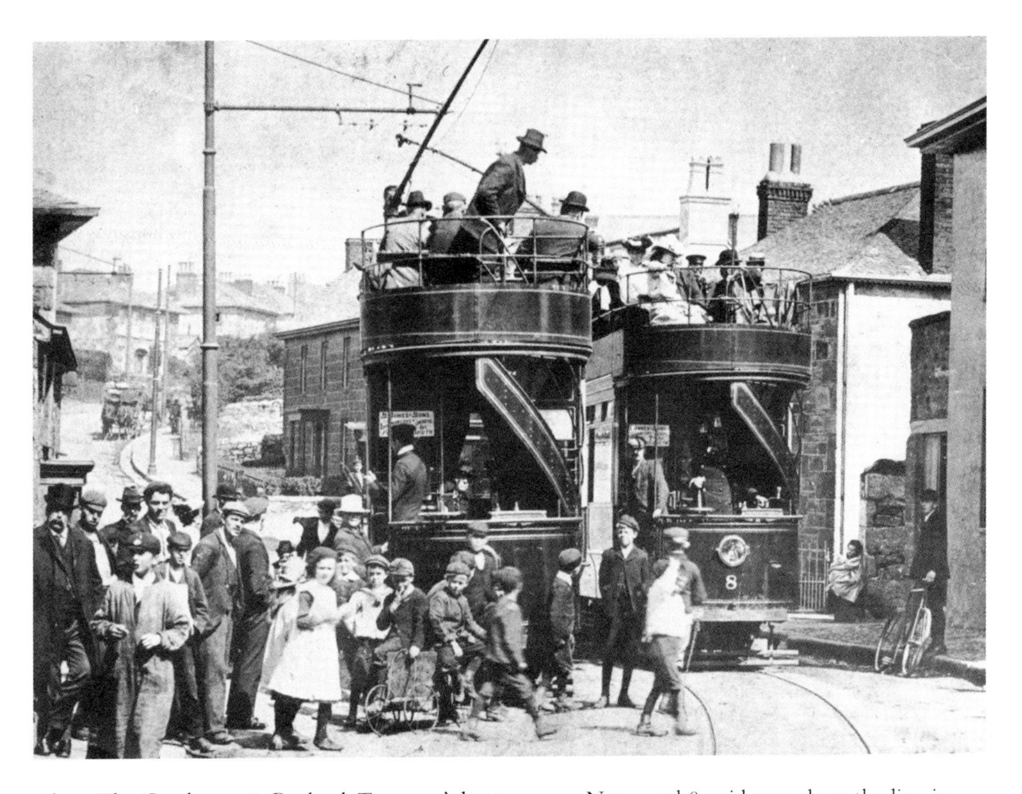

Above: The Camborne & Redruth Tramway's last two cars, Nos 7 and 8, mid-way along the line in the hamlet of Pool in the summer of 1903, shortly after these last two cars had been delivered to Cornwall's only tramway. Here the line was double-tracked for a short distance. *(Author's collection)*

Opposite: Edwardian trade advertisement for the British Thomson-Houston Co. Ltd.

Left: An enlargement of part of a postcard showing Camborne & Redruth No. 2 of 1902 in Roskear, near Camborne. Note the postbox next to the headlamp on the dash: a number of tramways offered this service to passengers (and others) whereby letters could be posted on the cars for onward sorting by the Royal Mail. *(Author's collection)*

Opposite above: Like other commercial concerns of the time, tramway companies issued decorative share certificates to investors, this example being one from the Cambridge Street Tramways Co. Today they are collectable items in their own right.

Closed: 18 February 1914
System: Cross
Length: 2.69 miles
Stock: 4 sd, 4 dd
Livery: Red & cream
Last Car: ?

Apart from the exceptional length of its main platform, the principal claim to fame of Cambridge's railway station is that it was built more than a mile from the city centre, at the insistence of the University authorities. Consequently, with the development of horse tramways, it was inevitable that sooner rather than later a proposal would be made to lay one to bridge that gap. In fact, two separate proposals were made, with that of the Cambridge Street Tramways Co. succeeding.

The first section of line opened ran from the station down Station Road, into Hills Road and then Regent Street to terminate outside the Post Office opposite Christ's College. In November 1880 a branch from the Hills Road/Regent Street junction (Hyde Park Corner) opened to Market Hill via Lensfield Road and Trumpington Street, quickly followed by a branch from Hyde Park Corner in the opposite direction along Gonville Place to East Road (and the depot), thus forming a simple + pattern thereafter worked as two separate routes. Both lines were single-track, except for a short stretch in Hills Road.

Proposed extensions to outlying parts of the city never materialised, nor did those for other routes through the city centre – opposed on account of the narrowness of the streets. Equally fruitless were the BET-backed proposals to electrify the tramway before it became an early casualty of motor bus competition. (In this and many other respects the system bore a striking similarity to that at OXFORD.)

No. 197

STC

THE
Cambridge Street Tramways Company

INCORPORATED BY THE CAMBRIDGE STREET TRAMWAYS ACT 1879
WHEREBY THE LIABILITY OF THE SHAREHOLDERS IS LIMITED TO THE AMOUNT OF THEIR SHARES

SHARE CERTIFICATE.

This is to Certify that Charles Finch Foster
of Mill Lane Cambridge
is the Proprietor of Ten Shares of £10 each
numbered 350 to 359 inclusive in The Cambridge
Street Tramways Company, subject to the Rules and
Regulations of the said Company.

Given under the Common Seal of the said Company
this 26th day of July 1881

Director.

Josiah Chater Secretary.

A locally-produced postcard poking gentle fun at Cambridge's tramways, out-moded even in 1905 (when this card was posted), some nine years before the system closed. *(Author's collection - compare with the similar Oxford example on p.139.)*

Another humorous Cambridge postcard, this time marking the demise of the horse trams. Such occasions were often marked locally by the publication of postcards, cartoon or photographic, of a semi-serious mourning aspect. *(Author's collection)*

Full details of the car fleet are not known, but it appears that the tramway operated a total of eight cars during its life, commencing services with double-deckers 1 and 4 and single-deckers 2 and 3 (both later converted to double-deckers). Prior to 1892 another two single-deckers were purchased and numbered 5 and 6; these were followed in 1894 by a Starbuck single-decker (No. 7) and in 1909 by another (No. 8). All eight were sold at auction following the tramway's closure to become garden sheds or whatever else their purchaser chose; the rescued lower saloon of one unidentified car, used as a cobbler's workshop in Ely, is displayed in an unrestored condition at the Ipswich Transport Museum.

Canvey Island Tramways

Authority: --
Gauge: Monorail
Traction: Horse
Opened: 1901
Closed: 1904?
System: Single line
Length: 3.03 miles
Stock: 1 sd?
Livery: ?
Last Car: ?

A superficial reading of the facts would suggest that the Canvey Island tramway was a typical example of its kind: a horse line is laid to serve a seaside property development – business grows and the line is electrified – financial pressures force its eventual closure. However, closer inspection soon reveals that at no time in its life could this line have been considered even faintly typical.

The tramway was promoted as a private venture by Frederick Hester who, at the end of the nineteenth century, was developing Canvey Island, on the Essex bank of the Thames estuary, as a seaside holiday resort and retirement area. In 1901 a horse monorail was laid from the north side of the island (where it connected with the ferry to Benfleet), past the proposed site of the Winter Gardens in the centre of the island and on to the beach at Leigh Beck on the southern coast. The monorail – known as the Mono-metal Tramway – was of the Caillet type whereby only one rail was used. As such it was a true monorail – the rail itself was laid on the ground upon which the tramway's small, open car(s) balanced on small, centrally mounted wheels. A rigid frame on one side of the car held a horse which half-pulled, half-pushed the vehicle along whilst at the same time keeping it upright.

The tramway – the only monorail tramway in the British Isles – was only intended as a stop-gap measure until a 'proper' 3ft 6in. gauge electric line could be laid on the same route as demand for Hester's building plots rose. In February 1904 BPs were contracted to build such a line and four single-deck cars were ordered from Brush. After their arrival at Benfleet station at least one, bearing the legend 'Canvey Island Electric Tramways', was taken to the island for trials on the short length of track and overhead actually installed. Severe flooding that year somewhat dampened would-be investors' ardour though, and the whole scheme collapsed. The electric car(s) went back to Loughborough and, despite being offered elsewhere, apparently the only service any of them saw was when two were used to test another BPs contract, the Llandudno & Colwyn Bay Electric Railway in Wales, before its 1907 opening.

In 1905 the unsold plots of land at Leigh Beck were sold to the Canvey Development Co. Ltd, a concern which also took over the monorail, though it is not known if the car(s) ever ran again. The 30-40ft-wide strip of land it occupied was divided up and sold at the end of the First World War and in 1919 a motor bus service began on the island, killing off any thoughts of a revival of the electric tramway scheme.

Carlton Colville: East Anglia Transport Museum

Run by members of the East Anglia Transport Museum Society, this museum occupies a small rural site outside Lowestoft, its genesis being the 1961 acquisition of LOWESTOFT No. 14 for preservation. A short, working 4ft 8½in. gauge overhead electric tramway was opened in 1972 and later extended as a single-track, out-and-back run some 500 yards in length.

Current stock (operational and non-operational) includes trams from Amsterdam, Blackpool, LONDON, Lowestoft and NORWICH. Buses, trolleybuses (operational) and other period road vehicles are also displayed, plus a short narrow-gauge railway. The museum opens in summer seasons only.

Above: The terminus of the short operational tramway at the East Anglia Transport Museum, Carlton Colville, with the car shed beyond. In service is ex-Blackpool No. 159 of 1927. *(Author)*

Left: An item of tramway-related street furniture at Carlton Colville: a sign warning motorists that the tram track in the centre of the road is about to run close to the kerb. *(Author)*

Opposite: The entrance to Chatham Dockyard, with workers leaving on their lunch-break – many of whom would no doubt use the waiting trams. *(Author's collection)*

Chatham & District Light Railways
Authority: Chatham and District Light Railways Order 1899
Gauge: 3ft 6in.
Traction: Overhead electric
Opened: 17 June 1902
Closed: 30 September 1930
System: Network
Length: 14.98 miles
Stock: 52 dd
Livery: Light green & ivory until 1927, then green & ivory
Last Car: ?

Promoted by the Rochester, Chatham, Gillingham & District Electric Railways Co. Ltd (registered 20 October 1897) to serve the Medway towns of its title, this system was authorised initially in a cut-down form on 17 August 1899 – the day the promoters cut down their name to the more manageable Chatham & District Light Railways Co. (a subsidiary of BTH, who acted as contractors for the project).

The original intention of linking the several towns and villages that make up this important port and dockyard conurbation on both sides of the River Medway was achieved only in stages. The first part opened was centred on Chatham and Gillingham: this was a kite-shaped circuit running from Chatham Town Hall, on the western corner, northwards along Dock Road to Brompton, then south-east to Gillingham High Street, then south to Jezreels Corner on Watling Street where it turned north-eastwards down the steep Chatham Hill back to the Town Hall. A branch ran south from the Town Hall along Railway Street and Maidstone Road to the Cemetery (with a spur to serve the LCDR station), a second branch continued up Dock Road in Brompton to serve the dockyard whilst a third ran along Gillingham High Street to Gillingham Green. A final branch doubled back south-eastwards from the bottom of Chatham Hill to Luton and the High Street depot just short of the terminus. Tracks were mainly double, and the first cars purchased were twenty-five Milnes open-toppers.

An agreement was quickly reached between the Company and Rochester City Council whereby the latter would build its own lines and lease them to the former, and on 22 December 1904 a branch off Railway Street westwards along New Road into Rochester as far as the foot of Star Hill was opened (with through cars running from Gillingham Green). To cope with the expected extra traffic ten Brush open-toppers (Nos 26-35) had been added to the fleet two years previously, and in 1905 five more were bought (Nos 37-41). On 13 May 1906 the line was extended southwards to Delce. (No. 36 was a Milnes car bought in 1903 to replace No. 19, damaged in a runaway accident in Old Brompton on 30 October 1902 and later rebuilt as a works car.)

The next addition to the system came on 25 August 1906 when a 3-mile, mainly reserved single-track extension was opened eastwards from Jezreels Corner alongside the main road to Rainham Mark and Rainham; the following year another five Brush open-toppers (Nos 42-46) were purchased.

On 16 April 1908 the Rochester end of the line was extended, as a double track, along the High Street and across the Medway bridge to a terminus some 200 yards beyond the Coach & Horses on the London Road in Strood Hill, whilst on 17 August a single-track extension of the Delce line to the village of Borstal was opened to complete the system. Two more open-top Brush cars (Nos 47 and 48) were added in 1912 and in 1914 three similar UEC cars joined the fleet (Nos 49-51). Only one other car – No. 52 – was

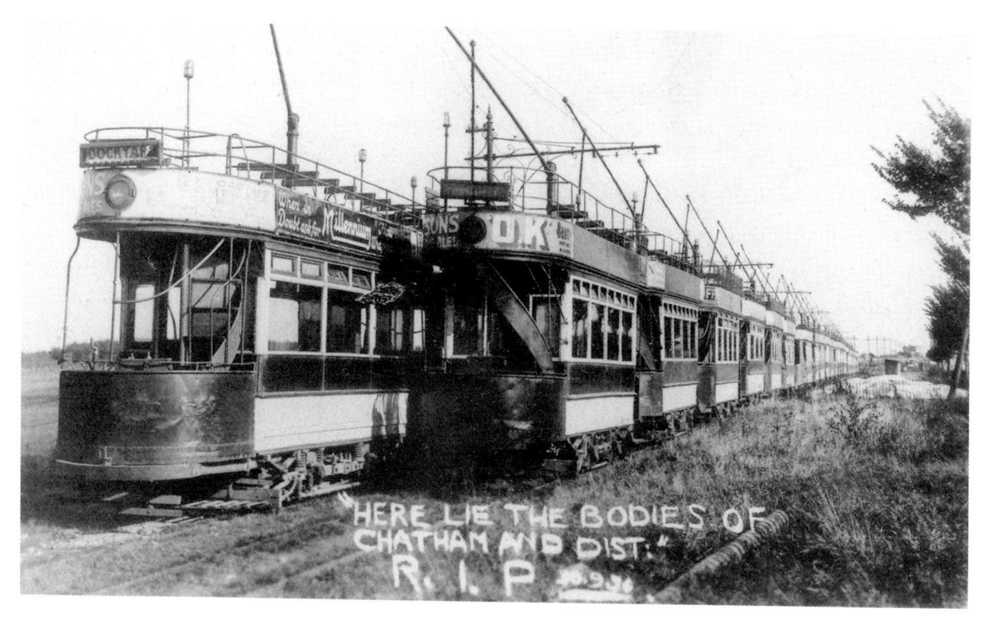

Souvenir postcard issued to mark the last day of services on the Chatham system. Such sights were sadly all too common during the 1930s, when many tramways were forced out of business by competition from other modes of public transport. *(Author's collection)*

thereafter acquired; this was previously MAIDSTONE No. 14, a small UEC 1907 open-topper purchased in 1928 when that system began trolleybus operations.

Inevitably, bus competition after the First World War threatened the existence of the tramway, and in 1927 BTH sold its interest in the Company to the Maidstone & District Motor Services Ltd; two years later the Company obtained the necessary authorisation to close the tramway and run its own buses, which it did from 1 October 1930 onwards.

Cheltenham & District Light Railway

Authority: Cheltenham and District Light Railway Order 1900
Gauge: 3ft 6in.
Traction: Overhead electric
Opened: 17 August 1901
Closed: 31 December 1930
System: Radial
Length: 10.44 miles
Stock: 2 sd, 23 dd
Livery: Dark red to 1903, dark red & dark brown to 1905, then medium lake & cream/primrose
Last Car: ?

The Cheltenham tramway system was promoted by an Irish-American entrepreneur, Thomas Nevins, who formed the Cheltenham & District Light Railway Co. in 1898 and obtained an initial LRO two years later. The first (and longest) route opened ran for nearly 6 miles in a north-easterly direction from the district of Lansdown along the Gloucester Road then past the adjacent Cheltenham stations of the MR and GWR on the Malvern Road. It continued through the town centre by way of St George's Road and St George's Place, past the GWR's Cheltenham St James station (where a one-way loop was soon put in around Ambrose Street, Lower High Street and Clarence Street) then out along Winchester Street and the Prestbury Road to Prestbury. The final part of its journey took it north along Southam Road to the village of that name and then north-east again on sleepered roadside track to the top of Cleeve Hill.

Services began with open-top double-deckers 1-8 from Stephensons, but the opening was overshadowed by a fatal accident on 29 July 1901 when one of the cars ran out of control down the 1:9 Cleeve Hill whilst on trials, and overturned, killing two workmen. The opening of the line was consequently delayed until 17 August, with a temporary terminus at Southam. Thereafter, passengers were not permitted to ride on the upper decks of cars on the hill and in 1902 a pair of single-deckers (Nos 9 and 10) were bought from Gloucester to help out. The system's formal opening ceremony took place on 22 August.

The system's other two routes from the town centre were opened on 28 March 1905 and ran via Bath Road and Leckhampton Road past the GWR's Leckhampton station to the village of that name in the south. It then travelled via the High Street, London Road, Copt Elm Road and the Cirencester Road to Charlton Kings in the south-east, terminating by that village's GWR station. Virtually the whole system was single-track with the depot (St Mark's) situated off the Gloucester Road by Lansdown station.

Cheltenham No. 20 of 1904 approaching the Leckhampton line terminus, on a postcard sent the following year. *(Author's collection)*

Two further Gloucester cars, open-toppers Nos 11 and 12, were added to the fleet in 1902 and two years later they were joined by eight BEC open-toppers (Nos 13-20) which had been bought to work the new routes. No more vehicles were added until 1921 when three EE open-toppers (Nos 21-23) were bought, followed in 1928 by Nos 24 and 25 (ex-Worcester open-toppers Nos 17 and 16), which took over the Leckhampton route services.

Sometime in the early 1920s No. 9 was converted into an open-top double-decker using the appropriate fittings from No. 12, which became a single-decker – as did No. 3 when No. 10 was scrapped about this time (and its number taken by No. 14 in 1927 when that car was rebuilt). No. 19 was similarly renumbered No. 1 the following year.

The Company – which had been taken over in 1914 by BB – decided at the end of the 1920s to replace the trams with trolleybuses, but local authority opposition to this idea resulted in the substitution of motor buses. Services ended quietly with the Cleeve Hill and Leckhampton routes closing in March 1930, the Lansdown-Charlton Kings route followed in the morning of the last day of the year.

Colchester Corporation Tramways

Authority: Colchester Corporation Tramways Order 1901
Gauge: 3ft 6in.
Traction: Overhead electric
Opened: 28 July 1904
Closed: 8 December 1929

Colchester High Street, with No. 3. of 1904 on the double-track section outside the Town Hall. *(Author's collection)*

System: Radial
Length: 5.74 miles
Stock: 18 dd
Livery: Maroon/dark brown & cream
Last Car: ?

The Colchester system was an unremarkable example of a municipally-owned tramway that, when major track and rolling-stock renewals were needed, was abandoned in favour of motor buses. The only real features of interest were that it was promoted slightly later than was usually the case (only after the private construction of a steam tramway had been abandoned in 1883 with ½ mile of track laid) and closed rather earlier than in many other towns.

The original sixteen cars were open-top ERTCW vehicles, joined in 1906 by a similar pair (Nos 17 and 18) from UEC. The first portion of the system opened consisted of a main, double-track axis 1 mile long running due south from the GER's Colchester station down North Station road (where the abortive steam tramway had been laid). From there it continued across the River Colne, then up North Hill past the High Street and into Head Street. Here it turned west to run as a single-track line down Lexden Road and Lexden Street to the suburb of that name. From the main axis a short, double-track section ran due east down the High Street then continued as a single track down East Hill to terminate in East Street just over the river. At the junction of the High Street and East Hill another short stretch of double tracks ran due south down Queen Street to St Botolph's station, then eastwards as a single track out to Hythe, terminating on the city side of the river. A final, single-track branch (the building of which occasioned the purchase of the line's last two cars) opened on 28 January 1906 and ran south-eastwards for ¾ mile from St Botolph's station to the Recreation Ground.

Croydon Tramways

Authority: Croydon Tramways Act 1878
Gauge: 4ft 8½in.
Traction: Horse
Opened: 9 October 1879
Taken over: 22 January 1900
System: Network
Length: 6.79 miles
Stock: 7 sd?, 24 dd?
Livery: Route colour

Formed by a group of local businessmen, the Croydon Tramways Co. began operations in October 1879, running over a single track 1½ miles from the depot at Thornton Heath Pond south along London Road to West Croydon station in North End, using five Starbuck single-deckers. The system was expanded gradually over the next three years, and on 2 August 1883 the Company amalgamated with the Norwood & District Tramways Co., a concern which was constructing a line in South Norwood to the north-east of Croydon. The Croydon & Norwood Tramways Co.'s resulting single-track system eventually resembled a letter Y, with a line from the Red Deer on Brighton Road in South Croydon running north along South End to the Crown (see below). At this point the original line carried on north to Thornton Heath Pond whilst a branch to the east, along George Street, led to East Croydon station and from there north-east through Addiscombe and Woodside to South Norwood. Two link lines and a short branch filled the gap between these two main arms of the network.

Two more Starbuck single-deckers (Nos 6 and 7) had been added to the stock by 1883 when the first double-deckers arrived. Full details of the cars are not available, though by 1897 the number series had reached 31, with all those after No. 7 probably double-deckers from a number of manufacturers. (Steam, oil and battery-electric traction were also experimented with at different times, without lasting success.)

On 25 October 1887 the Company went into liquidation and the system was cut back with the closure of unprofitable routes, and on the first day of 1890 a new concern, the Croydon Tramways Co., took over the line and its fourteen cars. By the end of the decade though, Croydon Corporation had decided to take over the system in order to electrify it, and in 1900 they did so under the provisions of the Croydon Tramways Act of that year (see below).

Croydon Corporation Tramways

Authority: Croydon Corporation Tramways Order 1894
Gauge: 4ft 8½in.
Traction: Horse, overhead electric

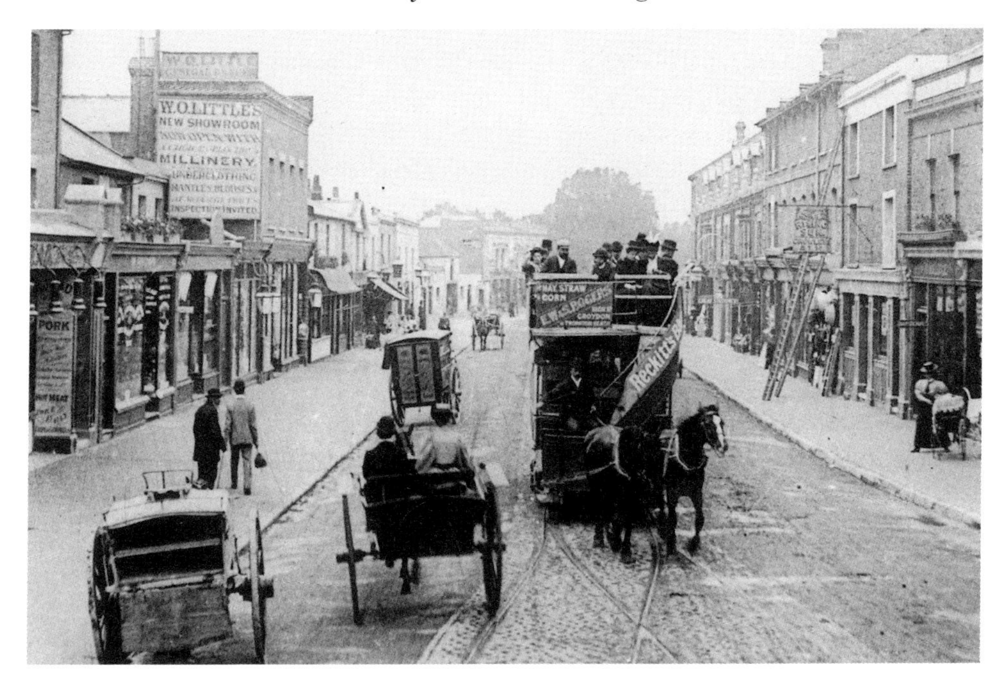

A Croydon double-deck horse car entering a passing loop in London Road. *(Author's collection)*

Took over: 22 January 1900
Taken over: 1 July 1933
System: Radial network
Length: 11.92 miles
Stock: 14? horse; 125 dd electric
Livery: Munich lake & ivory to 1928, then port wine & grey

Croydon Corporation began tramway ownership very modestly, with just 286 yards of track in the High Street linking the CROYDON TRAMWAYS hitherto unconnected sections in North End and South End (see above). This opened on 6 June 1897 and was leased to the Company. Two years later, the Corporation had decided to take over the whole system as soon as it was entitled to do so and lease it to the BET. The price paid was £50,000 and the agreement was signed on 22 January 1900 (though preparatory work on the electrification had already started).

The first section of the new system to be opened, on 26 September 1901, ran from Norbury station near the town's northern boundary, south along the London Road to Thornton Heath Pond (and the rebuilt depot). It then continued along the former horse route through South Croydon and on along the Brighton Road into Purley where it terminated at the town's southern boundary. The first cars were Nos 1-35, open-top double-deckers (as were all the cars) from Milnes, with similar bogie vehicles 36-45 arriving in 1902 as new routes were opened. (These latter cars were owned directly by the BET.) On 10 January 1902 the former horse link line from Thornton Heath Pond north-east to Thornton was reopened, followed on 24 January by the former route to Selhurst (extended on 14 March to South Norwood). The last horse cars were sold by auction on 17 February that year. Later in 1902 Nos 46-55, Milnes bogie cars, were added to the fleet, followed by similar vehicles 56-60, this time from Brush (and again BET-owned). A second depot was provided in Purley to cope with the growing number of cars.

In 1905 the Corporation decided to terminate the BET's lease – it was concerned about the Company's empire-building plans for the surrounding area – with 1 July 1906 as the expiry date. The BET promptly withdrew from the Croydon operation, taking its own trams with it, so to fill the gap the Corporation purchased a series of Brush bogie cars: Nos 36-60 in 1906, 61-70 a year later and 71-75 in 1911 – the last pre-First World War acquisitions.

Further routes were opened and, after relations with the BET's subsidiary the SOUTH METROPOLITAN TRAMWAYS had improved, through-running began on 24 June 1907 across the boundary at South Norwood to Penge High Street, and to the Crystal Palace via Anerley Road. (These two short branches had been built by the BET prior to its split with the Corporation.) On 17 February 1926, after years of negotiations, through-running over LONDON COUNTY COUNCIL metals began at Norbury (where a conduit plough had to be affixed to a Croydon car going through to the Victoria Embankment). The South Metropolitan meanwhile had opened two routes from Tamworth Road, opposite West Croydon station: north-west to Mitcham and on to Tooting, and south-west past Croydon Aerodrome to Sutton.

During 1927-28 a large-scale reorganisation of the car fleet took place. Surviving cars of the 1-35 batch were withdrawn, Nos 46-55 were fitted with top covers and renumbered 21-30, and Nos 43, 44, 62-64, 66, 67 and 69 were sold to the South Met. Nos 41 and 57 were scrapped whilst the remainder of the Brush cars, 36-75, were renumbered 1-20 (though in reverse order). At the same time twenty-five enclosed bogie double-deckers, Nos 31-55, were bought from HN.

On 28 March 1927 the short eastern Addiscombe route was closed and the trams were replaced by London General Omnibus Co. buses. Early in 1933 the track-doubling programme was completed (much of the system was so treated), just in time for the 1 July takeover by LONDON TRANSPORT.

Croydon: Tramlink

Authority: Croydon Tramlink Act 1994
Gauge: 1.435m.
Traction: Overhead electric
Opened: 10 May 2000
System: Branching
Length: 28.2km
Stock: 24sd
Livery: Red & white, some cars with overall adverts

Southern England's newest tramway, Tramlink is the happy outcome of a 1987 study (updated in 1990) into the transport needs of the Croydon and New Addington area. Authorised in 1994, preliminary preparation work began in the autumn of 1996 with

Southern England's newest tramway: Croydon Tramlink's western terminus inside Wimbledon railway station, with car No. 2538 at the buffer stop. Note the re-modelled railway platform edge catering for the narrower tramcars. *(Author)*

construction work commencing early the following year. Three years later it was ready to open, the completed system comprising roughly equal portions of street sections (with grooved rails set in concrete slabs) and refurbished former BR lines – still in use when conversion work began with the last trains between Wimbledon and Croydon running on 31 May 1997. The first test of a tram under power took place on 16 June two years later, though hopes of a November 1999 opening had to be abandoned.

The primarily double-track system is made up of three service routes, all with rail interchanges at their terminals and at some intermediate stops. Line 1 runs from Wimbledon station south-east to West Croydon, where there is a counter-clockwise circle known as the Centre Loop in the town centre, then on eastwards through East Croydon to Elmers End. Line 2 follows Line 1 east from the Centre Loop to just before Elmers End where it leaves to turn north then east to terminate at Beckenham Junction, while Line 3 runs from the Centre Loop to New Addington, turning south-east off Line 1 just beyond East Croydon. The route lengths are: Wimbledon to West Croydon – 9.4kms, Centre Loop – 4.2kms, the Elmers End/Beckenham Junction branch – 7kms and the New Addington branch – 7.6kms. The three routes opened on different days, in reverse order, with Centre Loop to New Addington being the first, Centre Loop to Beckenham Junction the second (23 May) and Wimbledon to Elmers End last of all, on 30 May. Possible extensions, at the time of writing, are envisaged to Crystal Palace and into Sutton.

The scheme was promoted jointly by LONDON TRANSPORT and the London Borough of Croydon, under the aegis of the government's Private Finance Initiative Scheme. The construction was (and operation is) by Tramtrack Croydon Ltd, a consortium

Croydon Tramlink No. 2538 again, this time at Dundonald Road, the first stop out from Wimbledon on the former BR alignment. *(Author)*

made up of the Royal Bank of Scotland (project finance), Sir Robert McAlpine and Amey Construction (construction joint venture), CentreWest Buses, a subsidiary of FirstBus (responsible for operation and maintenance), and Bombadier Eurorail (also maintenance), using a host of sub-contractors. Bombadier Eurorail also suppplied the tramway's fleet of three-section, six-axle articulated cars, all built at its Vienna works in 1998-99 to a Continental design. Fittingly, not only do these carry an up-dated version of the old London Transport tramway livery, but they also continue that body's numbering sequence (from 2530 to 2553). Each unit's theoretical passenger capacity is 208, though figures of more than 300 have been recorded during the rush hour! The one depot is at Therapia Lane, on the Wimbledon line.

The total estimated cost of getting the project up and running was some £200 million, with the government paying about £125 million and TCL the remainder. The first full year of service – 2001 – saw 18 million passengers carried, exceeding the promoters' original expectations. By 2005 the figure was 22 million.

Dartford Hospitals Tramway

A private 4ft gauge tramway once served the Long Reach, Orchard and Joyce Green isolation hospitals sited on the marshes between Dartford and the Thames estuary. It was built in 1897 by the Metropolitan Asylums Board and ran from a loading stage on the river, through Long Reach Hospital on the bank then across a causeway to serve the other two sites. The line was single-track with various branches added throughout its life as the whole complex evolved from the temporary huts of the 1890s to the permanent buildings of the 1900s, making for a total track length of 3.4 miles.

The system was apparently used only for the carriage of coal and other goods, not patients, until 27 February 1902 when four second-hand HARROW ROAD & PADDINGTON TRAMWAYS single-deck horse cars (Nos 5-8) were put into service to cope with the influx of patients caused by a smallpox epidemic, followed in 1905 by a purpose-built ERTCW single-deck ambulance tram (No. 1). Four similar vehicles (Nos 3-6) were added in 1909 (from UEC). Also in 1902, four double-deck steam trailers were acquired – two from Burnley and two from Huddersfield – but, being of the wrong gauge and far too heavy for horse-haulage, these were removed from their bogies and used as shelters in the hospital grounds.

The original cars 5-8 are thought to have been withdrawn from service in 1906 (Nos 5 and 6), 1925 (No. 8) and 1931 (No. 7); horse traction ceased in 1925 and from then on the surviving cars were towed by Talbot motor ambulances. Regular services ceased in October 1930 though the system saw occasional use until (probably) 1936, the surviving tramcars being sold after the system was formally closed two years later. The rails were lifted in 1943 to help with the war effort.

Dartford Urban District Council Light Railways

Authority: Dartford and District Light Railways Order 1902
Gauge: 4ft 8½in.
Traction: Overhead electric
Opened: 14 February 1906
Taken over: 1 July 1933
System: Radial
Length: 6.55 miles
Stock: 1 sd, 12 dd
Livery: Maroon/chocolate & cream/yellow

Although constructed and originally operated by the firm of J.G. White & Co. Ltd, this small system was owned by Dartford UDC, who leased it out to BB from 1909. It was essentially a single-track line running from the municipal boundary with BEXLEY in the west through Crayford to Dartford where it turned north-east along the Dover Road to the district of Horns Cross. A short branch in Dartford ran northwards to the SECR station and the depot whilst a slightly longer one ran south to the village of Wilmington.

The original passenger fleet comprised UEC open-top double-deckers 1-12 of 1905, which were joined in 1915 by an MV demi-car 13 purchased from ERITH. Two years later, on the Bank Holiday of 7 August 1917, the depot burned down and all thirteen cars were destroyed. Temporary replacement vehicles were provided by Bexley UDC (the wartime importance of the local munitions industry saved the tramway from closure), an authority which operated the line on behalf of BB until 1921 when the latter's lease ran out. From April 1921 the two UDCs operated both systems as a joint enterprise under the Bexley Council Tramways and Dartford Light Railways Joint Committee, with through-running to Woolwich. This state of affairs lasted until 1 July 1933 when both were taken over by LONDON TRANSPORT – who closed them in favour of trolleybuses two years later.

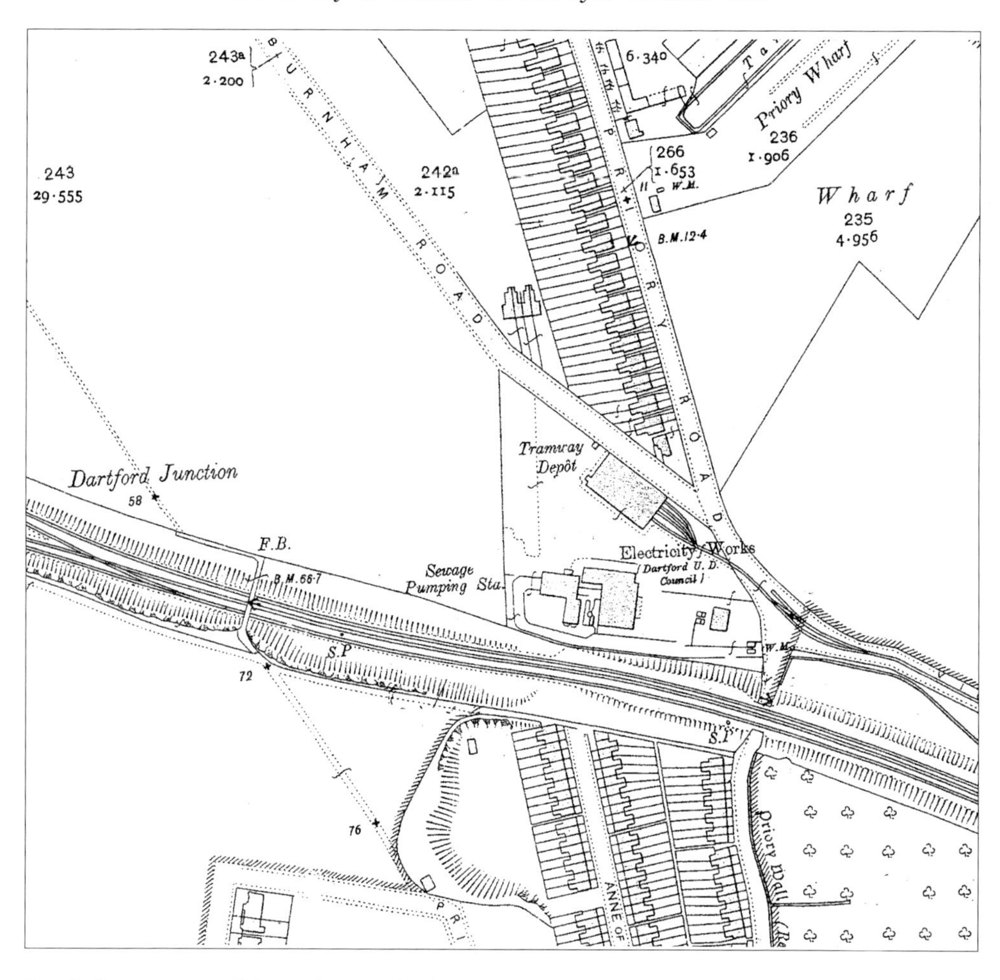

Dartford's Victoria Road depot, destroyed by fire in 1917, on the 1909 Ordnance Survey 25" to 1 mile map.

Deptford *see* London, Deptford & Greenwich

Devonport & District Tramways

Authority: Devonport Corporation Tramway Order 1899
Gauge: 3ft 6in.
Traction: Overhead electric
Opened: 26 June 1901
Taken over: 20 October 1915
System: Network
Length: 9.2 miles
Stock: 33 dd
Livery: Chocolate & cream/yellow to 1915, then sage green & cream

The last of the three tramway companies to begin operations in the PLYMOUTH area, the Devonport & District Tramways Co. Ltd (registered 1898) was part of the BET group and had the advantage over the others of starting out with an electric system. Initial authorisation was for 5 miles of routes within the borough boundaries, from the town centre west to Morice Town, north through South Keyham, North Keyham and Keyham to Camel's Head, north-east to the depot at Milehouse, and east to Victoria Park. To work the line twenty open-top double-deckers were ordered from Brill.

In 1902 five Brush open-toppers (Nos 21-25) were purchased, followed later by eight similar Brush cars obtained second-hand from the City of Birmingham Tramways, Nos 26-29 of 1904 (delivered in the winter of 1910/11) and Nos 30-33 of 1902 (No. 30 being originally a SHEERNESS car) delivered a year later. Meanwhile, in 1900 Devonport Corporation, wishing to see the system extended, had obtained powers for another 4 miles of lines to Tor Lane, Peverell and Saltash Passage and, having constructed the last two routes, leased them to the D&D. The line from North Keyham east to Milehouse and Peverell was connected to the main system but the Saltash Passage route to Camel's Head, just north of Keyham, was not. This was largely because a wooden bridge over Weston Mill Creek would not support the cars; this isolated section was worked for a short while by Nos 20 and 24 from a small depot at Camel's Head until a connecting embankment was built.

In October 1914 the Plymouth local authority area was enlarged to include Devonport and the D&D was then purchased by PLYMOUTH CORPORATION, the final takeover coming twelve months later.

Dover Corporation Tramways

Authority: Dover Corporation Tramways Order 1896
Gauge: 3ft 6in.
Traction: Overhead electric
Opened: 6 September 1897
Closed: 31 December 1936
System: Branching
Length: 4.29 miles
Stock: 45 dd
Livery: Medium green & ivory to 1920, emerald green & ivory to 1927, then dark red & ivory*
Last Car: No. 10

In layout, the municipally-owned and operated Dover system formed a crooked Y with its two branches meeting in the town centre from where a single line ran first down to the harbour, then along its boundary. It was constructed by DK, and originally ran northwards from the shore end of the Admiralty Pier (Clarence Place) via Strond Street, Snargate Street and Northampton Street, then north-west away from the harbour via Bench Street to the Market Place. From there it continued through the town by way of Biggin Street, High Street and London Road as far as Buckland Bridge (where it crossed the River Dour); a branch from Biggin Street ran south-west along the Folkestone Road to Maxton. Total route length was just over 3 miles – virtually all single track – and, unusually for such a small system, there was a depot at the end of each northern branch.

Dover Corporation No. 18 of 1905, with its proudly-posing crew. *(Author's collection)*

Ten Brush open-top cars, Nos 1-10 (of which 8 and 10 ran as trailers for a few months), were ordered for the opening, the date of which made the line an electric pioneer in southern England. Six similar cars were purchased in 1898, Nos 11-14 from Milnes and Nos 15 and 16 from Brill. By this time the system had undergone its first route change with the abandonment of 200 yards or so of track at the Admiralty Pier end of the line. (This section only opened at the beginning of 1898 and was closed in April of that year to avoid trams being held up at a level crossing over the railway line on to the pier there; from then on services started at Strond Street by the LCDR's Dover Harbour Station.) In 1902 another open-topper (No. 17) was bought, this time from ERTCW.

In 1905 the Buckland route was extended for just over a mile up Crabble Hill, down Crabble Road and thence over a private right of way to the village of River. The opening of this new double-track section took place on 2 October; part of the purpose of its construction was to alleviate local unemployment. At the same time four further ERTCW open-toppers (Nos 18-21) were purchased and these were followed in 1912 by three similar Brush cars (Nos 22-24).

In 1920 the line's last new open-toppers, from EE, were bought and numbered 25-27; thereafter second-hand vehicles were obtained as replacements for its older cars, these being Nos 8 and 9 in 1926 (formerly Darlington 17 and 18 of 1913), Nos 1-5 in 1927 (West Hartlepool 1-5 of 1913), Nos 11 and 12 in 1928 (Birmingham & Midland 15 and 17 of 1915), Nos 6, 7, 10, 14 and 17 in 1930 (B&M, again, of 1904) and lastly Nos 19-22 in 1933 (Birmingham Corporation of 1905, which retained their Birmingham blue and cream livery at Dover).

In 1936 the trams gave way to bus competition after the East Kent Road Car Co. Ltd reached a financial agreement with the Corporation allowing it to operate within the town.

Dulwich *see* London, Camberwell & Dulwich

East Anglia Transport Museum *see* Carlton Colville: East Anglia Transport Museum

East Ham Corporation Tramways
Authority: East Ham Improvement Act 1898
Gauge: 4ft 8½in.
Traction: Overhead electric
Opened: 22 June 1901
Taken over: 1 July 1933
System: Branching
Length: 8.34 miles
Stock: 76 dd
Livery: Chocolate & cream*

The municipally-owned tramway system of East Ham was the central one of a close group of five in south-west Essex, close to London. In layout, it comprised a main north-south route from Wanstead Park Avenue (by the City of London Cemetery) running along Forest Drive through Manor Park, the High Street (North and South) through East Ham itself to Beckton. From there it carried on via Manor Way to a terminus in Cyprus Place just short of the Woolwich boundary by the Royal Albert Dock. Running east from this main line were branches from Manor Park Broadway along Romford Road to Ilford Hill to connect with the ILFORD system, and from East Ham Town Hall along Barking Road to connect with the BARKING tramways. Opposite branches west from Manor Park Broadway and the Town Hall formed connections with the WEST HAM system at Green Street (and through it to LEYTON in the north), as did a central, parallel branch running from the Burnell Arms on High Street North along Plashet Grove.

Services began with DK open-top cars 1-15, quickly joined by Nos 16-20, over the completed sections of Beckton-Manor Park, Broadway-Ilford and Barking boundary-West Ham Town Hall, some 4½ route miles in all. The depot was in Nelson Street by the Town Hall and the routes were a mixture of single and double tracks (although most of the single sections were later doubled). The northern ¾ mile from Manor Park Broadway to the Cemetery opened on 24 March 1902 and that year DK supplied car Nos 21-30, again open-top double-deckers. That November the Plashet Grove route opened, whilst in March 1903 the main line was extended slightly past the Cemetery to Wanstead Park Avenue at the northern end, and from Beckton to Cyprus Place in the south. Later that year similar DK cars Nos 31-35 arrived, after which a top-covering programme was begun.

In 1905 top-covered cars 36-40 were bought from DK and on 17 November that year the service to Barking was extended over that Corporation's metals to Barking station. This left the Manor Park Broadway-West Ham section to be added to the system. This section had been worked (as a through-route from Stratford up to February 1905) by the NORTH METROPOLITAN TRAMWAYS as a horse line; now only the section within East Ham remained, and in 1908 the Corporation purchased it for £8,000 and reopened it that June for electric working. Through-running with West Ham and LONDON

COUNTY COUNCIL saw car Nos 17, 19 and 21-33 adapted for the latter's conduits, as were DK top-covered Nos 41-45 of 1910. Car No. 46 was ex-Barking No. 9, purchased in 1915 (and which retained its old livery), whilst Nos 47-52 and 37-40 were top-covered Brush vehicles of 1921 (when scrappings had begun). Brush 51-60 were top-covered bogie cars of 1927, also equipped for dual working, with similar cars 61-70 joining the fleet in 1928, five years before LONDON TRANSPORT absorbed it.

Eastbourne Electric Tramway

This miniature tramway was the previous incarnation of the SEATON TRAMWAY, operating before that line and after the one at Rhyl (see Volume 2). With the move from Wales in 1953-54 to a larger site, a wider gauge of 2ft was chosen to allow the construction of more spacious cars. The new line was laid at Princes Park, Eastbourne, with a single track running from a terminus at Royal Parade to the Crumbles (part of the route having been used for a short demonstration line in September 1953 for the benefit of local Councillors and Chief Officers whose permission was needed to construct the tramway).

The line was constructed by Claude Lane's company, Modern Electric Tramways Ltd, during 1954-55 with the first section opening on 4 July 1954 and the official opening the following Whitsun. Two new cars were built to help Rhyl Nos 3 (Edwardian-style open-topper) and 225 (Blackpool 'Boat'), both regauged from 15in to work the line. The new cars were also based on Blackpool prototypes: No. 226 (another 'Boat') and No. 238 (a model of a 'Balloon' but without the internal upper floor). Further cars were to

The Eastbourne miniature tramway depot, with (from left to right) Nos 226 of 1954, 238 of 1955 and 6 of 1956. Note that although technically miniature in scale, No. 6 still manages to dwarf its crew. *(Author's collection)*

Eastbourne No. 6 again, this time underway on the tramway's pleasant little out-and-back run. *(Author's collection)*

follow: freelance design bogie open-toppers Nos 6 (1956) and 7 (1958), and No. 4 in 1961, another 'Boat'. These last three cars all incorporated parts such as seats and controllers from withdrawn British full-sized tramcars.

By 1958 the track had reached its final limit at the borough boundary (1 mile in all) and, although MET's five-year concession was extended, it became clear that the local authority's plans might affect the tramway – and so it proved when, in 1967, formal notice was given that the line would be severed by a new roadway. The Company accordingly began looking for yet another site, the search resulting in the removal of the whole operation to Seaton after its closure on 14 September 1969, at the end of its last summer season. The last car built for Eastbourne, in 1968, was No. 8 – similar in design to Nos 6 and 7 but a larger, narrow-gauge rather than miniature vehicle built with conversion to 2ft 9in. gauge in mind.

Erith Urban District Council Tramways

Authority: Erith Tramways and Improvement Act 1903
Gauge: 4ft 8½in.
Traction: Overhead electric
Opened: 26 August 1905
Closed: 9 November 1935
System: Branching
Length: 4.7 miles
Stock: 2 sd, 19 dd
Livery: Apple green & primrose to 1917, then dark red & ivory*
Last Car: ?

Erith's 'First Tram' inaugurating the municipal system, with the official party of dignitaries – and their wives – in proud attendance at the depot. *(Author's collection)*

This system was promoted by Erith UDC to link the Thameside towns of north-east Kent with the LONDON COUNTY COUNCIL system at Plumstead, some 3 miles to the west. However, the completed version was somewhat more modest; it comprised a double-track main line from the end of Erith High Street which ran along West Street, Lower Road and Abbey Road, only as far as the UDC boundary at Abbey Wood (which the LCC reached with its own extension from Plumstead in 1908).

From Erith the main line continued in the other direction as a mainly single-track route south-westwards down Walnut Tree Road (past the depot) and the Bexley Road to meet the BEXLEY system at Northumberland Heath (with an end-on connection to permit through-running). A ½-mile mainly double-track branch from the Erith end of Bexley Road running south to North End completed the system; services to both the other terminals started from here.

To work the tramway fourteen double-deck cars were purchased from Brush in 1905: Nos 1-6 and 9 were open-topped and Nos 7, 8 and 10-14 were balcony cars. It quickly became obvious that it was better to work the system as a single route from Abbey Wood to Northumberland Heath, with a shuttle service from Erith to North End (commencing 18 September 1905). To make further economies on this latter section two MV single-deck demi-cars (Nos 15 and 16) were bought in March 1906, but the route still proved unprofitable and services were reduced, until 31 August 1910 when they were withdrawn altogether. In 1915 No. 15 was sold to DARTFORD and No. 16 to Doncaster Corporation. However, by then the boom in the local munitions industry brought on by the outbreak of war had produced an upsurge in traffic (and the tramway's first profit), and four 1902 Milnes open-top cars were hired in 1915 from LONDON UNITED

TRAMWAYS to help cope with the increasing demand. In 1919 these were purchased outright and renumbered 15-18 (LUT 187, 192, 221 and 252); in 1916 ex-Hull balcony car No. 101 was bought (and later renumbered 19). This car retained its Hull colours of maroon and cream which, in 1917, were closely matched by a new Erith livery.

After the war the tramway's losses began again and bus competition became serious, leading to the demise of the system as an independent concern when it was taken over by LONDON TRANSPORT from 1 July 1933 for just £4,667. For the rest of their operational lives the formerly separate tramways of Erith, Bexley and Dartford were operated as a single entity. Only then, on 18 December 1933, was the long-awaited connection at Abbey Wood made when a short link was laid to facilitate stock movements. Less than two years later the whole route from Abbey Wood to Bexleyheath closed, to be replaced by a trolleybus service.

Exeter Corporation Tramways

Authority: Exeter Tramways Act 1881
Gauge: 3ft 6in.
Traction: Horse/overhead electric
Opened: 6 April 1882
Closed: 19 August 1931
System: Radial
Length: 4.95 miles
Stock: 8 sd, 4 dd horse; 37 dd electric
Livery: Chocolate & yellow horse; dark green & cream to 1925, then light green & cream electric
Last Car: No. 14

The Exeter system began life as a private concern with three single-deck cars operated by the Exeter Tramway Co. over a ½-mile route running eastwards from the Bude Hotel, at the northern end of the High Street, along Paris Street to the Diocesan Training College in Heavitree Road. In 1883 the line was extended northwards across the High Street and along New North Road to the GWR's Exeter St David's station, and eastwards from the High Street out along Sidewell Road to Pinhoe Road. All lines (totalling just 2.34 route miles) were single-track and the depot was in New North Road. Three more single-deckers were bought to help work the new routes, followed by another pair a year later.

In 1896 two replacement double-deck cars were purchased for the tramway – now operated by the Tramway Purchase Syndicate – and another two in 1900 from PLYMOUTH CORPORATION TRAMWAYS, though by now the steep and winding St David's line had been closed as too expensive to maintain. The Company was in fact having financial problems all round and in 1899 offered the system to the Corporation; after much negotiation a price of £6,749 was agreed and ownership was transferred on 1 February 1904. The Corporation immediately put in hand extension and electrification plans with the last horse and the first electric trams both running on 4 April 1905. The new car fleet comprised Nos 1-12 (open-top double-deckers from ERTCW) and Nos 14 and 15 (similar cars from UEC); these were followed by another six from UEC the next year (Nos 16-21).

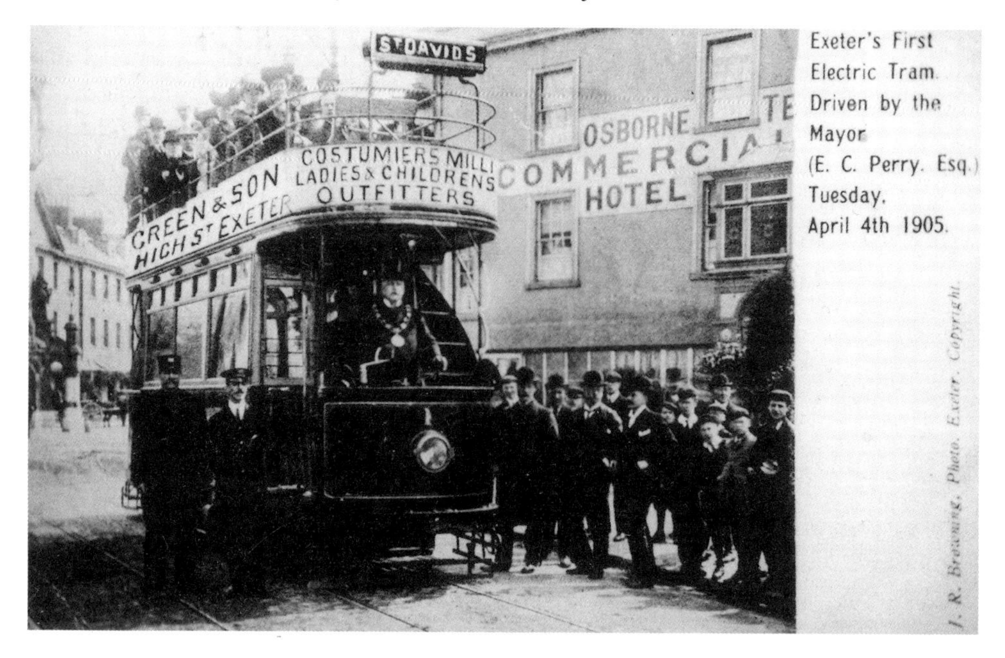

Commemorative postcard of Exeter Corporation's first electric tramcar, No. 1, inaugurating the new service. *(Author's collection)*

New routes ran from St David's station to the High Street via Queen Street (the old New North Road section having been abandoned), and from the Guildhall at the southern end of the High Street out east along Heavitree Road. This latter route was extended further: to the Cross Park Terrace/Fore Street junction in Heavitree and, at the other end, westwards across the River Exe on a new bridge, past the GWR's Exeter St Thomas station to just past the football ground in Cowick Street. The depot for the electric cars was at the junction of Paris Street and Heavitree Road.

On 22 September 1906 the last branch opened, from just south of the river bridge out south along the Alphington road to Stone Lane. All routes were mainly single tracks, with short sections of double or interlaced track.

The car fleet stayed unchanged until 1914 when replacement cars 22-25 were supplied by Brush, followed after the First World War by Nos 26 and 27 in 1921, Nos 28-30 in 1925, Nos 31-34 in 1926 and Nos 1-4 in 1929. All of these cars were open-toppers from the same firm (with some of the original cars then being renumbered). By this time though, the inevitable bus competition was making itself felt, and in April 1929 the Corporation entered the bus business itself and made that its transport priority. In April 1931 cars 26-34 were sold to PLYMOUTH and (Brush replacement cars) 1-4 to Halifax before the system closed later that summer.

Car No. 21 (previously 19 of 1906) now runs in a new guise at SEATON.

Fareham *see* Gosport & Fareham

Farnborough *see* Aldershot & Farnborough

The opening of Exeter's last route, on 22 September 1906, with new UEC open-toppers bearing assorted dignitaries. *(Author's collection)*

Felixstowe Pier Railway

Not a tramway but a 3ft 6in. gauge centre rail electric railway, the Felixstowe Pier Railway opened with the ½-mile pier in August 1905 operated by the Coast Development Co. Ltd (a concern which operated a similar line on the pier at Walton-on-the-Naze just down the coast). It was eventually closed on the outbreak of the Second World War; the original stock comprised two powered cars and one trailer, all roofed toastracks mounted on Peckham trucks. The railway is included here because in 1926 an ex-IPSWICH CORPORATION TRAMWAYS double-decker was purchased (delivered minus its top-deck fittings), this being Brush-built No. 34 of 1904 vintage; the body became a waiting room at the pier head and its truck was used as a replacement for one from a powered car. The other two cars were scrapped five years later. After closure the pier was irrevocably damaged by the sea and following the end of the war it was demolished completely to make way for a shorter, concrete structure; the fate of the ex-Ipswich body and truck is unknown.

Folkestone, Hythe & Sandgate Tramways

Authority: Folkestone, Sandgate and Hythe Tramways Act 1884
Gauge: 4ft 8½in.
Traction: Horse, mule
Opened: 18 May 1891
Closed: 30 September 1921
System: Branching
Length: 3.36 miles

Stock: 5 sd
Livery: SER carriage lake
Last Car: ?

The idea of linking the south Kent coastal resorts of Hythe and Sandgate with a tramway was first mooted seriously in 1880 and four years later an Act was obtained for a horse-worked standard gauge line. Further Acts followed to obtain extra time and alter the route, and it was not until 1889 that construction began. The first completed section ran from the Sandgate School terminus, near St Paul's church, along Sandgate High Street and Esplanade to the Seabrook (now Imperial) Hotel on Hythe sea front. The short completing section into Hythe proper (via South Road, Stade Street and Rampart Road to the Red Lion Square depot) opened on 6 June the following year. A short spur midway along the Esplanade ran up to serve the SER's Sandgate station whilst a longer, ½-mile branch led from Princes Road up Canongate Road to Hythe station. This was never used for passenger traffic though, and had in fact begun life as a standard gauge railway siding laid to help in the construction of Princes Parade (opened in 1883).

In 1893 the SER – which already had a financial interest in the tramway's owner, the Folkestone, Sandgate & Hythe Tramways Co. – purchased the line outright and, for some reason, rearranged the place-names of its title in non-topographical order. Despite the continuing presence of 'Folkestone' in the tramway's name, the short stretch of terrain from Sandgate into that town was considered too steep to permit an extension of the line in that direction, nor was the local authority there willing to countenance such a venture from outsiders. Without the traffic a terminus in Folkestone would have generated, and with increasing competition from firstly horse brakes and then motor buses, it was only a

The Folkestone, Hythe & Sandgate winter saloon No. 3 of 1892, built by the SER. *(Author's collection)*

By way of contrast, the F.H.&S.'s last car, toastrack No. 5 of 1897, also built by the SER and doubtless popular on warm summer days. *(Author's collection)*

matter of time before the tramway was forced to close; this occurred shortly after the end of the First World War with various schemes for electrifying it having come to nothing. (It had already closed for the duration of the war and, reopening for Whitsun 1919, made use of ex-army mules for a while until horses could be obtained. They were not a success, proving true to type in being more than unusually stubborn and wilfully disobedient!) The end came in 1921, the SER bowing to the concerns of Sandgate UDC over the poor state of the track.

The tramway's first two cars were Milnes toastracks (No.1 was roofed from the start and No. 2 from c.1897); these were joined in 1892 by two vehicles built by the SER of which No. 3 was a winter saloon and No. 4 a roofed toastrack. In 1897 the SER supplied the line's last car, No. 5, another open toastrack.

City Of Gloucester Tramways

Authority: Gloucester Tramways Order 1878
Gauge: 4ft
Traction: Horse
Opened: 24 May 1879
Taken over: 1 January 1903*
System: Radial
Length: 3.43 miles
Stock: 16 sd
Livery: ? to 1881, then blue & cream and red & cream

The first Gloucester tramways were promoted by the Gloucester Tramways Co. Ltd, an IMPERIAL TRAMWAYS subsidiary, and worked by six single-deck horse cars (a mixture of closed saloons and roofed summer toastracks). There were five routes radiating from the city's central Cross: north along Northgate Street, Worcester Street and Kingsholm Road to Kingsholm, north-east along Northgate Street and London Road to the Fleece Inn at Wotton, south-east along Eastgate Street and Lower Barton Street to India Road (and the depot), south-west along Southgate Street and Bristol Road as far as Theresa Place, and north-west along Westgate Street as far as St Nicholas' church. A short branch from Eastgate Street served the city's neighbouring GWR and MR stations.

The tramway was not a financial success. The multiplicity of short routes could not have helped matters, and in July 1881 it was sold for £8,000 to a new concern, the City of Gloucester Tramways Co. Ltd. Subsequently both the very short Westgate and stations branches were abandoned. Six new Starbuck cars were bought and two of the old ones withdrawn. Thereafter things improved sufficiently to warrant a short extension, down the Bristol Road to Tuffley Avenue, which opened on 10 July 1897, and a Light Railway Order was applied for in order to extend, and electrify, the whole undertaking.

The electrification proposal was approved by the City Corporation which, on 30 September 1902, purchased the concern for £26,000 in order to carry out the work itself, although the Company continued as operator until the end of the year. (See below.) By now another four cars – believed to have been numbered 11-14 – had been added to the fleet, probably all from the local Gloucester builders. One car, identity unknown, is currently on show in Gloucester Transport Museum whilst undergoing long-term restoration.

Gloucester Corporation Tramways

Authority: Gloucester Tramways Order 1878
Gauge: 3ft 6in.
Traction: Horse/overhead electric
Took over: 1 January 1903
Closed: 11 January 1933
System: Radial network
Length: 9.75 miles
Stock: 14 sd horse; 30 dd electric
Livery: Crimson lake & cream to 1915, then battleship grey*
Last Car: ?

On 9 November 1903 work began on rebuilding the Gloucester horse lines (see above) to the narrow gauge electric 'standard' 3ft 6in. and horse services were slowly curtailed, finishing completely on 17 March the following year. The car fleet by then comprised fourteen open and closed single-deckers, including vehicles from Gloucester and Starbuck.

The rebuilt system – a mixture of single and double-track routes – opened to the public on 29 April 1904 (with an official ceremony on 3 May 1904) with services operated by

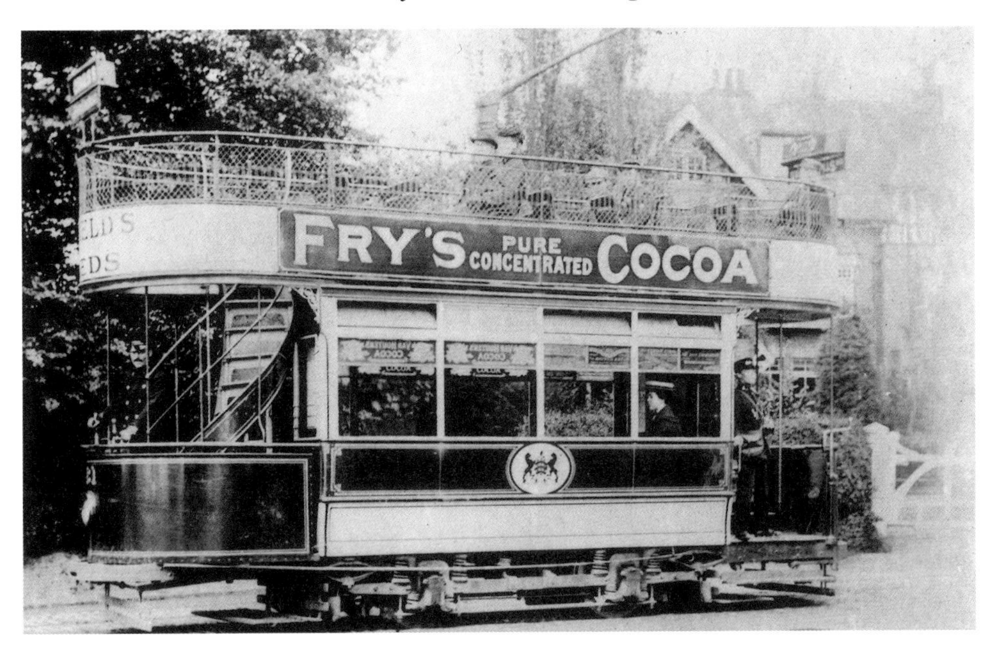

An early shot of Gloucester Corporation No. 21 of 1904, a typical Brush product of the period typifying Edwardian tramcar design. *(Author's collection)*

Brush open-toppers 1-20; these were joined shortly after by another ten similar cars, with no further additions thereafter. (As on many systems, the trams were painted light grey during the First World War as a consequence of restrictions on paint supply but, unlike elsewhere, they were never repainted in their former livery.) All the horse tram routes were rebuilt (the first of these to reopen being the Bristol Road line) with the exception of the stations branch. The following extensions were also laid: Barton Street and Painswick Road to Cemetery Road, and the Westgate Street line as far as the other side of the River Severn. In addition, a branch was laid from the end of Bristol Road where it met Southgate Street along Stroud Road to Reservoir Road, Tuffley (also opened on 29 April), with a link line from it to Barton Street via Parkend Road. These new lines were authorised by the Gloucester Corporation Light Railways Order 1903 whilst the County of Gloucester (Gloucester and Brockworth) Light Railways Order of the same year authorised a 2-mile extension from the Fleece Inn across the city boundary and along Barnwood Road and Ermine Street to Hucclecote. This last line opened on 3 May 1904, with the other routes following by mid-June. Although owned by the County Council, the Hucclecote line was worked by the Corporation as an integral part of the system and was extended in 1917 to serve a new aerodrome at Brockworth; this was laid as a reserved track beside the roadway using the rails from the Westgate Bridge route (which closed on 12 August that year). Although of great importance as it was very busy during the war, it was closed on 1 October 1924 when traffic no longer warranted its staying open. A spur off the London Road to the GWR goods yard was also laid in 1917 to handle war material for the aerodrome, this being transported by car No. 14, specially modified for the purpose.

The next sections to close were the Stroud Road-Barton Street link in 1927 and, on 8 September 1929, the Cemetery Road route. The Corporation had already decided to replace the trams with buses and that same month closed the Kingsholm and Tuffley routes as well, leaving just the Bristol Road-Hucclecote line to survive another few years whilst it still remained profitable.

Gorleston *see* Yarmouth & Gorleston

Gosport & Fareham Tramways

Authority: Gosport Street Tramways Act 1879
Gauge: 3ft/4ft 7¾in.
Traction: Horse/overhead electric
Opened: 17 July 1882
Closed: 31 December 1929
System: Branching
Length: 7.75 miles
Stock: 8 sd, 1 dd horse?; 18 dd electric
Livery: Emerald green & cream (some cars grey & white 1914-18)
Last Car: No. 8

This tramway opened as a single-track, single line operated by the Gosport Street Tramways Co., a subsidiary of PROVINCIAL TRAMWAYS (who already had interests across the harbour in PORTSMOUTH). The first section, of just over 1½ miles, ran from the beach at Gosport Hard westwards past the depot in the High Street, then in a roughly north-westerly direction along Clarence Road and Mumby Road, past the LSWR station and along Forton Road to Ann's Hill. Services were worked by four single-deck cars, joined shortly afterwards by four more.

At the end of January 1883 (or possibly the beginning of February) the line was extended further northwards for 1¼ miles up Brockhurst Road to the junction with Elson Road in Brockhurst, making an official route length of 2.62 miles. In June that year the first double-deck car was put into service, the intention being to eventually replace the single-deckers. Later that year the Company was amalgamated with the various Portsmouth concerns to become part of the Portsmouth Street Tramways Co.

In 1900 Gosport and Alverstoke UDC decided to buy the line, however the Company raised objections although in a remarkable about-turn they offered to sell the line a year later to the UDC, but without success! Undaunted, in 1901 and again in 1903 Provincial obtained Parliamentary approval to electrify and extend the tramway as far as Fareham, under the name Gosport & Fareham Tramways. The first portion opened, on 20 December 1905, was basically the old line, reconstructed to the 4ft 7¾in. gauge of the other Portsmouth-area lines; it is not known when the horse trams ceased to run. There was a remodelled Gosport Hard terminus and a 4-mile, mainly reserved roadside extension at the northern end up the Fareham Road to Hoeford Depot and from there along its continuation, Gosport Road, to Fareham where the line swung west along West Street to terminate by the LSWR station.

Gosport & Fareham No. 11 of 1905 outside Fareham Post Office. Such a location was common as a terminus or stopping place on many tramway systems. *(Author's collection)*

Another postcard view of the G&F, this time of No. 6 of 1905 passing the Hoe Ford Inn, just south of Fareham. *(Author's collection)*

Electric services began with Brush open-toppers 1-12, these being joined by similar MV cars 13-22 in 1906 to help work a 1-mile branch (opened 13 October) running westwards from the end of Gosport High Street along Walpole Road and Stoke Road, then past the LSWR's Gosport Road & Alverstoke station into Foster Road and Bury Road to terminate by the Wiltshire Lamb at Bury Cross. No further routes were opened (though more than half the track was eventually doubled).

Proposals to construct other routes – and even to link the tramway to the Portsmouth system – came to nothing and in late 1929 the Bury Cross branch was closed, as was that part of the main line between Fareham and St Ann's Hill. 1929 also saw the PST Co. change its name to the Gosport & Portsmouth Omnibus Co. before promptly closing the last section of the line in favour of buses. After the closure seven of the cars were transferred to the PORTSDOWN & HORNDEAN LIGHT RAILWAY and six to the Great Grimsby Street Tramways, two other Provincial concerns.

Gravesend, Rosherville & Northfleet Tramways

Authority: Gravesend, Rosherville and Northfleet Tramways Order 1881
Gauge: 3ft 6in.
Traction: Horse, conduit electric*
Opened: 15 June 1883
Closed: 30 June 1901
System: Single line
Length: 2.19 miles
Stock: 5 sd, 4 dd horse; 2 sd electric*
Livery: Various?
Last Car: ?

The first 1½ miles of this grandly-named tramway opened in 1883 as a horse line using five single-deck cars. The operator was the Gravesend, Rosherville & Northfleet Tramways Co. Ltd and the single-track line ran from the depot by the Leather Bottle Inn in Northfleet, eastwards along the London Road past Rosherville station, on the LCDR, to the Clock Tower in King Street, Gravesend. A westwards extension of nearly ¾ mile along Northfleet High Street was authorised in 1884 but not opened until 1889, it having been built by DK as the contractors for the Series Electrical Traction Co. as a demonstration line for the Short-Nesmith system of conduit electricity supply, for which it held the rights. (The system involved the use of positive and negative cables in a conduit, the entrance to which was the gap formed by a bullhead running rail and a second rail laid just inside it; the other running rail was of the usual grooved tramway pattern.) The extension, which ran from the Leather Bottle down The Hill and along the High Street as far as Huggens College opposite Station Road, was supposed to have opened to the general public on 16 April 1889. However, it appears to have been used only for trial runs with school children (possibly from March 1889), and by November 1890 the two electric saloon cars had been replaced by horse trams. Both electric cars were built by Falcon; their subsequent use or disposal is unrecorded.

In 1898 four double-deck horse cars were purchased (probably second-hand) to replace the five single-deckers, two of which were sold the following year to Lincoln;

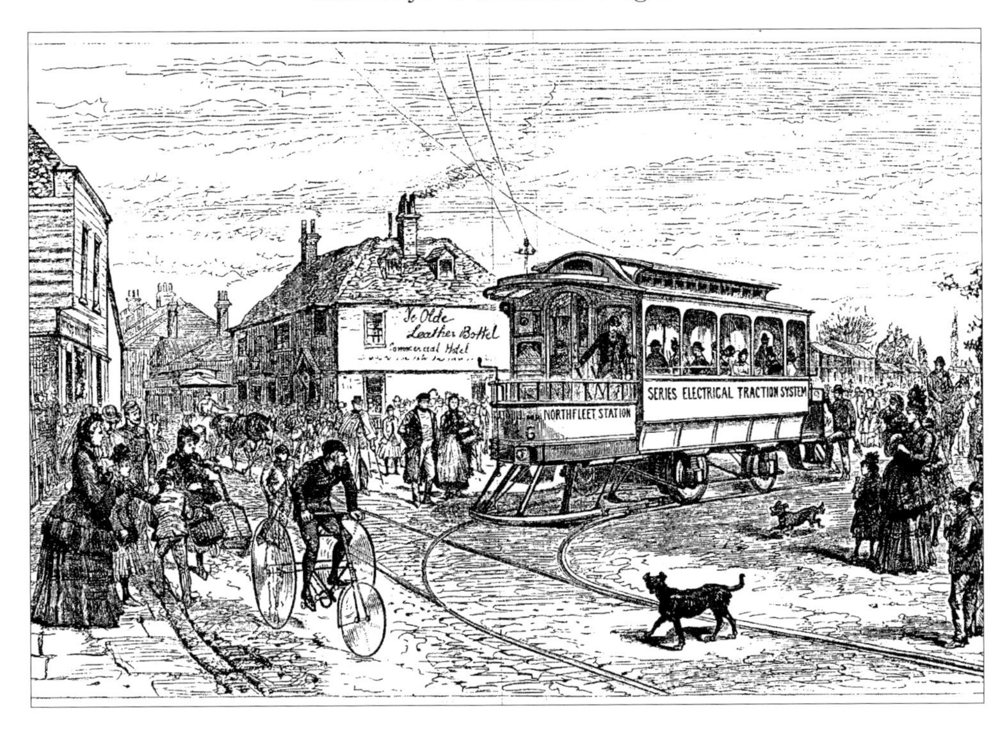

The Series Electrical Traction Co.'s experimental conduit car on the Gravesend, Rosherville & Northfleet line, as drawn for *The Illustrated London News* of 6 April 1899.

1899 also saw the Drake & Gornham Electric Power & Traction Syndicate Ltd acquire a controlling interest in the Company. As implied by the new owner's title, the intention was to electrify the line and also extend it, on a new gauge of 4ft 8½in., to be able to link it with the DARTFORD system. It was resold to the BET on 1 January 1901, and on 18 April of that year the Gravesend & Northfleet Electric Tramways Ltd was registered to build and operate the new line. The old one was then closed shortly after.

Gravesend & Northfleet Electric Tramways

Authority: Gravesend, Rosherville & Northfleet Tramways Order 1899
Gauge: 4ft 8½in.
Traction: Overhead electric
Opened: 2 August 1902
Closed: 28 February 1929
System: Network
Length: 6.47 miles
Stock: 4 sd, 26 dd
Livery: Maroon & cream to 1921, then cherry red & ivory
Last Car: ?

Construction work on the new Gravesend system commenced with the former horse line (see above), the work being carried out by William Griffiths & Co. with the Clock Tower-

Leather Bottle section being the first to reopen. This was followed on 22 September 1902 with extensions eastwards along Milton Road to Denton, westwards along the London Road to Swanscombe, and southwards down Pelham Street in Gravesend. This last line was extended on 30 January 1903, up the Dover Road past the new depot to rejoin the main route at the Leather Bottle. A final 5-furlong section, opened on 4 December 1903, ran from King Street (near the Clock Tower) southwards down Windmill Street to the Old Prince of Orange pub. (The hoped-for link to DARTFORD never materialised, the 1½-mile gap between the two systems being the result of opposition to such a connection by the SECR.)

The original stock comprised twenty ERTCW open-toppers, of which Nos 1-10 were bogie vehicles and 11-20 shorter four-wheelers. However, it soon transpired that the fleet was too large, the bogie cars proved too costly to run for such a small undertaking and four were sold to Swansea in 1904. A further two went to the SOUTH METROPOLITAN two years later, two more to the South Metropolitan in 1907 and the final two to Jarrow in 1909 (precise identities uncertain). Two Brush one-man operated single-decker replacements for use on the Windmill Street and Dover Road routes were bought in 1904 (and given the vacated numbers 9 and 10 in the fleet list). In 1905 replacement Nos 1-4 were obtained from Brush: these were open-top double-deckers followed in 1909 by two slightly smaller Brush cars (Nos 5 and 6) from Jarrow; these had been built in 1906 as Jarrow Nos 5 and 6 (not necessarily respectively).

This restructured fleet ran until 1921 when Nos 9 and 10 were replaced by two ex-TAUNTON single-deckers (renumbered 7 and 8), whilst Nos 15-20 were fitted with top covers.

As an isolated system, with ageing rolling-stock, the Gravesend tramway was no match for the growing number of local bus companies. Indeed it had been running its own bus service under the title North Kent Motor Services since 1913 (merged with the BET's Maidstone & District Motor Services Ltd in 1920), and it came as no surprise when the tramway was taken over by the M&D at the beginning of 1929 as a prelude to its abandonment.

Great Yarmouth *see* Yarmouth

Greenwich *see* London, Deptford & Greenwich

Hanham *see* Bristol

Harrow Road & Paddington Tramways *see* London: Harrow Road & Paddington Tramways

Haslar Hospital Tramway

On Spithead in Hampshire, a 400 yard-long standard gauge private tramway (built in 1877) linked the Haslar Royal Naval Hospital (opened 1753) with a landing stage on Haslar Creek near Gosport. The one tramcar, used to ferry in-coming patients on stretchers up to the hospital, was a four-wheeled single-deck saloon built in 1877 by Metropolitan which, when in use, was manually propelled by six or eight sailors; it was also used to convey visiting senior officers and dignitaries. The tramway is believed to have fallen out of use sometime between the wars. Utilising dual gauge track, an 18in. gauge railway from the hospital took the same route to the shore, where it forked: with one branch going to Fort Blockhouse and the other to the neighbouring Zymotic Wing of the hospital where infectious cases were treated. This line (presumably also manually-powered) was used for transporting materials to repair the sea wall, and also patients to the Zymotic Hospital. These were moved on a vehicle likened to an 'upright piano' – perhaps carrying stretchers stacked vertically? – a practice which appears to have ceased shortly before the outbreak of the First World War.

Hastings & District Electric Tramways

Authority: Bexhill and St Leonard's Light Railway Order 1900; Hastings Tramway Act 1900
Gauge: 3ft 6in.
Traction: Overhead electric, surface-contact, petrol-electric
Opened: 31 July 1905
Closed: 15 May 1929
System: Network
Length: 17.78 miles
Stock: 65 dd
Livery: Maroon & cream
Last Car: ?

The first of the two main components of the Hastings tramway layout was the Circle, a long, circular route which ran inland from Hastings to Baldslow and back via Ore. The second was a long, east-west route on or close to the seafront from Hastings through its twin town of St Leonard's to beyond Bexhill. (All routes were principally double-track, except for the northern half of the Circle.)

The system emerged after competition between a number of (often conflicting) proposals, the PROVINCIAL Co. eventually winning the day with an authorising LRO and Act of Parliament, both in the same year. Before construction could start however, Provincial sold its interest in the scheme to the Hastings & District Electric Tramways Co., incorporated in 1904, with track-laying beginning in December that year.

The first two routes to be opened were the Circle, which ran (clockwise) from the Albert Memorial in Hastings north-west up Bohemia Road to Silverhill (and the depot) then continued north-east along Sedlescombe Road to Baldslow before turning south-east down London Road through St Helens to Ore, then finally westwards behind West Hill to the Memorial, plus a 1-mile branch north up Battle Road from Silverhill to Hollington. Of the original order of thirty open-top ERTCW cars, twenty-two arrived on time for the opening and the remaining eight the next day.

A third route, from Ore south-east along Harold Road for a mile to Hastings Old Town, with a terminus by the Market Cross in the High Street, opened on 21 August 1905 and soon after another ten ERTCW open-toppers (Nos 31-40) were delivered. The next route

Hasting's first service tram, No. 10 of 1905, with an escort of small boys, on a postcard marking the occasion. *(Author's collection)*

to open, on 9 April 1906, was a separate section from St Leonard's to the Metropole Hotel in Bexhill via Bexhill Road and De La Warr Road; this was extended to Cooden Beach on 28 July, about 3 miles from St Leonard's, and was worked by eleven cars shedded at Bulverhythe Depot just outside St Leonard's. That year another twenty open-toppers (Nos 41-60) were supplied by UEC, followed by similar cars Nos 61-65 the following year. Also on 28 July 1906, another route from Silverhill, this time due south down London Road to the seafront Grand Parade, was opened.

All that remained to complete the system was a seafront link between St Leonard's, the Grand Parade and the Memorial. The obstacle to completing this was the refusal of Hastings Corporation to countenance overhead wires on the seafront, an action legally enshrined in the 1903 Act authorising the route. Accordingly, the Dolter stud system was employed on this section and the line opened on 12 January 1907 using cars from the 1906 batch that had been equipped for both systems of current collection. As was found elsewhere (see TORQUAY), the Dolter system was not a satisfactory or reliable one and in 1913 the BoT instructed the Company to find an alternative. Consequently the adapted cars were fitted with Tilling-Stevens 24hp petrol engines and dynamos and, in this form, they operated the seafront service until March 1921 when, the Corporation having relented, overhead wires were brought into use.

Barely had the system been unified as regards current collection than the Company decided to deal with the problem of increasing bus competition by switching to trolleybuses. On 1 April 1928 the trolleybuses took over the Hollington branch, followed on 21 May by the London Road route to the Grand Parade, and to Bexhill Marina and the Memorial on 30 July. The Cooden extension went the same way on 18 September that year. The Circle was then so treated, in sections, with the last piece to go being the northern half from Silverhill to St Helens.

Hellingly Hospital Railway

Built to aid the construction of the East Sussex County Asylum (later Hellingly Hospital), this standard gauge branch line ran for just over a mile north-east to the hospital from a platform and sidings at Hellingly station on the LBSCR's Eridge-Polegate line. The asylum opened on 20 July 1903 and it is thought that the private branch opened for passenger traffic at the same time (it having been used previously by the building contractor). The railway is included here because it was electrified with a tramway-style overhead after the construction work was finished. Passengers were conveyed, until 1931, in a tiny, single-deck four-wheeled Brush saloon car supplied by Robert W. Blackwell & Co. Ltd of London with freight services worked, until 1959, by a small four-wheeled steeple cab locomotive (of possibly German origin) again supplied by Blackwell (who also electrified the line).

Herne Bay Pier Tramway (1)

Authority: --
Gauge: ?
Traction: Sail, manual
Opened: 13 June 1833?
Closed: 1864
System: Single line
Length: *c.*0.68 miles
Stock: 1 sd?
Livery: ?
Last Car: ?

Opened in June 1832 by the Herne Bay Pier Co. to serve the General Steam Navigation Co.'s traffic from London, the 3,613ft-long Herne Bay pier incorporated a tramway that had probably been used during its construction. When the pier opened to the public, so did the tramway (of which no mention is made in the pier's 1831 authorising Act), with hand-propelled four-wheeled wagons used to carry passengers' luggage to and from the boats. It is doubtful that the passengers themselves were carried until 13 June of the following year when a sail-propelled carriage – grandly named *Old Neptune's Car* – made its maiden run. The idea for such a vehicle came from Sir Henry-Chudleigh Oxenden, the pier's local financial backer and an ice and land yacht enthusiast; when the wind was not favourable the car was man-handled along the pier by two or three porters.

The pier closed in 1864 and with it the tramway. Its demise was brought about partly by the cessation of the steamer trade two years earlier and partly by thirty years of general decay on the part of the wooden structure, though this was by no means the end of the story. (See below.)

Car No. 3 on the Herne Bay Pier Tramway. The conduit for the electricity supply is next to the right-hand running-rail. *(Author's collection)*

Herne Bay Pier Tramway (2)
Authority: Herne Bay Pier Order 1891
Gauge: 3ft 4½in.
Traction: Conduit electric/petrol-electric/battery electric
Opened: 1 April 1899
Closed: 3 November 1939
System: Single line
Length: *c.*0.74 miles
Stock: 3 sd electric; 1 petrol-electric railcar; 1 battery railcar
Livery: Green & cream
Last Car: Hibberd railcar (+ trailer?)

After the closure of the original Herne Bay pier (see above), plans were made for a replacement. In 1871 the old pier was demolished and the following year work began on a new structure, which opened in August 1873. As originally built it was just 320ft long but in 1891 authority was obtained by the Herne Bay Pier Co. to extend and lay a tramway for both the construction work and passenger traffic. The line was built by BTH and the greatly-lengthened pier (now 3,930ft long) was opened in June 1898, the tramway opening the following year with a single Brush-bodied car (No. 1) supplied with electricity via an off-centre conduit. In May 1901 this vehicle was joined by Nos 2 and 3, a pair of ex-BRISTOL horse toastracks (Nos 46 and 47 of probably late 1870s vintage), which were converted for use as trailers to serve the recommenced steamer traffic.

In February 1905 the pier was placed in receivership and sold on 5 November 1908 to Herne Bay UDC. The First World War interrupted both the steamer and tramway services and the tramway did not reopen until the 1925 August Bank Holiday, this time with services handled by a petrol-electric vehicle built locally by Strode Engineering. (The old

Herne Bay Pier Tramway again, this time looking towards the terminus outside the ornate pier head pavilion. *(Author's collection)*

car bodies are believed to have been used as shelters on the pier for a while before being scrapped.) The new car proved unreliable however, and was converted in 1934 to serve as a trailer to accompany a new Hibberd battery railcar.

The outbreak of the Second World War saw the suspension of the steamer service once again and following the last day of tramway operations the pier was breached in two places as an anti-invasion measure. Although the breaches were repaired and the pier reopened after the end of hostilities, the tramway was not so lucky and the cars were sold for scrap. (In 1968 much of the pier was closed as unsafe and in 1978 it was breached again, this time by a gale, never to be repaired.)

Highgate Hill Tramways *see* London: Highgate Hill Tramways

Horndean *see* Portsdown & Horndean

Hundred of Manhood & Selsey Tramway

Commonly known as the Selsey Tramway, this standard gauge West Sussex line was, despite its title, a typical light railway of the Colonel H.F. Stephens empire. Starting from its own little station next to the LBSCR's Chichester station (where there was a physical connection), it ran due south for 7¾ miles through Hunston, Chalder and Sidlesham to Selsey. It opened on 27 August 1897, was extended a further ½ mile to Selsey Beach the following year (a station closed in 1904) and in 1924 changed its name to the West Sussex Railway. Operated with a typical motley crew of Stephens' collection of second-hand tank engines and carriages (plus two primitive railcar sets), it was closed on 19 January 1935 and the stock sold.

Hythe *see* Folkestone, Hythe & Sandgate

Ilford Urban District Council Tramways
Authority: Ilford Improvement Act 1898
Gauge: 4ft 8½in.
Traction: Overhead electric
Opened: 14 March 1903
Taken over: 1 July 1933
System: Radial
Length: 7.4 miles
Stock: 57 dd
Livery: Crimson lake & cream to 1918, sage green & ivory from 1916

Ilford UDC operated 6.66 miles of its own tramways and 0.74 miles which were leased from BARKING UDC. Its four routes radiated from Ilford Broadway west to the borough boundary on Ilford Hill, south along Ilford Lane to the Barking boundary at Loxford Bridge (opened 22 May 1903), east along High Road to the boundary at Chadwell Heath, and north along Ley Street and Horns Road through Newbury Park to Tanners Lane, Barkingside. The first and last of these routes were mainly single-track.

The first cars were HN open-toppers 1-12 and bogie open-toppers 13-18, all shedded just off Ley Street; these were joined later in 1903 by Nos 19-22, four more single-truck HN vehicles. All these cars were later top-covered, and were joined in 1910 by top-covered Brush cars Nos 23-26, then in 1914 by No. 27 (ex-Barking No. 10) and a year later by No. 28 (ex-Barking No. 8). Between 1920-23 twenty Brush top-covered cars were bought, partly as replacement vehicles, and they took the numbers 1-20 (with surviving old cars being renumbered higher in the series). Three similar bodies were bought in 1929 for fitting with existing trucks, and numbered 21-23; these were followed three years later by Nos 33-40, eight top-covered Brush cars of a new design – the last additions to the fleet before it became part of the new LONDON TRANSPORT.

The tramway was connected in the west to the EAST HAM CORPORATION TRAMWAYS which, after 1 April 1905, worked the short Ilford Hill line with cars running through to the Broadway (and from 25 May 1910 by WEST HAM and LONDON COUNTY COUNCIL trams as well). In the south it was connected to the Barking system at Loxford Bridge where a similar arrangement, from 6 June of that same year, saw Ilford working a short, isolated route on behalf of Barking.

Imperial Tramways
The Bristol-based Imperial Tramways Co. Ltd (1878-1930) owned, at one time or another, the tramways at BRISTOL, Darlington, GLOUCESTER and READING. They also owned the Middlesborough, Stockton & Thornaby system and the LONDON UNITED TRAMWAYS (formerly the WEST METROPOLITAN TRAMWAYS); in addition it owned the Dublin Southern District Tramways in Ireland and the narrow-gauge Corris Railway in Wales.

Ipswich Tramway
Authority: Ipswich Tramways Order 1879
Gauge: 3ft 6in.
Traction: Horse
Opened: 13 October 1880
Closed: 6 June 1903
System: Network
Length: 4.25 miles
Stock: 6 sd, 3 dd
Livery: Maroon & cream
Last Car: ?

Although the Ipswich horse tramway system ended its days under Corporation ownership, it began as a private concern, promoted and built by S.A. Graham of Manchester. The first line opened ran for ¾ mile from the GER's Ipswich station up Princes Street to Cornhill in the town centre and was worked by single-deck Starbuck cars Nos 1 and 2. The depot was off Princes Street in Quadling Street, on the west side of New Cardinal Street, about ¼ mile from the station (and later moved to the other corner of New Cardinal Street).

A second Order of 1880 led to the construction of a branch from just north of the depot spur along Portman Road and Norwich Road to Brook Hall. A year later, under the Ipswich Tramways Act of 1881, the Ipswich Tramway Co. was formed to take over the two lines and provide a link between them from Cornhill along Westgate Street and St Matthews Street, thus producing a triangular layout. That same year a Starbuck double-decker (No. 3) and another single-decker (No. 4), possibly also from Starbucks, were acquired to work the growing tramway, followed by single-deckers Nos 5-7 in 1883, again possibly from Starbucks (and rebuilt as double-deckers in the late 1890s). An eastwards extension from Cornhill to Derby Road station in 1884 completed the system, with another double-decker, No. 8, added – again possibly from Starbucks. The final car acquisition was No. 9 in 1894, a double-decker possibly from Milnes. All lines were single tracks.

Under its 1900 powers (see below) the Corporation purchased the system on 1 November 1901 to provide the basis for its planned electric tramways and, as the system was now operating at a loss, closed it down as soon as possible.

Ipswich Corporation Tramways
Authority: Ipswich Corporation Tramways Act 1900
Gauge: 3ft 6in.
Traction: Overhead electric
Opened: 23 November 1903
Closed: 26 July 1926
System: Network
Length: 10.82 miles
Stock: 36 dd
Livery: Dark green & cream electric
Last Car: ?

Left: One of Ipswich Corporation's fleet of Brush open-toppers by the Town Hall, on the corner of Westgate Street and Princes Street, its crew posing for the camera in the otherwise empty roadway. *(Author's collection)*

Below: In contrast, a rather more crowded scene: one of the popular 'Last Car' cartoon postcards, in this case overprinted for sale in Ipswich. *(Author's collection)*

Under its 1900 Act the Corporation was empowered to take over the existing Ipswich horse tramways (see above), as well as to electrify and extend them. This it set about doing, more than doubling the size of the old system with seven basic routes, all primarily single-track, radiating out from Cornhill to serve most parts of the town. Services began with Brush open-toppers Nos 1-16, which were quickly followed by ten more (Nos 17-36) a year later. The car shed and power station were in Constantine Road, just off Portman Road.

The first section of the system to close was the very short branch in Bath Street, which was used only to link the railway station with the Quay when GER steamers docked there; this closed in 1917. It was followed in 1923 by the stations Cornhill and the Princes Street-Mill Street lines, these former horse routes replaced by Corporation trolleybus services. Three years later the rest of the system went the same way (with the Corporation not adopting motor buses until the 1950s). Following the closure, seven cars were sold to Scarborough and one (No. 34) to FELIXSTOWE PIER. Car No. 33 is currently on display at Ipswich Transport Museum whilst undergoing restoration, along with a locally-constructed permanent way handcart of similar vintage.

Isle of Thanet Electric Tramways

Authority: Isle of Thanet Light Railway Order 1898
Gauge: 3ft 6in.
Traction: Overhead electric
Opened: 4 April 1901
Closed: 27 March 1937
System: Split single line
Length: 10.84 miles
Stock: 60 dd
Livery: Maroon & cream to 1927, then crimson & ivory; 1918-20 some sage green & ivory
Last Car: No. 20

Despite the failure of the abortive RAMSGATE & MARGATE tramway, interest remained high in the idea of a line linking the major towns on the Isle of Thanet in the north-eastern corner of Kent. Of the various proposals made, that of William Murphy proved the successful one. On 3 March 1896 he formed the Isle of Thanet Light Railways (Electric) Co. Ltd – the name was changed on 11 March 1899 to the Isle of Thanet Electric Tramways & Lighting Co. Ltd – and two years later he obtained the necessary LRO.

The line was constructed by the Thanet Construction Co. Ltd, another Murphy company – he had interests in several British tramways, including Dublin United where he became Chairman – with some nine-tenths of it being double-track. It commenced in Canterbury Road, Westbrook on the western edge of Margate and from there ran along the seafront past the LCDR's Margate West and the SER's Margate Sands stations. It then turned east inland, then south, through Cliftonville to cross the Isle of Thanet, partly on road and partly on reserved sections, to Broadstairs on its eastern coast. Here the main line ran through the town via the High Street and Dumpton Park Road whilst a 'top road' provided a bypass route to the west. South of Broadstairs, Ramsgate was reached, where

Isle of Thanet No. 38 of 1901 dropping down towards the harbour in Ramsgate. This steep section – Madeira Walk – was a noted accident blackspot on the tramway. *(Author's collection)*

Isle of Thanet No. 4 of 1900, one of the tramway's original cars. In place of the more usual system name, the car side sports the legend MARGATE BROADSTAIRS RAMSGATE. *(Author's collection)*

the line followed the seafront before swinging back on itself north up Grange Road, then east along Park Road, to terminate by the SER's Town station.

The first section to open – the bulk of the line in fact – was from the Margate stations to Ramsgate Harbour via the top road, the main line through Broadstairs and the short end sections opening on 6 July that same year. The original car fleet comprised open-toppers Nos 1-20 from the St Louis Car Co. of the USA, but it quickly became clear that these would not be sufficient and another twenty (Nos 21-40), of larger capacity, arrived in July 1901, followed by Milnes open-toppers 41-50 later that year. A final ten, similar cars (Nos 51-60) were purchased in 1903 from BEC.

The system was plagued by problems in its early years on account of the number of steep hills in the towns and accidents were frequent, culminating in car No. 41 going over the cliff at Ramsgate on 3 August 1905. Amazingly, the driver was the only person seriously injured, but the car had to be scrapped. In the early 1920s Nos 42 and 45 had their stairs removed as part of their conversion to one-man operation (though only No. 45 had its top deck removed as well).

Although the Company (known as the Isle of Thanet Electric Supply Co. from June 1924) had been operating motor buses since 1913, it seems that pressure from the local councils led to the tramway's demise in 1937, to be replaced by East Kent Road Car Co. buses – the firm which had purchased the tramway's bus operation the previous year.

Landport & Southsea Tramway *see* Portsmouth Street Tramways

The northern end of the Isle of Thanet line: the seaside resort of Margate, complete with such necessary accoutrements as bandstand, pleasure gardens and carriages for hire. *(Author's collection)*

Lea Bridge, Leyton & Walthamstow Tramways
Authority: Lea Bridge Leyton and Walthamstow Tramways Act 1881
Gauge: 4ft 8½in.
Traction: Horse
Opened: 13 May 1883
Taken over: 1 June 1905
System: Branching
Length: 4.8 miles
Stock: 10 sd?, 28 dd?
Livery: Brown & white to 1884?, red & white from 1889

Formed by a group of local dignitaries, the Lea Bridge, Leyton & Walthamstow Tramways Co. had the aim of providing a means of easy access from London to the northern part of Epping Forest. The project got off to a shaky start – it was offered to the NORTH METROPOLITAN TRAMWAYS in October 1881 but turned down – but the financial situation appears to have then improved and construction went ahead. The first section to be opened ran north-east as a single line from Lea Bridge, on the London/Leyton boundary, past the depot in Russell Road and along Lea Bridge Road (just inside the Leyton/Walthamstow boundary) to Whipps Cross on the edge of the forest, a distance of some 3 miles. The first cars were ten Merryweather vehicles, all thought to be single-deckers, bearing the legend 'Epping Forest'.

A further ½ mile of line, from Lea Bridge Roadalong Forest Rise to the Rising Sun in Epping Forest, had also been built. However, this stretch was not opened as the contractors had not been paid so would not hand it over (!), and the Company was wound up on 13 December 1884, services having ceased some months earlier (probably at the beginning of October). Again it was offered unsuccessfully to the North Metropolitan, and only in 1888 was it transferred to a new company, the Lea Bridge, Leyton & Walthamstow Tramways Co. Ltd (registered 19 October 1888). Twelve second-hand double-deckers were acquired, possibly from the North Metropolitan and probably numbered 1-12. They were then housed in a new depot across Lea Bridge Road from the old one.

Services recommenced on 13 May 1889, now going all the way to the Rising Sun. However, connections were urgently needed to other systems to make the line pay and authorisation was sought and obtained for these. (At the same time the Company was dissolved and the statutory Lea Bridge, Leyton & Walthamstow Tramways Co. incorporated.) On 31 March 1890 a 1½-mile branch was opened south from the Baker's Arms (by the depot) along Leyton Road to the GER station in Leyton where it terminated opposite Maud Road; about half the line was double-track. The system was completed on either 21 or 22 April 1892, with the opening of a ½-mile westwards continuation (again, half double-track) of the line across the Lea Bridge and along Lea Bridge Road into London, terminating at the corner of Cornthwaite Road in Clapton.

More cars were bought to cope with the increasing traffic – the purchase probably comprised six second-hand ones numbered 37-42 (lower numbers being taken by horse buses) – and a track-doubling programme started. In 1896 cars 51-54 were purchased, again probably second-hand, followed in 1904 by the ex-North Metropolitan double-deckers

Nos 55-60. (An associated concern, the Great Eastern London Suburban Tramways & Omnibus Co. Ltd was set up in 1900 to take over the bus side of the business, as it was illegal for the LBLWT Co., as a statutory tramway company, to run it.) With the tramway's twenty-first anniversary imminent, complicated negotiations resulted in the 1905 takeover of the line by LEYTON URBAN DISTRICT COUNCIL, effective from 1 June.

The Company's 748 yards of line across the boundary in London were leased to Leyton UDC for a down payment of £8,640 and rent of 1s a year until LONDON COUNTY COUNCIL were permitted to buy it (from 5 April 1911). The UDC accordingly continued the horse service, but only until 30 July 1908 when the line was sold by the Company to the LCC, with the agreement of the UDC. It was then reconstructed for electric working, the horse cars finishing on 9 December that year and the electric cars commencing the next day (see below). The Company quickly went into voluntary liquidation.

Leyton Urban District Council Tramways

Authority: Leyton Urban District Council Act 1898
Gauge: 4ft 8½in.
Traction: Horse, overhead electric
Opened: 1 June 1905
Taken over: 1 July 1921
System: Network
Length: 9.52 miles
Stock: 31? horse; 60 dd electric
Livery: ? horse; dark green & primrose electric

The first (horse) trams in Leyton were operated in the 1870s by NORTH METROPOLITAN TRAMWAYS. They had a standard gauge line from Stratford running north up Leytonstone High Road from West Ham into Leyton as far as the Green Man Hotel in the town. Then, in 1890-92, the LEA BRIDGE, LEYTON & WALTHAMSTOW TRAMWAYS Co. (see above) opened a standard gauge single-track line from Cornthwaite Road in Clapton, Hackney. This line ran north-eastwards along Lea Bridge Road, crossing the borough boundary formed by the River Lea and on to the Baker's Arms at the junction with Leyton Green High Street. (Beyond this point it was already open for ¾ mile along Lea Bridge Road to its junction with Whipps Cross Road, then along Forest Rise and Woodford New Road to the Rising Sun Inn in Epping Forest; a branch opened in 1890 ran from the Baker's Arms south down the High Street to the GER's Leyton station.)

By the end of the nineteenth century Leyton UDC had obtained powers to operate its own horse or mechanical tramways. Under the Leyton Urban District Council Act of 1904 it further gained the power to operate electric ones. On 1 June 1905 it purchased the LBLWT lines within its boundaries, together with twenty-eight cars and the depot by the Baker's Arms. The line was promptly rebuilt (and doubled) and a connection made to the WALTHAMSTOW system at the Baker's Arms.

The North Metropolitan line within the borough was taken over on 1 June 1906 as soon as its lease ran out, together with fifteen cars (which the Council never used), and again promptly relaid (mainly with double tracks) and extended further north from the Green

Man up Whipps Cross Road to meet the Lea Bridge Road line. At the same time the Leyton station branch was extended south down Leyton High Road then east along Crownfield Road by the borough boundary to the Thatched House, where it joined the Leytonstone High Road line. Three ex-LONDON COUNTY COUNCIL cars were bought to work this line in the short term. Finally, an eastern extension of the branch from the Thatched House was laid along Cannhall Road and Dames Road to the boundary at Vansittart Road. However, this section was never worked by horse cars, being without a service until 1 December 1906 when electric working started (with through-running from WEST HAM).

Electric services began with MV top-covered cars Nos 11-50 based at a new depot by the Baker's Arms. (Numbers 1-10 were used for the slimmed-down fleet of horse cars used on the Hackney through service, that portion of the LBLW line not having been converted.) The system was now complete, with some 6 miles of former horse lines and 3 miles of new routes. A further twenty MV cars (Nos 51-70), similar to Nos 11-50, were ordered in 1907 to cope with demand. The last horse tram ran on 9 December 1908 and through-running with the LCC commenced, followed ten days later by through-running from Vansittart Road south over West Ham metals via Forest Road and Woodford Road, through Forest Gate to Woodgrange Road. Through-running to Chingford via Walthamstow began on 8 October the following year, and in 1910 cars 31-70 were fitted with plough carriers for conduit working over the LCC's tracks beyond Clapton. By the end of the First World War though, both track and car fleet were in very poor shape and in 1921 the LCC was forced to take over the tramway.

London

The history of London's tramways is that of England's tramways in microcosm. In the early 1860s G.F. Train of Birkenhead fame opened three experimental street railways in the capital, but such was the opposition from the local authorities that all were closed within months. After a few years' hiatus, other promoters constructed more conventional tramways to usher in a period of piecemeal horse, steam and cable systems, grander visions being hampered by the fragmentary nature of the city's local government structure. Gradually though, the various companies coalesced through a series of mergers and takeovers until 1933 when the entire network was taken over by the London Passenger Transport Board to become part of LONDON TRANSPORT – the largest single tramway system in the British Isles. By then electrically worked, the tramways had been gathered into the hands of three major operators: LONDON COUNTY COUNCIL, LONDON UNITED TRAMWAYS and the METROPOLITAN ELECTRIC TRAMWAYS, all of whom had already extended their lines well beyond the growing capital's boundaries into the surrounding counties. In chronological order of opening, the London tramways were:

London: Train's Tramways

Authority: Local authority permission
Gauge: 4ft 8½in.?
Traction: Horse
Opened: 23 March 1861
Closed: 20 June 1862

The opening of G.F. Train's first tramway in London, as portrayed by *The Illustrated London News* of 20 April 1861 in this scene near Marble Arch.

System: Three single lines
Length: *c.*3 miles
Stock: 5 sd
Livery: Various
Last Cars: ?

The first three tramways in London were all unsuccessful promotions by the flamboyant American entrepreneur George Francis Train. In 1860 he had opened a line in Birkenhead (which was to fare better than his London efforts) and, turning his attention to the great metropolis, persuaded the local authorities – not without some difficulties – to permit him to construct three separate tramways. The first of these ran from Marble Arch for 1 mile along the Bayswater Road as far as Porchester Terrace and was opened on 23 March 1861, with Charles Dickens and William Thackeray among the assembled dignitaries and onlookers. It was worked by the Marble Arch Street Rail Co. Ltd with two single-deck cars, built by Prentiss of Birkenhead, named *Princess Royal* and *Her Majesty*.

The second line, opened on 15 April 1861, ran from Victoria Station up Victoria Street to Parliament Square and was operated by the Westminster Street Rail Co. Ltd, with one car named *The People*. The third tramway, opened on 15 August that same year, ran from the other side of Westminster Bridge past Lambeth Palace to Kennington Gate and was operated by the Surrey Side Street Rail Co. Ltd with two cars. Like the first tramway, both were single-track lines about a mile in length.

FIGURE 1.
VICTORIA
BAYSWATER
NAPOLEON
LITHOGRAPH OF TRAMCARS AT MARBLE ARCH, 1861.
This shows one of the first street tramways in London. It was laid by Mr. G. F. Train from the Marble Arch to Notting Hill Gate in 1861. Four-wheeled single and double-decked cars were employed, each drawn by two horses.
The Science Museum, London. No. 195.

An artist's fanciful impression, issued more than four decades later as a postcard, of what Train's tramway might have looked like. The cars have been given (erroneously) the names *Victoria* and *Napoleon*. *(Author's collection)*

Public opinion was sharply divided over the tramways. Those who used them – numbering in the tens of thousands a week – liked them, but residents and other road users (especially omnibus operators) did not. Matters were not helped by Train's use of tramroad-style step rails – that is, rails with raised edges protruding above the road surface to keep the cars on track – and the authorities soon ordered their removal. The Bayswater line was closed by mid-September 1861 and the Victoria Street line went the same way on 6 March the following year; the tramway south of the Thames perforce closed on 20 June 1862 when the Sheriff's workmen lifted the rails whilst the cars were running, after Train had defied a court order to do so himself!

London: North Metropolitan Tramways

Authority: North Metropolitan Tramways Act 1869
Gauge: 4ft 8½in.
Traction: Horse, battery electric
Opened: 9 May 1870
Closed: 28 April 1908
System: Network + single line
Length: 56.77 miles
Stock: 16 sd? 730+ dd? horse; 4 locos, 6 dd electric
Livery: Route colour
Last Car: ?

In 1869 the North Metropolitan Tramways Co. (incorporated 12 July that year) obtained powers to build 7 miles of horse tramways in east London. Construction began that November and the following May the first 2½ miles of double tracks between Whitechapel church and Bow Bridge opened with five Stephenson double-deckers working the services. From this small beginning sprang a major tramway system; eventually reaching Aldgate, London Docks and the West India Dock in the south, Holloway, Stamford Hill and Finsbury Park (in Middlesex) in the north, Holborn, Bloomsbury and Islington in the west and Leytonstone, Manor Park and Plaistow (all in Essex) in the east.

In 1878 the Company began production of its own cars at its Leytonstone Works (eventually becoming a major supplier of tramcars to other British systems), and by 1883 it had sixteen single-deckers and 225 double-deckers in service. Steam traction had been experimented with by then, a Merryweather tram locomotive having been tried at Stratford for a month before being sent to WANTAGE. A compressed-air loco. was tested in 1881 whilst the following year a horse car was converted into a battery electric vehicle for trials. In 1883 another battery car was tested and three years later an Elieson patent electric loco. from the Electric Locomotion Power Co. Ltd was put on trial. This machine evidently proved more successful for, on 4 August 1887, two of these entered public duty on the Stratford-Manor Park route, each hauling a horse car as a trailer. Two more locos were added but the service lasted only a year before being abandoned; this was not the end of this form of traction though, for on 14 June 1889 six self-contained, open-top double-deck battery cars began operating on the Canning Town-Plaistow route. (This 1¼-mile line along Barking Road, opened in September 1886, was always isolated from the rest of the system to the north and west.) The use of the battery cars, rented from the General Electric Power & Traction Co. Ltd, ceased on 27 July 1892 following a disagreement over their hire charges.

By 1891 the Company was operating nearly 400 double-deckers (the single-deckers apparently having been withdrawn). Six years later, on 14 October 1897, it took over operation of the LONDON STREET TRAMWAYS system, this having been purchased the previous day by the LONDON COUNTY COUNCIL and leased to the North Metropolitan. The network remained at this level of omnipotence for just five years, for on 26 November 1902 the METROPOLITAN ELECTRIC TRAMWAYS, took over the 7 miles of line in Middlesex, whilst on 1 July the following year WEST HAM bought its 4 miles of line in the locality. On 1 April 1906 LEYTON took over its lines with the entire London network passing to the LCC that same day. All the Company was left with was its line to Manor Park in East Ham, depots in Romford Road and Barking Road, six trams and the Leytonstone car works. EAST HAM CORPORATION then offered £8,000 for the Romford Road line and successfully took it over at this price, the last services running on 28 April 1908 and the last cars and horses being auctioned in May. The Company was liquidated on 15 February 1913 after disposing of its remaining properties.

London Tramways

Authority: Metropolitan Street Tramways Act 1869; Pimlico Peckham and Greenwich Street Tramways Act 1869

Gauge: 4ft 8½in.

Traction: Horse, cable
Opened: 2 May 1870
Taken over: 1 January 1899
System: Network + single line
Length: 24.37 miles
Stock: 330+ sd & dd horse; 50 tractors, 76 dd cable*
Livery: Route colour*

Following the failure of Train's Surrey Side Street Rail line (see LONDON: TRAIN'S TRAMWAYS) the first successful tramway south of the Thames was opened in 1870 by the Metropolitan Street Tramways Co., this time using conventional grooved rails. The first section to be opened ran from Gresham Road in Brixton north for 1¼ miles along Brixton Road to The Horns in Kennington. This was extended on 5 October up Kennington Road to Westminster Bridge Road (and a short extension opened from Gresham Road south to Brixton church) and, on 22 October, westwards along Westminster Bridge Road to the river. On 7 December a second route was opened; this was a branch heading south-west from St Mark's church, Kennington, down Clapham Road to the Swan at Stockwell. It was extended on 1 May 1871 to the Plough at Clapham. On 11 September 1871 a ¼-mile branch was opened eastwards off Kennington Road to St George's Circus.

While all this expansion was going on a second concern, the Pimlico, Peckham & Greenwich Street Tramways Co., had been running trams from Blackheath Road in Greenwich westwards along New Cross Road since 13 December 1870. This was followed up on 4 March 1871 with the opening of a branch north-east from Blackheath Road to Christchurch in Greenwich. During 1871 this system crept further westwards, on 1 September reaching St George's Circus where it was connected ten days later with the Metropolitan's metals. Other lines were added over the next three years to form a network of routes centred on the Elephant & Castle and St Mark's church, with one short line (opened on 20 October 1873) isolated on the north side of the Thames. This line ran from Vauxhall Bridge up Vauxhall Bridge Road to the Windsor Castle by Victoria railway station. Shortly after this, under the provisions of the London Tramways Company Limited Purchase Act of 1873, the two concerns were bought by the London Tramways Co. Ltd (registered 12 December 1870) in order to rationalise matters.

The combined system continued to grow slowly, including an extension of the Clapham line to Tooting Bec Road (on 15 December 1888) and then to Tooting (16 December 1890). A cable line was also constructed to continue the Brixton route up Brixton Hill and Streatham Hill whereupon it was decided, in 1890, to convert the existing horse line as far back as the major tramway centre at Kennington Gate, a total distance of 2¾ miles. Accordingly, a winding house was constructed at Telford Park on the top of Streatham Hill and double tracks laid with a continuously-wound cable running at 8mph in a central conduit in each. The rebuilt line opened on 11 August 1891 for struggling horse-haulage until (probably) 7 December 1892, when cable working began with thirty tractor cars hauling horse trams. These tractors, or 'dummies' as they were known, were small, open-sided four-wheeled vehicles fitted with driver-controlled grippers to engage the cable. Most were housed in the winding house with one or more shedded at Kennington.

The Elephant and Castle, on a postcard sent in 1912: this was a major hub of the London tramway system, from horse car days onwards, south of the Thames. *(Author's collection)*

The construction and equipping of the cable line was by DK who, in 1895, extended it a further ¾ mile down the other side of Streatham Hill to Streatham village, terminating by the Tate Library. This section was officially inspected on 23 November that year and presumably opened shortly afterwards, again using tractors (of which fifty were eventually acquired). In 1898 however, work began on rebuilding some of the double-deck horse cars specifically for dual horse/cable-working, and between then and 1900 seventy-six of them had been fitted with grippers. Like the dummy-towed horse cars, they could now be horse-hauled onwards from Kennington after leaving the cable section. Presumably they proved more popular with the local residents than the dummies which, because of complaints about the noise they made, had had to be fitted with tanks for watering the track.

The MST's first horse cars, housed in the first depot at Brixton, were open-toppers supplied by Starbuck, Stephensons, Metropolitan and the Danish firm of Rowan of Randers (numbers unknown). The original livery is thought to have been blue and white with later cars taking different colour schemes as new routes opened. The PPGST cars (of which there were at least nine) were again double-deckers, probably from Messrs Drew & Burnett of Fountainbridge in Edinburgh. With the amalgamation of the two concerns, a score or so of depots were built round the system to house the growing fleet of single and double-deck vehicles supplied by a wide range of builders. There was also a fleet of horse buses, one of their functions being to link the two portions of the system across Vauxhall Bridge.

By the early 1890s LONDON COUNTY COUNCIL had already made its intentions plain; it wished to take over the tramways as and when their twenty-one years were up

Postcard (sent 1909) of the LUT's terminus at Hampton Court with car No. 296 of 1903, one of the batch bought to work this route. *(Author's collection)*

– much against the wishes of the Company. Not until 1898 was agreement reached on a total package deal of nearly £1 million, the transfer of control occurring at the start of the following year.

Car No. 284 is currently on display at the London Transport Museum, Covent Garden, in fully restored condition.

London Street Tramways
Authority: London Street Tramways Act 1870
Gauge: 4ft 8½in.
Traction: Horse*
Opened: 27 November 1871
Taken over: 13 October 1897
System: Network
Length: 13.45 miles
Stock: 140+ dd?
Livery: White & route colour

Until its takeover in 1897 by LONDON COUNTY COUNCIL, the London Street Tramways Co. ran a small network of lines in north London, with routes from Holborn and Farringdon in the south meeting at King's Cross from where a branch east along the Pentonville Road led to the Angel, Islington. A line north from King's Cross went up the Caledonian Road whilst a line north-west went to Camden Town and Kentish Town. Lines from Camden Town led north-east to Hampstead and south to Euston Road whilst branches north from Kentish Town went to Parliament Hill and the Archway Tavern on Junction Road.

The Hampstead line opened on 27 November 1871 before it had been inspected by the BoT. In spite of this and – an adverse inspection report – the Company continued to operate services, claiming that it was entitled to do so under its Act of Parliament. Further line openings followed, authorised by further Acts and Orders in the 1870s and 1880s. The next decade saw the LCC ready to begin taking over those parts of the system now twenty-one years old but this was opposed by the Company. The dispute could only be resolved by going to independent arbitration, then to the courts and finally to the House of Lords who found, on 30 July 1894, in favour of the Council. The 4¼ miles of line in question were thereupon leased back, as from 1 April 1895, to the Company. After this, negotiations were entered into by the LCC with the NORTH METROPOLITAN TRAMWAYS Co. with a view to that company working all the Council's lines, and on 27 May 1897 the buy-out of the LST was agreed, the purchase by the LCC becoming effective as of that October.

Details of the car fleet are sketchy. The vehicles were probably all double-deckers; furthermore they were from more than one manufacturer, with 139 of them being transferred to the NMT in 1897. However, it is not clear whether older cars had already been withdrawn or not; seven depots were spread around the system near the various terminals to house them all. Trials were carried out on the Caledonian Road with at least one compressed-air car (built by Lancaster for the British Mekarski Improved Air Engine Co. Ltd) entering service in 1883, but for how long they continued, and how many of these open-top double-deck cars were put into public service – if any – is not known.

One side of car No. 39 is currently on display in restored condition at the National Tramway Museum, Crich.

London: West Metropolitan Tramways

Authority: Southall Tramway Order 1873
Gauge: 4ft 8½in.
Traction: Horse
Opened: 1 June 1874
Taken over: 6 August 1894
System: Branching + single line
Length: 8.74 miles
Stock: 49+ sd & dd?
Livery: Various

This system was the forerunner of the LONDON UNITED TRAMWAYS of west London and, in turn, had its origins in a line opened in 1874 by the Southall, Ealing & Shepherd's Bush Tram Railway Co. Ltd (incorporated 12 May 1870). This line ran westwards for just over a mile along Uxbridge Road between Uxbridge Road station in Shepherds Bush and Askew Crescent in Acton Vale. The two cars used are thought to have been Starbuck double-deckers. The single-track line was constructed by Reid Bros of City Road and, after it closed for financial reasons on 23 February 1875, they took it over, reopening it on 21 September and extending it another 1½ miles to Acton Lane (18 February 1878) with a third (and later fourth) car added. On 6 March 1882 the tramway was acquired by the West Metropolitan Tramways Co. Ltd (incorporated 12 August 1881), who had a number of other routes planned.

On 18 March 1882 a 1½-mile line from Shepherds Bush station, worked by Falcon single-deckers, was opened along Goldhawk Road south-west to Young's Corner at the junction with King Street, and extended westwards on 16 December through Chiswick to the Star & Garter at Kew Bridge, terminating north of the river crossing. Then, on 17 April of the following year, a 2-mile line was opened south of the Thames from Kew Bridge to Lower Mortlake Road, Richmond (the bridge itself not being crossed on account of its narrowness). Finally, on 14 July 1883, the northern route to Kew Bridge was extended back eastwards for a mile from Young's Corner to the Hammersmith boundary. (This whole route from Hammersmith to Kew Bridge was doubled over the next ten years.)

Although other routes were planned and the possibilities of electric traction were investigated, the Company was failing and in 1893 a Receiver was appointed. As a direct consequence, on 13 June 1894 everything was put up for auction – only to attract no bids at all, such was the state of the assets. Rescue was at hand though, for on 6 August it was sold privately, to an agent for IMPERIAL TRAMWAYS for the sum of £30,000. It was then reconverged on 20 July to the London United Tramways Co. Ltd, a company which had been incorporated the day before, for rebuilding. From the auction details it would appear that the tramway was worked by at least forty-nine cars, of which the youngest were the fifteen Milnes double-deckers. The main depot was off Chiswick High Street with smaller ones at Shepherds Bush and in Kew Road, Richmond.

LUT No. 87 of 1901, outside Shepherds Bush tube station. *(Author's collection)*

London, Deptford & Greenwich Tramways

Authority: Southwark and Deptford Tramways Act 1879
Gauge: 4ft 8½in.
Traction: Horse, oil-gas
Opened: 28 October 1880
Taken over: 7 July 1904
System: Network
Length: 6.87 miles
Stock: 42+ sd & dd horse?; 1 loco. oil-gas
Livery: Route colour

Built by the Southwark & Deptford Tramways Co., this south-east London single track system began with a short line in Bermondsey running north-east along Spa Road. It then continued along Jamaica Road, Union Road and Lower Road through Rotherhithe to the depot by the bridge carrying the LBSCR's Deptford Wharf branch line. On 5 June 1881 the track was extended along Evelyn Street to the Noah's Ark in Deptford High Street, followed by an extension at the other end along Grange Road and Bermondsey New Road to the Bricklayers Arms. There was also a branch west from Jamaica Road along Parker's Row to Tooley Street, along with a branch south from the Red Lion on Lower Road along Rotherhithe New Road to Canal Bridge, which lay just short of the LONDON TRAMWAYS line in the Old Kent Road, and finally a short link between Rotherhithe New Road and Grange Road.

Services were worked by an unknown number of single and double-deck cars, at least some of which were supplied by Metropolitan. Official returns give a total of forty-two in 1904 though this figure probably includes replacements for withdrawn cars. That year saw the sale of the system by the Company, which had been renamed the London, Deptford & Greenwich Tramways Co. in 1893, to LONDON COUNTY COUNCIL for £91,363 plus costs. There was also an oil-gas locomotive, built by Weyman & Co. Ltd of Guildford, used on the Rotherhithe New Road line from the end of 1892 until (probably) October 1895. This was a small, double-ended, four-wheeled vehicle similar in shape and size to a steam or battery electric tramway loco., equipped with side windows and with 'The Connelly Motor' emblazoned on the side.

London: South London Tramways

Authority: The South London Tramways Act 1879
Gauge: 4ft 8½in.
Traction: Horse
Opened: 1 January 1881
Taken over: 22 November 1902
System: Network
Length: 12.87 miles
Stock: 28 sd?, 67 dd?
Livery: White & route colour

Postcard of the ceremonial opening, by the Prince of Wales on 15 May 1903, of the first section of LCC electrified tramway from the Thames out to Tooting. *(Author's collection)*

Above: When trams ruled the road: the LCC route over Westminster Bridge, with at least two single-deckers and six double-deckers visible – and very little other traffic. *(Jan Dobrzynski collection)*

Opposite: The corner of Westminster Bridge and the Thames Embankment with the central conduit used by the LCC for supplying current clearly visible on each track. *(Jan Dobrzynski collection)*

The South London Tramways Co. operated a long, thin network of lines on the south bank of the River Thames in the Battersea area. The first to open ran from (probably) the Princes Head at the junction of Battersea Park Road and Falcon Lane, along Battersea Park Road and Nine Elms Lane to the Royal Rifleman. On 5 January 1881 the short stretch on from here to the Coal Wharf Gates was opened, followed on 21 March by a short section in Falcon Lane.

Within two years the single-track system was complete. The final layout comprised a main line running south-west from London Bridge down Southwark Bridge Road, then Lambeth Road, from the Albert Embankment to Vauxhall station and Vauxhall Bridge. The route continued along Nine Elms Lane, Battersea Road, York Road and North Street with branches off north towards the Thames serving Southwark Bridge, Waterloo station (via Waterloo Road), Westminster Bridge (via Stangate), and Chelsea Bridge (via Queen's Road). Two southern branches opposite Waterloo Road served the Elephant & Castle. A second, parallel main line left the first line to the west of Vauxhall station to follow Wandsworth Road, Lavender Hill and St John's Hill; this was linked to the first line via Queen's Road and Falcon Lane.

The tramway is recorded as opening with twenty-eight cars – possibly all single-deck vehicles – though at the time of its takeover by the LONDON COUNTY COUNCIL in 1902 ninety-five cars were transferred. These were mainly double-deckers based in depots at Southwark Bridge Road, Queen's Road and Falcon Lane. Horse bus feeder services were also operated from March 1882 onwards.

In 1891 the Company leased its Waterloo Road section to LONDON TRAMWAYS, so when that concern was taken over by the LCC on 1 January 1899 the Council negotiated to buy that line too, doing so on 11 August for the price of £5,276. The remaining 12.73 miles of the system were purchased two years later for £¼million as part of the LCC's tramway acquisition and electrification policy.

London: North London Tramways

Authority: North London Suburban Tramways Order 1879
Gauge: 4ft 8½in.
Traction: Horse, steam
Opened: 10 April 1881
Taken over: 1 August 1891
System: Branching
Length: 8.37 miles
Stock: 20 sd horse; 25 locos, 27 dd steam
Livery: Dark green & white

Promoted and built by the North London Suburban Tramway Co. Ltd (registered on 14 December 1878 but dissolved and replaced in 1882 by the North London Tramways Co.), the first section of this Middlesex system to be opened ran south along the Hertford Road from the depot in Tramway Avenue, Ponders End, for 2 miles through Edmonton to the boundary with Tottenham. The line through Tottenham was opened on 16 May 1881 for 1½ miles to High Cross and, on 4 June, for another mile through Seven Sisters to Stamford Hill where it made an end-on connection with the NORTH METROPOLITAN TRAMWAYS line. On 7 January 1882 a northern extension of 1 mile took the mainly single-track tramway to close to the boundary with Hertfordshire at Waltham Cross.

Services began with twelve Eades patent reversible single-deck cars, they were joined later in 1881 by eight more. On 1 April 1885 steam working began with Merryweather tram locomotives 1-14 and open-top bogie trailers 1-20 from Falcon (with horse working lasting until the end of May). These were joined by loco. No. 15 from Merryweathers in 1885 and Nos 16-25 from DK in 1886-87, plus another seven Falcon trailers.

A ½-mile branch from Seven Sisters south-west to the Manor House opened on 24 October 1885, extended by another ½ mile on 12 December to Finsbury Park. A third route, north from the Manor House to Wood Green Town Hall (again, single-track), opened on Christmas Eve 1887, by which time the short Seven Sisters Corner-Stamford Hill section had fallen into disuse. The Company too was ailing – service was poor because of track and mechanical problems – and in 1890 it went into receivership, being purchased a year later for £22,600 by the North Metropolitan, who worked it with its own horse cars. The old stock was sold for scrap, two of the locos finding their way to the Dewsbury, Batley & Birstal line nine years later.

London: Woolwich & South East London Tramways

Authority: Woolwich and Plumstead Tramways Order 1880
Gauge: 3ft 6in.
Traction: Horse
Opened: 4 June 1881
Taken over: 1 June 1905
System: Branching
Length: 4.96 miles

Stock: 35 dd
Livery: Light blue & primrose/yellow, later dark maroon & cream

The authority for this line was secured by the Woolwich & Plumstead Tramways Co., which was then bought almost immediately by a new concern, the Woolwich & South East London Tramways Co. Ltd. As it was built, the original line ran roughly east-west from Plumstead church along the High Street and Plumstead Road, through Beresford Square and on along Beresford Road to Woolwich High Street where it terminated by the Free Ferry in Nile Street (1½ miles), with a branch of 328 yards heading in the same direction from Beresford Square along Powis Street just south of the main line. The narrow gauge, unique for horse lines in London, was chosen on account of the narrow, winding streets the tramway occupied.

Services began with three Metropolitan double-deckers, shortly after to be joined by three more. In 1881 an Act was obtained for an eastwards extension of 2¾ miles past the dockyards and the Royal Arsenal to Greenwich. This was to run by way of Church Street, George Street, Albion Street and Woolwich Road to a terminus adjacent to the LONDON TRAMWAYS line. This mainly single-track extension opened on 21 November 1882, with six more Metropolitan cars having been added to stock. These were followed by another ten cars just two years later, another five in 1895-96, six in 1900-01 and two in 1902 – probably a mixture of new and second-hand vehicles. The depot was in Cage Lane off Plumstead High Street. The only significant alteration made to the system came in 1903 when the Plumstead terminus was moved a few yards further east to meet the new electric line from BEXLEY, though no track connection could be made on account of the difference in gauges.

By the early 1900s LONDON COUNTY COUNCIL was permitted to purchase the tramway, in 1905 it did so for the arbitrated total price of £46,667 for the assets, including the thirty-two surviving cars.

London Southern Tramways

Authority: London Southern Tramways Act 1882
Gauge: 4ft 8½in.
Traction: Horse
Opened: 7 December 1883
Taken over: 20 December 1906*
System: Radial
Length: 5.75 miles
Stock: 33 dd?
Livery: Route colour (red, blue, brown) & cream

The London Southern Tramways Co.'s small system linked Vauxhall, Camberwell Green, Brixton and West Norwood with four, mainly single-track routes radiating from 'Loughborough Junction', where Coldharbour Lane met Hinton Road and Loughborough Road. The first sections opened were an east-west line from Camberwell

The Embankment entrance to the Kingsway Subway immediately after its 1908 opening, an LCC single-decker exiting beneath Waterloo Bridge with the top of Somerset House just visible beyond. *(Author's collection)*

The same view, this time in January 2006, with John Rennie's 1817 bridge replaced in the 1930s by one designed by Sir Giles Gilbert Scott and the original Subway exit, moved in 1937 to directly below the bridge, now obliterated. *(Author)*

Green along Coldharbour Lane to Brixton church, and part of the northern route off Coldharbour Lane along Gresham Road towards Vauxhall. The first part of the southern route from Loughborough Junction south down Milkwood Road to Herne Hill station opened on 30 May 1884, followed on 10 July by its extension along Thurlow Lane (now Norwood Road) to Tulse Hill. On 4 June 1885, the remaining portion along Church Street to Thurlow Place in West Norwood was opened.

The system was completed on 21 August 1887 with the opening of the rest of the Vauxhall line from the Swan Inn at Stockwell, along Stockwell Road and South Lambeth Road. This route crossed the lines of the LONDON TRAMWAYS Co. twice, in Brixton Road and Clapham Road, before connecting with those of the SOUTH LONDON TRAMWAYS on the other side of the LSWR's Vauxhall station. Services were worked by an unconfirmed number of double-deck cars (the returns of 1902 give thirty-three); the first batch were probably all from Falcon with later ones being constructed by the Company, all based at depots off Stockwell Road and Thurlow Place.

The tramway was bought by LONDON COUNTY COUNCIL for £62,085 in 1906, with the Council formally taking over operations on 2 October 1906 (but not ownership until 20 December that year).

London: Highgate Hill Tramways

Authority: Highgate Hill Tramways Order 1882
Gauge: 3ft 6in.
Traction: Cable
Opened: 29 May 1884
Closed: 23 August 1909
System: Single line
Length: 0.71 miles
Stock: 3 tractors, 8 dd
Livery: Blue & cream
Last Car: ?

Operated by the Highgate Hill Tramways Co. (a successor to the Steep Grade Tramways & Works Co. Ltd who had obtained the original authority), this short, single-track line ran up the road of its title, on a 1:11 gradient, from the Archway Tavern to Highgate Village. However, it went no further – plans to extend it another 6½ miles to Finchley, New Barnet and Chipping Barnet came to nothing. Opened by the Lord Mayor of London, Sir Robert Fowler, the line was worked in true cable tramway fashion with a constantly-moving cable in a conduit and grippers on the cars which could be engaged or disengaged by their drivers. Three types of cars were used on the line, the original fleet being made up of (passenger-carrying) single-deck tractor cars Nos 4-6 hauling open-top double-deck trailers Nos 1-3, plus driver-controlled bogie open-toppers Nos 7-9 (soon joined by Nos 10 and 11), all from Falcon.

An accident on 5 December 1892 saw the tramway closed down; this was only one in a series of (mainly financial) problems which eventually resulted in the liquidation of the Company later that same month, to be replaced the following February by the Highgate Hill Tramways Co. Ltd. On 14 August 1896 the line was sold to a new concern, the Highgate Hill Tramways Ltd, and was reopened on 19 April (Easter Monday) the following year. The Company apparently considered converting the line into a standard gauge electric tramway but got nowhere with the idea, caught as it was in the middle of London and Middlesex County Council rivalry, making it difficult for the Company to gain the necessary authority. In 1909 it was agreed that the LCC would buy its portion of the line for £13,099, effective from 24 August, and the MCC would purchase its 400 yards at the village end for £6,377, which it would then lease back to the LCC for working. The day before the takeover the tramway was closed for reconstruction as part of LONDON COUNTY COUNCIL TRAMWAYS, reopening eight months later in its new, electric guise. The cars were sold for scrap.

London: Harrow Road & Paddington Tramways

Authority: Harrow Road and Paddington Tramways Act 1886
Gauge: 4ft 8½in.
Traction: Horse
Opened: 7 July 1888
Taken over: 16 August 1906
System: Branching
Length: 2.85 miles
Stock: 21+ dd?
Livery: Red/brown & white

This short, mainly single-track line was owned and operated by the Harrow Road & Paddington Tramways Co. A main line ran in a south-easterly direction from the Royal Oak Inn, Harlesden Green, along the Harrow Road to Lock Bridge over the Grand Junction Canal at Amberley Road, Paddington. In addition a short branch off to the north just before this terminus ran for a little over ½ mile up Chippingham Road into Cambridge Road. Services began with twelve Milnes double-deckers. Details of later cars are incomplete: by 1901 twenty-one were recorded but, bearing in mind the length of the system, some of the later additions (from Falcon) were almost certainly replacements for older vehicles. The depot was in Trenmar Gardens, off the Harrow Road about ¾ mile from the Royal Oak.

No extensions were made to the tramway, though several were planned and authorised, and during the early 1890s the Chippingham Road branch fell into disuse (but a car was occasionally run over the bridge to preserve the Company's rights regarding it). In 1903 the Company obtained an Act permitting electrification, and another the following year to authorise the sale of the line to the METROPOLITAN ELECTRIC TRAMWAYS. This took place two years later for a price of £36,921 and the MET ran the tramway with the existing stock as reconstruction work went ahead, the residual horse service ceasing on 1 September.

London: South Eastern Metropolitan Tramways

Authority: South-Eastern Metropolitan Tramways Act 1888
Gauge: 4ft 8½in.
Traction: Horse

Opened: 11 October 1890
Taken over: 1 April 1902
System: Single line
Length: 2.56 miles
Stock: 10 dd
Livery: White

After nearly twenty years of proposals a short, isolated horse tramway was finally built in Lewisham in south-east London as the last such private venture to be authorised in the city. The one, mainly single-track line ran south from South Street in Greenwich along Lewisham Road, Lewisham High Street and Broadway to terminate at the depot by the Black Horse in Rushey Green. After a few months' delay upon completion, the grandly-named South Eastern Metropolitan Tramways Co. opened the line with ten open-top cars built by the NORTH METROPOLITAN TRAMWAYS.

In 1899 the Company obtained an Act authorising electrification of the line – on the face of it not a viable proposition considering the length of the tramway and the fact that it connected with no other system. The real purpose behind the move was probably to ensure a better price in the event of a likely LONDON COUNTY COUNCIL takeover. This came three years later, the Council paying £50,000 for the concern.

London United Tramways

Authority: London United Tramways Order 1895
Gauge: 4ft 8½in.
Traction: Horse, overhead electric
Took over: 6 August 1894
Taken over: 1 July 1933
System: Network + single line
Length: 53.75 miles
Stock: 70+ horse?; 4sd, 386 dd electric
Livery: Chocolate & cream to 1909, then blue & yellow horse; route colour & white to 1918, then scarlet & white electric

Formed in 1894 to take over the WEST METROPOLITAN TRAMWAYS, the London United Tramways Co. Ltd set about turning round the ailing fortunes of that concern. New cars were ordered and old ones scrapped, whilst in 1895 authorisation was obtained for new lines and the Shepherds Bush-Acton line was doubled, then on 31 August extended ¾ mile to the top of Acton Hill. Further Acts and LROs were obtained with a view to building a sprawling electric tramway system covering west and south-west London, on both sides of the Thames, stretching out as far as Uxbridge, Maidenhead, Staines, Hampton Court and Tooting.

The first electric routes – Shepherds Bush to Acton and Shepherds Bush to Hammersmith and Kew Bridge – reopened on 4 April 1901 after the reconstruction work had been completed and inspected. This was followed by a formal inauguration on 10 July (and the opening of the Acton line extension through Ealing and Hanwell to Southall). Services began with eighty cars from the initial order of Nos 1-100; these were open-top bogie double-deckers from HN, and they were followed in 1902 by similar cars Nos 101-211 and 237-300 from Milnes, and 212-235 from BEC. (Some fifty of these were later top-covered.) The main depot and power station were off Chiswick High Road beside the West Met horse depot, with additional depots being opened at Acton, Hanwell, Hillingdon, Isleworth and Fulwell.

An extension from Kew Bridge through Brentford and Isleworth to Hounslow opened on 6 July 1901, followed by new lines and extensions from Isleworth south to Twickenham and on via Teddington or Hampton to Hampton Wick and across the Thames to Kingston. Kingston soon became the focal point for lines radiating south to Surbiton, Ditton and Tolworth, north to Ham Boundary and Richmond Park Gates, and east to Kinsgton Hill, Wimbledon, Tooting and Summerstown. (This last branch, opened on 27 June 1907, was the final part of the system to be put in place.) The northern portion of the network was completed by a long westwards extension of the Southall line through Hayes and Hillingdon to Uxbridge, together with link lines to the Hammersmith-Hounslow Heath line to the south. (The authorised lines to Staines and Maidenhead were never built.)

In 1906 UEC supplied top-covered cars Nos 301-340 to meet the tramway's increasing needs, with no further vehicles being added until after the First World War when, in 1924, the Company put four single-deck one-man cars into service. These were No. 341 (which was a rebuilt ex-METROPOLITAN ELECTRIC TRAMWAYS car, No. 132 of 1905) and Nos 342-344 (rebuilds of double-deckers Nos 175, 178 and 275). In 1928 the MET's

The present-day northern exit of the Strand Underpass, taking traffic via the Subway from the Strand onto Kingsway. *(Author)*

experimental bogie enclosed car No. 319 'Poppy' was bought (and renumbered 350), to be followed three years later by Nos 351-396, 'Feltham' bogie enclosed cars from the Union Construction & Finance Co. Ltd, to complete the fleet.

Horse car services lasted until 20 April 1912, on the West Met's former Kew Bridge-Richmond route, which was always isolated from the rest of the system and, because of local opposition, never electrified. By the time of its closure, the horse car fleet (which had grown from the thirty-three cars inherited from the West Met to fifty-nine in 1899) had dwindled to single figures. Ten years later, on 2 May 1922, LONDON COUNTY COUNCIL took over those sections of the system within its boundaries (in Hammersmith and Shepherds Bush), and on 5 July that same year the Hounslow Heath route was cut back to Hounslow. On 1 October 1924 the Richmond Bridge-Twickenham line closed, and between 1931 and 1933 (when LONDON TRANSPORT took over the tramway) the routes south of there centred on Kingston were converted to trolleybus operation.

London: Alexandra Park Electric Railway

Authority: --
Gauge: 4ft 8½in.
Traction: Overhead electric
Opened: 13 May 1898
Closed: 30 September 1899
System: Single line
Length: 0.38 miles
Stock: 4 sd
Livery: Dark green?
Last Car: ?

To this short, short-lived line goes the honour of being the first electric tramway in the capital. Although sited wholly within Alexandra Park in north London, it was not a pleasure line as such but had a real transport function conveying visitors to the various events held in Alexandra Palace from the Park Gates, opposite Wood Green railway station, some 660 yards to the building's eastern entrance.

At the close of the nineteenth century the Palace and Park were leased to Thomas Hawkins, who allowed the Berlin firm of Elektrizitäts-gesellschaft Wandruska to construct and work the tramway, a double-track line laid with grooved rails on wooden sleepers on a continuous slope (as steep as 1:9.75) up to the Palace, generating station and car shed. The line's four semi-open cars were constructed by Waggonfabrik Falkenried of Hamburg.

The tramway was also intended to be a showcase for the Company and its Engineer, Victor Wandruska, and it might well have lasted longer than it did (from 13 May to 5 November, and Christmas week, in 1898 and 31 March to 30 September the following year) had Hawkins not gone bankrupt. However, Hawkins' bankruptcy led to the tramway being seized and sold by a creditor after it closed for the winter, the cars eventually making their way to the Great Grimsby Street Tramways.

London, Camberwell & Dulwich Tramways

Authority: Peckham and East Dulwich Tramways Act 1882
Gauge: 4ft 8½in.
Traction: Horse
Opened: Early 1896
Closed: 1900
System: Branching
Length: 2.89 miles
Stock: 4 sd
Livery: ?
Last Car: ?

Details of this small system are tantalisingly vague. A minor tramway in every sense, it was built by the Peckham & East Dulwich Tramways Co – extremely tardily – as the only portion of a grand scheme for a network of lines in the Peckham Rye area of south London. Construction began soon after authorisation was obtained, though the single-track tramway did not open until early 1896, making it the last of its kind to be inaugurated in London. It was worked with (probably) four roofed and curtained Midland toastracks, more suited to a seaside line.

The main route ran south along Hollydale Road, west along Brayards Road and Choumert Road (to the south of Peckham Rye railway station), then south again down Maxted Road, Adys Road and Crystal Palace Road to terminate by the Plough Inn in Lordship Lane. A short branch ran east off Adys Road along East Dulwich Road to the Kings Arms (and depot) where it swung north along Peckham Rye before terminating at the Heaton Arms in Rye Lane.

No connections were made to other tramways and in 1900, after an unprofitable existence not helped by the expense of promoting four Acts of Parliament between 1882 and 1887 (to keep its powers alive), services ground to a halt (after weekdays-only running in the latter days). The Company – grandly renamed the London, Camberwell & Dulwich Tramways Co. in 1887 – went into receivership and the line was bought by the LONDON COUNTY COUNCIL (see below) for just £6,500, with part of it earmarked for possible incorporation into the LCC's own expanding electric empire.

London County Council Tramways

Authority: London County Tramways Act 1896
Gauge: 4ft 8½in.
Traction: Horse, cable, conduit electric, overhead electric, petrol-electric
Took over: 1 January 1899
Taken over: 1 July 1933
System: Network
Length: 167.18 miles
Stock: 500+ horse?; 50 tractors, 29 dd cable; 50 sd, 2,282 electric; 3 dd petrol-electric
Livery: Various/route colours horse and cable; purple lake & primrose to 1926, then crimson & cream electric*

STAR POST CARDS
YORKSHIRE RELISH
L.C.C. TRAM WITH ARCH ROOF AND PASSENGER QUEUE.

LCC Class B car of 1903, originally open-topped. These cars were fitted later with top-covers as protection for the passengers, a practice carried out on many systems as a response to growing motor bus competition. *(Author's collection)*

The London County Council's tramway system – one of the 'Big Three' in the capital during the first quarter of the twentieth century – came about as a consequence of the Council's decision to buy up the independent tramways within its boundaries in order to unite, extend and electrify them. Its first takeover as an operator, as of the beginning of 1899, was of the LONDON TRAMWAYS system, thereby acquiring 24.38 miles of route, nine horse cars based on a main depot at Penrose Street off Walworth Road (plus numerous small depots), fifty tractors and twenty-nine cable cars. (The Council, incorporated in 1889, already owned the LONDON STREET TRAMWAYS and the NORTH METROPOLITAN TRAMWAYS lines within its boundaries, having bought them on 24 June 1896, but these were leased back to those concerns for operating purposes.)

Subsequent system acquisitions were of SOUTH LONDON (22 November 1902), the SOUTH EASTERN METROPOLITAN (1 April 1904), the LONDON, DEPTFORD & GREENWICH (7 July 1904), the LONDON, CAMBERWELL & DULWICH (15 August 1904), the WOOLWICH & SOUTH EAST LONDON (1 June 1905), the LONDON SOUTHERN (2 October 1906) and the HIGHGATE HILL cable line (24 August 1909). Also bought was the London County section of the LEA BRIDGE, LEYTONSTONE & WALTHAMSTOW LINE (1905), though this was then leased to LEYTON URBAN DISTRICT COUNCIL for three years.

By the time the above purchases had been completed, the electrification programme was well under way. Electric services, using the conduit system of current supply as pioneered at Blackpool, began on 15 May 1903 on the lines in the Westminster Bridge/Waterloo Station/Blackfriars Bridge area. They continued out through Kennington and Clapham to Tooting some 8½ miles away, after which the conversion work proceeded apace, firstly south of the Thames and then north of it. The resulting network spread right across London in all directions with river crossings via (from east to west) the Southwark, Blackfriars, Westminster, Vauxhall, Battersea and Putney bridges. Connections were made with, or terminals sited close to, other systems in the north and west (METROPOLITAN ELECTRIC), the west (LONDON UNITED), the south (SOUTH METROPOLITAN), the south-east (BEXLEY and ERITH), and the east (WEST HAM and LEYTON).

A notable feature of the LCC system was the only underground section of tramway in the British Isles, the Kingsway Subway. Opened in stages between 1906 and 1908 to link Southampton Row in Bloomsbury, just north of High Holborn with the Victoria Embankment, this incorporated gradients of up to 1:10 and ran for $^{2}/_{3}$ mile beneath Kingsway and Aldwych, new thoroughfares which had been built after slum clearances. Underground tramway stations were provided at Holborn and Aldwych and fifty single-deckers bought to operate services through it. Rebuilt in 1930-31 to allow the passage of double-deck trams, the subway closed for good on 6 April 1952, just three months before the rest of what was left of the London network; eleven years later much of the southern half was converted as part of a one-way underpass for road traffic from the Strand to Kingsway. (The northern portion, the old entrance ramp of which is used for storing road mending materials, is opened to the public on special occasions.)

Another 1903 Class B car, No. 106, which escaped scrapping and can now be seen restored to working order at the National Tramway Museum at Crich in Derbyshire. *(M. Donnison)*

A car from one of the last batches of trams built for the LCC, the E/3 Class of 1930, seen here in London Transport livery. *(Author's collection)*

The last horse cars ran on 19 July 1913 in Liverpool Road, Islington (this route was not electrified), whilst the Highgate Hill cable line was not operated in that form by the LCC but closed upon takeover in 1909. It eventually reopened on 25 March 1910 as part of the electric network; the Brixton cable line was operated as such until 5 April 1904, when it too was closed for rebuilding.

The LCC's first electric car was No. 101, a Milnes open-top bogie car of 1900, purchased for conduit trials after the London Tramways Exhibition of that year, but after the First World War it was converted to a single-decker, renumbered 110 and withdrawn c.1926 for scrapping. From 1903 onwards, with the introduction of electric services, the car fleet was assembled as follows:

Nos 1-100:	ERTCW bogie open-toppers of 1903 (Class A)
Nos 102-201:	ERTCW open-toppers of 1903 (Class B)
Nos 202-301:	Brush open-toppers of 1903 (Class C)
Nos 302-376:	Brush bogie open-toppers of 1904 (Class D)
Nos 377-401:	BEC Class D of 1904
Nos 402-551, 602-751:	HN top-covered cars of 1906 (Class E)
Nos 552-567:	UEC bogie single-deckers of 1906 (Class F)
Nos 568-601:	Brush bogie single-deckers of 1906 (Class G)
Nos 752-1001:	HN top-covered bogie cars of 1907-8 (Class E/1)
Nos 1002-1051:	LCC Class E/1 of 1907-08
Nos 1052-1426:	HN Class E/1 of 1908-9
Nos 1477-1676:	Brush Class E/1 of 1910-11

No. 1427: LCC open-topper of 1909 (Class M)
Nos 1428-1476, 1677-1726: HN Class M of 1910
Nos 1727-1776: HN Class E/1 of 1921-22
Nos 1777-1851: Brush Class E/1 of 1921-22
No. 1852: LCC experimental top-covered bogie car of 1929 (Class HR/1)
No. 1853: LCC similar car of 1929 but Class HR/2
Nos 1854-1903: EE Class HR/2 of 1930
Nos 1904-2003: HN enclosed bogie cars of 1930 (Class E/3)
Nos 101-160: HN Class HR/2 of 1931
Nos 161-210: EE Class E/3 of 1931 for use in Leyton

Classes F and G were rebuilt in 1929-30 as double-deckers with new EE bodies. The last car built for the system was No. 1 of 1932, an experimental, enclosed bogie car nicknamed 'Bluebird' on account of its royal blue and ivory livery. (That same year, No. 795 was clad

Another LCC tram in LT livery: No. 1622 of 1911, restored and running at the National Tramway Museum, Crich. It is seen here on the interlaced section of track beneath the Bowes-Lyon Bridge. *(Author)*

briefly in unpainted aluminium panels as an experiment.) Sold to Leeds in 1951, No. 1 survives at the National Tramway Museum, Crich.

On 1 July 1921 the LCC took over the Leyton municipal system, inheriting sixty top-covered cars (Nos 11-70) that were gradually withdrawn over the next twelve years to be replaced by E/1 and later E/3 Class cars. Trailer cars were operated for a while, beginning in 1913 with eight suitably converted ex-North Metropolitan double-deck horse cars (and renumbered T1-T8). They were joined in 1915 by purpose-built Brush open-top trailers T9-T158, the use of which (almost exclusively south of the Thames) lasted until 1924, after which they were broken up. (The body of one, T24, currently forms the basis of a Dublin-style replica open-topper, numbered 224, on show in the National Museum of Transport at Howth Castle outside Dublin.) During 1913 three petrol-electric cars joined the fleet: Nos P1-P3, again conversions of former horse cars, with 40hp petrol engines supplied by W.A. Stevens Ltd of Maidstone, but their period of service lasted only from May to December of that year.

The principal problem encountered by the LCC after the system's electrification was that the neighbouring operators all used overhead wires to supply current to their cars, not conduits, thus through-running became impossible. A solution was found however, whereby those operators seeking through-running agreements equipped some of their cars with carriers that could be fitted with conduit ploughs at special change pits where the two systems connected. The LCC likewise equipped many of its cars for overhead working. In addition, some 27 miles of the Council's peripheral routes were constructed with overhead wires rather than conduits to simplify matters somewhat. (A surface-contact method of current supply via studs set into the roadway was experimented with on the Aldgate-Bow Bridge route in 1908, but the trials lasted less than a month and the studs were replaced by a mixture of overhead and conduit sections.)

In all, twenty-two electric car depots were employed around the system, with most surviving until the 1933 incorporation of the tramways into the new LONDON TRANSPORT network. The Central Car Repair Works (opened in March 1909) was on Woolwich Road, Charlton, and had a rail connection to the nearby SECR line complete with its own steam shunting locomotive.

Car No. 106 can be seen restored to operational condition at the National Tramway Museum, Crich, as can No. 1622, whilst No. 1858 operates at the East Anglia Transport Museum, CARLTON COLVILLE (though the last two are in LT guise). No. 1025, also in LT guise, is on show at the London Transport Museum, Covent Garden.

London: Metropolitan Electric Tramways

Authority: County of Middlesex Light Railways Order 1901
Gauge: 4ft 8½in.
Traction: Horse, overhead electric
Took over: 26 November 1902
Taken over: 1 July 1933
System: Network
Length: 53.51 miles
Stock: 62 horse; 20 sd, 362 dd electric
Livery: Vermillion & ivory*

MET bogie car No. 156 of 1906, in Wood Green. *(Author's collection)*

The Metropolitan Electric Tramways Ltd was a BET subsidiary operating lines in the north and north-west of London. It began life as the Metropolitan Tramways & Omnibus Co. Ltd (incorporated 21 November 1894), which was taken over by the BET in 1901 (and the name changed), the intention being to buy the NORTH METROPOLITAN horse lines and, working in partnership with Middlesex County Council, extend and electrify them. The North Metropolitan was accordingly purchased in 1902 and work began on the reconstruction.

The first routes to reopen, with electric services beginning on 22 July 1904, were the MET's line from Finsbury Park running north-east along Seven Sisters Road to Seven Sisters Corner, and the branch north from the Manor House to Wood Green. The first MCC-built tramway was a new line from Wood Green east along Lordship Lane and Bruce Grove to Tottenham, which opened on 20 August that year.

Over the next six years the system grew to form a sprawling network of double-track lines of which the Company itself owned less than 9½ miles. This was largely made up of the Wood Green route and the line to Seven Sisters (which continued northwards up the High Road to Tottenham and on via Fore Street through Edmonton and then along the Hertford Road to Ponders End). Hertford County Council owned 1½ miles (the north-western extremity of the system from the county boundary at New Barnet to Chipping Barnet church), and the MCC the remainder of a network stretching to Sudbury via Willesden and Wembley in the west, to Edgware and Barnet in the north-west, to Enfield and Waltham Cross (from Ponders End) in the north, to Tottenham in the east, and to Paddington and Acton in the south. The last section opened, on 20 February 1911, was a branch west from Ponders End to the GER's Enfield Town station.

Horse car services in Tottenham ceased in 1904 and the cars were sold back to the North Metropolitan (which retained a nominally separate existence) for use on the lines it still

A Cynicus 'Last Car' postcard (sent 1907) relating to the area served by the MET. Examples of this artist's work – including the similar 'Last Train' variety – appear with numerous different localities printed on them. *(Author's collection)*

leased from LONDON COUNTY COUNCIL, whilst the last horse services in Edmonton probably ceased on 18 July 1905, the day before electric cars began running there.

Electric services began with Brush open-top bogie cars Nos 1-70, which were joined in 1904-05 by similar vehicles Nos 71-130; most of these were later top-covered. In 1905 Brush supplied single-deckers Nos 131-150 for use on the two short branches to Alexandra Palace and, a year later, bogie open-top cars Nos 151-165 (later top-covered) and Nos 166-190, four-wheeled open-toppers. In 1907 Brush open-topper 191 entered service; this had been a 1903 sample car built for Leicester Corporation (where the tender had not been won) bought by the MET in 1904 and used briefly as an engineers' inspection car. In 1908 the same firm supplied bogie open-toppers Nos 192-211 (again, later to be top-covered) and enclosed-top bogie cars Nos 212-216, followed a year later by bogie open-toppers Nos 217-236 (also later top-covered).

Between 1909 and 1912 Brush provided a further batch of enclosed-top bogie cars, Nos 237-316 (nicknamed 'Dreadnoughts'), after which the First World War put a stop to acquisitions until 1921 when the Company built open-top bogie car No. 317 (later top-covered). This car had the distinction of being, before its withdrawal in 1938, the last MET car in service. Between 1924 and 1925 the Company constructed enclosed-top bogie cars Nos 2, 12, 22, 31, 46 and 82 to replace withdrawn trams (some parts of which were incorporated into the new cars). In 1927 it produced experimental car No. 318, a fully-enclosed bogie vehicle with a rear entrance and a front exit, nicknamed 'Bluebell' on account of its pale blue and white livery. A companion car, No. 319, painted dark red and white and known as 'Poppy', was constructed for the Company by the London General Omnibus Co. but sold in 1928 to LONDON UNITED TRAMWAYS.

In 1928 the Union Construction & Finance Co. Ltd built two enclosed bogie cars, Nos 320 ('Blossom') and 330 ('Cissie'), designated 'Experimental Felthams' after that company's works. In 1930 No. 331 was added, which had a centre entrance and stairs. These were followed by 'Felthams' Nos 319, 321-329 and 332-375 from 1931 onwards, just before the whole system became part of LONDON TRANSPORT. The fleet was housed in five depots: Edmonton, Finchley, Hendon (the main works), Stonebridge Park and Wood Green.

The system was connected at several of its southern terminals to the LCC network and through-running began on 1 August 1912, for which the Council had to fit a number of its cars with trolley poles for overhead current collection. The MET also had work to do: some of its cars were fitted with plough carriers to enable them to run over the LCC's conduit tracks.

The Company also operated buses through its subsidiary, the Tramways (MET) Omnibus Co. Ltd, which was registered on 13 January 1912. Later that year this combined with the MET and the LUT under a holding company, the London & Suburban Traction Co. Ltd, with links (though the LUT) to the Underground Group. The SOUTH METROPOLITAN ELECTRIC TRAMWAYS joined the group the following year, thus paving the way for a city-wide unified transport system twenty years before the London Passenger Transport Board came into existence and took it over.

Car No. 331 is now at the National Tramway Museum, Crich (after seeing service as LT No. 2168 and Sunderland Corporation No. 100), whilst No. 335 of 1931 (latterly LT No. 2099 and Leeds No. 501) is on display at the London Transport Museum, Covent Garden; car No. 94 of 1904, much rebuilt, can be seen running at SEATON.

London Transport

Authority: London Passenger Transport Act 1933

Gauge: 4ft 8½in.

Opposite: MET Type B No 6. of 1904, which survived to become London Transport No. 2498 following the 1933 takeover. *(Author's collection)*

Right: The last night of London Transport tramways: appropriately-numbered car 1952 on the final Plumstead-Woolwich service. *(Author's collection)*

Traction: Overhead electric
Took over: 1 July 1933
Closed: 5 July 1952
System: Network
Length: 328.45 miles
Stock: 19 sd, 2,611 dd
Livery: Red & cream
Last Car: No. 1951*

The London Passenger Transport Board was established in 1933 to provide a single body responsible for the whole of the capital's public transport on and below its streets. The existing tramways were to be unified – including any systems outside the city's boundaries but connected to those of the London operators. The Board therefore assumed control of the LONDON COUNTY COUNCIL lines, the METROPOLITAN ELECTRIC TRAMWAYS and, as part of the Underground Electric Railway Co., LONDON UNITED TRAMWAYS. Not only did they acquire these companies but also the systems of BEXLEY, CROYDON, EAST HAM, ERITH, ILFORD, LEYTON, WALTHAMSTOW, WEST HAM and the SOUTH METROPOLITAN TRAMWAYS.

With the above lines came the operators' surviving cars – all 2,630 of them – to be merged into a single fleet. More than half were ex-LCC vehicles and these retained their old numbers, as did the ex-MET and ex-LUT cars, whilst the others were given temporary suffixes to their fleet numbers thus: Bexley – C, Erith – D, Croydon – E, Ilford – F, East Ham – G, West Ham – H, Walthamstow – K and Southmet – S. Withdrawals of unwanted vehicles began immediately and a renumbering programme began, this eventually taking the number series up to 2529, the cars being lettered 'London Transport'. During the next twenty years no further passenger cars were added to stock; instead, many of the inherited cars were rebuilt and modernised as the fleet continued to shrink. Seventy trams went in the first twelve months, after which the withdrawal rate accelerated: 87, 150 and 263 went during the next three years, including all the cars inherited from Bexley, Croydon, Erith and the Southmet.

The reduction in fleet size was accompanied by a rationalisation of the depot arrangements and, ominously, by an increase in the size of the Board's trolleybus fleet. During the first twelve months of the LPTB's operations however, just 3 miles of route were trimmed from the tramway network and no further cuts were made until 1935-36 when 40 miles were abandoned to the trolleybuses; over the next twelve months another 58 miles went. By mid-1939 the car fleet had shrunk by almost exactly half and stood at 1,316 vehicles operating over 135 route miles – both of these figures were comfortably exceeded by the corresponding trolleybus totals. The abandonments and withdrawals continued during the Second World War, hastened by the damage sustained during the Blitz and, at the end of 1946, only 913 cars were operating over 102 miles of route.

In January 1948 the Board's operations were nationalised with the London Transport Executive assuming control to oversee what it became clear were the tramways' final days. It was announced in July 1950 that the trams were to be replaced by trolleybuses over the next two years. So it proved, with the last service car running from Woolwich on the night of 5 July 1952, arriving at New Cross in the early hours of the following day. (This car, No. 1951, was designated the official 'Last Car', with its attendant ceremonies and publicity, though ex-Leyton No. 187 arrived after it – while ex-East Ham No. 87 was still in service on its way to Abbey Wood Depot.)

LT cars Nos 1 (static) and 1622 (operational) can be seen at the National Tramway Museum, Crich, No. 1025 is on display at the London Transport Museum, Covent Garden, whilst No. 1858 is operated at the East Anglia Transport Museum, CARLTON COLVILLE.

Lowestoft Corporation Tramways

Authority: Lowestoft Corporation Act 1901
Gauge: 3ft 6in.
Traction: Overhead electric
Opened: 22 July 1903
Closed: 8 May 1931
System: Branching
Length: 4.08 miles
Stock: 4 sd, 15 dd
Livery: Tuscan red/chocolate & primrose/cream
Last Car: ?

A somewhat unlikely subject for an early twentieth century Christmas card: a trio of Lowestoft trams in London Road South on a bright summer's day! *(Author's collection)*

The Lowestoft system was owned and worked throughout its life by the Corporation, although the local authority's original intention had been to build the tramway and then lease it to a private company. The system was principally a single, mainly single-track route which ran, like the Suffolk town itself, in a north-south direction roughly parallel to the shore from Yarmouth Road (by the GER's Lowestoft North station), down the High Street and London Road to cross the narrow harbour entrance – roughly the mid-way point – by means of a swing bridge. The route then continued down London Road South (the 'touristy' hotels and Esplanade part of the town) to a southern terminus at the corner of Pakefield Street in the district of that name. A 1-mile branch on the northern side of the harbour ran inland past Lowestoft Central station to the depot in Rotterdam Road; the intention had been to continue the tramway on around the back of this northern, older part of the town but the idea never came to fruition. The original stock comprised open-toppers 1-11 and single-deck saloon cars 21-24, all from Milnes. The gap in the number sequence was presumably left to accommodate more double-deckers, and indeed another four similar vehicles (Nos 12-15) were purchased a year after the opening.

By the end of the 1920s it was time for the Corporation to face the problem of whether to modernise the tramway or replace it with a bus service. It opted for the latter course of action and the section north of the harbour bridge closed in April 1931, with the southern half going the same way the following month. The body of No. 14 survives not too far from home as a static exhibit at the East Anglia Transport Museum, CARLTON COLVILLE.

Luton Corporation Tramways

Authority: Luton Corporation Tramways Order 1905
Gauge: 4ft 8½in.
Traction: Overhead electric
Opened: 21 February 1908
Closed: 16 April 1932
System: Radial
Length: 5.25 miles
Stock: 1 sd, 12 dd
Livery: Grass green & white/ivory
Last Car: No. 7

This little system – Bedfordshire's only tramway – comprised five mainly single-track routes (none much more than a mile in length) radiating from the Town Hall. The route north went along Manchester Street and New Bedford Road to Wardown Park, the north-east route took passengers along Midland Road and High Town Road to Stockingstone Lane in Round Green. The south-east track proceeded along George Street and Park Street to Bailey Street and the depot, while the southern route went off George Street to the London Road via Chapel Street, Hibbert Street and Ashton Road. Finally the north-western route took its passengers along Upper George Street and the Dunstable Road. The whole system opened as one with UEC open-toppers Nos 1-12, of which Nos 1, 2, 4 and 5 were later top-covered. The only other car added to the fleet was No. 13 (ex-Glasgow 118), a single-deck horse car and later electrifc passenger then parcels

George Street, Luton, looking towards the Town Hall, the hub of Bedfordshire's only tramway system. *(Author's collection)*

Another Luton postcard, this time of No. 9 passing the Market Cross. *(Author's collection)*

car bought in 1923 when Luton Corporation took over the running of the system itself from 21 February. It had been operated previously on lease, first by J.G. White & Co. Ltd (the constructor and then, from 1909, by BB).

The system was closed by the Corporation in 1932 in favour of its own motor buses; the London Road, Dunstable Road and Wardown Park routes went on 28 February, leaving just the Round Green-Depot route to survive another few weeks. The cars were sold for scrap to a London dealer, who disposed of the bodies locally.

Lynton & Lynmouth Cliff Railway

Although not a tramway as such, this water-powered funicular railway was built with one fascinating tramway feature. Officially opened on Easter Monday, 7 April 1890, as a double-track 3ft 9in. gauge line nearly 300 yards long linking the twin Devon towns of its title on a gradient of 1:1.75, it was the brainchild of the publisher Sir George Newnes (who had a residence nearby). Newnes worked in conjunction with the Birmingham consulting engineer and patent agent, George Croydon Marks, who was the project's Hydraulic Engineer. The two cars had triangular underframes holding the water tanks used to move them, and upon each frame was mounted a small, locally-built tramcar (not an integral body), on its own set of narrow-gauge L-section rails, which could be run-off at either terminus to allow the bare underframe platform to be used for the conveyance of goods and motor vehicles, an especially important feature in the early years. This ingenious idea, patented in 1889 by Newnes, Marks and Bob Jones, the Lynton-based builder of the railway, was never adopted by any other British cliff railway though it could, in theory, have been used as part of a tramway system to connect routes on two different levels (as indeed it did in Cincinnati in the USA, for example). The car bodies were rebuilt in 1947, but retained their flanged wheels.

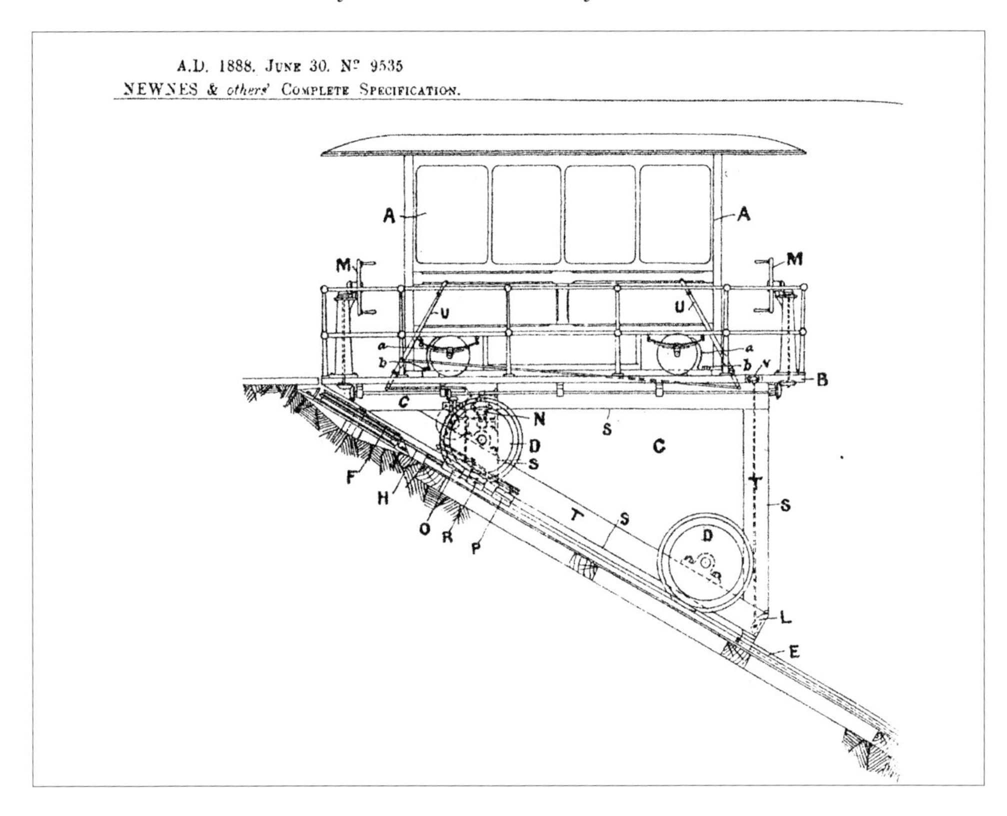

Above: Diagram from Newnes, Marks and Jones' 1889 patent, as applied on the Lynton funicular, showing the wheeled tramcar body on its triangular underframe.

Left: A postcard (sent 1905) of the Lynton & Lynmouth Cliff Railway, showing the converging run-off tracks for the wheeled cars – a funicular/tramway invention that progressed literally no further than this in Britain. *(Author's collection)*

Official Opening
OF THE
Maidstone Tramway,
July 14th, 1904.
Photo by De'Ath & Dunk
Week Street, Maidstone

A commemorative postcard of the official procession of cars at the opening of the Maidstone tramways. The sender has written: 'Can you recognise me in the picture?'! *(Author's collection)*

Maidstone Corporation Light Railways

Authority: Maidstone Corporation Light Railways Order 1903
Gauge: 3ft 6in.
Traction: Overhead electric
Opened: 14 July 1904
Closed: 11 February 1930
System: Radial
Length: 5.25 miles
Stock: 1 sd, 17 dd
Livery: Golden ochre & off-white to 1918, then ochre & off-white
Last Car: No. 2

Maidstone's first authorised tramway was a 2-mile street line running westwards from the High Street across the River Medway and out along the Tonbridge Road to the village of Barming (where the depot was situated). Six open-top double-deck cars were supplied by ERTCW to work it, with an identical car (No. 7) bought a year later. A second route opened on 16 October 1907, running southwards from the High Street and out along Loose Road for 2 miles to the village of that name, while a third, shorter line came off the Loose route just south of the High Street to run south-westwards to Tovil paper mill. Opened on 9 January 1908, it completed the mainly single-track system. (Only the two main routes in the centre of the town were double-tracked.) To work the enlarged system ten further cars were purchased from UEC in 1907 and numbered 8-17; these were similar to Nos 1-7 but slightly smaller. Single-deck UEC demi-car No. 18, bought in 1909, completed the passenger car fleet.

Maidstone No. 3 passing St Michael's church on the Tonbridge Road, on another 1904 postcard. *(Author's collection)*

In 1924 the Corporation started operating motor buses, followed by trolleybuses which, on 1 May 1928, began by taking over the Barming route (though the tramway track was left *in situ* to enable the depot to be reached). The next closure came on 1 August 1929 when motor buses replaced the Tovil trams (one of these, No. 14, being sold to CHATHAM) with the Loose service succumbing to trolleybuses the following February.

Marble Arch Street Railway *see* London: Train's Tramways

Margate *see* Isle Of Thanet; Ramsgate & Margate

Metropolitan Electric Tramways *see* London: Metropolitan Electric Tramways

Metropolitan Street Tramways *see* London Tramways

Mono-Metal Tramway *see* Canvey Island Tramway

Mousehold Light Railway *see* Norwich Electric Tramways

National Electric Construction Co. Ltd

Established in 1897 (renamed in 1903) the NEC, among its other interests, at one time or another owned the English tramway systems of Dewsbury, Ossett & Soothill Nether (which it operated directly), OXFORD, Mexborough & Swinton and TORQUAY. In addition, it owned the Rhondda system in Wales and that at Mussleburgh in Scotland.

Newport Pagnell & District Tramways

A late 1880s tramway that almost but not quite made it, this was to have been a steam-worked 3ft 6in. gauge line, 6.14 miles in length, between the LNWR station in the north Buckinghamshire market town of Newport Pagnell and the MR station in the smaller town of Olney to the north. Some 5 miles of track were laid by a local contractor, Charles Herbert Wilkinson, for the Newport Pagnell & District Tramways Co. and a new bridge over the Great Ouse was built, but the project foundered when the BoT refused to sanction running along the main street through the village of Emberton just south of Olney. (The rails were not lifted until at least 1893, so some hope of buying the land needed to bypass the village was kept alive for a while.) If it had been completed, it would have provided an interesting partner to its close neighbour (and other Wilkinson line), the WOLVERTON & STONY STRATFORD TRAMWAY, which opened in 1887, the year the NPDT Co. obtained the authority, in the form of the Newport Pagnell and District Tramways Order, for its own line.

North Metropolitan Tramways *see* London: North Metropolitan Tramways

Northfleet *see* Gravesend & Northfleet; Gravesend, Rosherville & Northfleet

Norwich Electric Tramways

Authority: Norwich Electric Tramways Act 1897
Gauge: 3ft 6in.
Traction: Overhead electric
Opened: 30 July 1900
Closed: 10 December 1935
System: Radial network
Length: 15.16 miles
Stock: 52 dd
Livery: Maroon & ivory
Last Car: No. 10

After a number of unsuccessful attempts from the 1870s onwards to provide the city with horse or cable tramways – despite the popular perception of Norfolk as being 'very flat', Norwich has its fair share of steep hills – it was not until the last year of the century that tramcars appeared on its streets. This followed unsuccessful proposals by the BET in 1896 and, in 1897, by the owner of the Coventry and the Douglas Southern tramways, the New General Traction Co. Ltd.

Construction began in June 1898 and routes were opened in batches, from July 1900 until the year's end, by the Norwich Electric Tramways Co. Originally, all services began and ended at Orford Place in the city centre (where a magnificent circular tram shelter was erected), but in 1901 more convenient through-services were introduced. In all, eleven radial routes, with some cross-connections between them, served the suburbs, the Barracks and all three of the city's railway stations and, apart from a short connecting line laid in 1919, the passenger network was complete. As regards the carriage of goods however, a notable development came in 1918 with the construction of just over ½ mile of sleepered track across Mousehold Heath – a high point overlooking the city to the north – from the existing terminus there to a munitions factory. (The rails for this line, known as the Mousehold Light Railway, came from lifting one of the double tracks in the narrow King Street.) Two powered trucks were built by the Company (but Government-owned) to serve the factory, which was now connected, via the passenger line down Gurney Road and Riverside Road, to exchange sidings beside the GER's Norwich Thorpe Station.

A postcard view of Orford Place in the centre of Norwich, shortly after the 1900 opening of the city's tramways. *(Author's collection)*

Postcards of night scenes were popular souvenirs during the Edwardian period: this one is of the Norwich Market Place, in front of the Guildhall, with an open-topper skirting its lower edge. *(Author's collection)*

In 1914 the Company obtained powers to operate bus services, which would be less obstructive in the city's narrow medieval streets, and these began in 1915; in 1918 the first prunings of the tramway system began, though improvements to the rest of it continued to be made. It was clear however, that the system had reached that critical age when wholesale track relaying and stock modernisation would be needed if it were to survive, but these options were not viable on the scale required and little-used routes were slowly shortened or abandoned altogether with their trams replaced by buses. By 1932 the City Council was in favour of buying the concern but a public poll the following year swayed it against the idea. Instead, the Eastern Counties Omnibus Co. Ltd purchased the NET Co. in 1933 and set about closing the tramways, the last route to go being Newmarket Road-Cavalry Barracks.

The original fleet of rolling stock comprised Brush-powered cars Nos 1-40 and ten trailers (Nos 41-50), all open-top double-deckers. In 1901 two similar powered cars (Nos 41 and 42) were transferred from Coventry to Norwich – the trailers with those numbers becoming Nos 51 and 52 – and in 1910 five Norwich cars (Nos 7, 9, 16, 32 and 36) made the return journey. In 1923 Nos 7 and 9 were built by EE – again open-toppers – using the electrical equipment and trucks from the former Mousehold Light Railway freight cars, and between then and 1930 thirty-two of the original powered cars were rebuilt by the same company.

Norwood *see* Croydon

City Of Oxford & District Tramways

Authority: Oxford Tramways Order 1879
Gauge: 4ft
Traction: Horse
Opened: 1 December 1881
Closed: 7 August 1914
System: Radial
Length: 5.25 miles
Stock: 12 sd? 20 dd?
Livery: Dark red & white/cream, some later chocolate brown & white/cream
Last Car: ?

Like its Cambridge contemporary – which also closed in 1914 – this small, 4ft gauge horse tramway system was never electrified, although for the last half-dozen years of its life such a move was proposed by various interested bodies. It was promoted by the Oxford Tramways Co. Ltd (incorporated 20 November 1879 but opened by the City of Oxford & District Tramways Co. Ltd (incorporated 14 December 1880), the latter company having taken over the powers of the former. Starting with just a single line running eastwards from the twin GWR (Oxford) and LNWR (Oxford Rewley Road) stations through Carfax in the city centre to Cowley Road, by 1898 three branches had been added: south from Carfax via St Aldates and Abingdon Road to Lake Street, New Hinksey (15 March 1887), north-east from Carfax to Kingston Road via Beaumont Street and Walton Street

(15 July 1884) and, thirdly, north from Carfax via St Giles and the Banbury Road to South Parade, Summertown (opened to Rackham's Lane on 28 January 1882 and through to South Parade on 5 November 1898).

Rolling-stock details are sketchy. Services commenced with four single-deck cars, soon joined by several more, after which a number of double-deckers were bought, some new from Milnes and a dozen or so second-hand from various LONDON operators.

With electrification proposals never coming to fruition, the tramway was soon killed off by motor bus competition – competition in which the City of Oxford Electric Tramways Ltd, an NEC subsidiary and the 1908 successor to the City of Oxford & District Tramways Co. Ltd, itself joined. Services to Walton Street and New Hinksey were withdrawn on 27 January 1914, with the remaining services following later that year.

Paddington *see* London: Harrow Road & Paddington

Peterborough Tramways

Authority: Peterborough and District Light Railway Order 1900
Gauge: 3ft 6in.
Traction: Overhead electric
Opened: 24 January 1903
Closed: 15 November 1930*
System: Radial
Length: 5.31 miles
Stock: 14 dd
Livery: Lake-brown & cream to 1914, then holly green & cream
Last Car: No. 12

Huntingdonshire's only tramway was operated by the BET-owned Peterborough Electric Traction Co. Ltd, and constructed after the failure of a number of proposed horse tramway schemes. It was an urban street tramway made up of three long, single-track branches to the northern outlying areas of Walton, Dogsthorpe and Newark diverging from a short stem leading south to the Market Place. The line's first twelve cars (Nos 1-12) were open-toppers built in 1902 by Brush, and they were followed two years later by two more (Nos 14 and 15). The depot was in Lincoln Road on the Walton route.

From 1913 onwards the Company supplemented the trams with motor buses; these first complemented and then, inevitably, replaced the trams services entirely, the Company becoming a co-founder of the Eastern Counties Omnibus Co. Ltd in 1931. Although the last public services ran on 15 November 1930, all routes had been abandoned to the buses in all but name from the Bank Holiday Monday (4 August) of that year and, until the closure proper, car No. 12 – nicknamed the 'Ghost Tram' – toured each route in turn throughout the day until the necessary authority to dispense with the service completely had been obtained.

Pimlico, Peckham & Greenwich Street Tramways *see* London Tramways

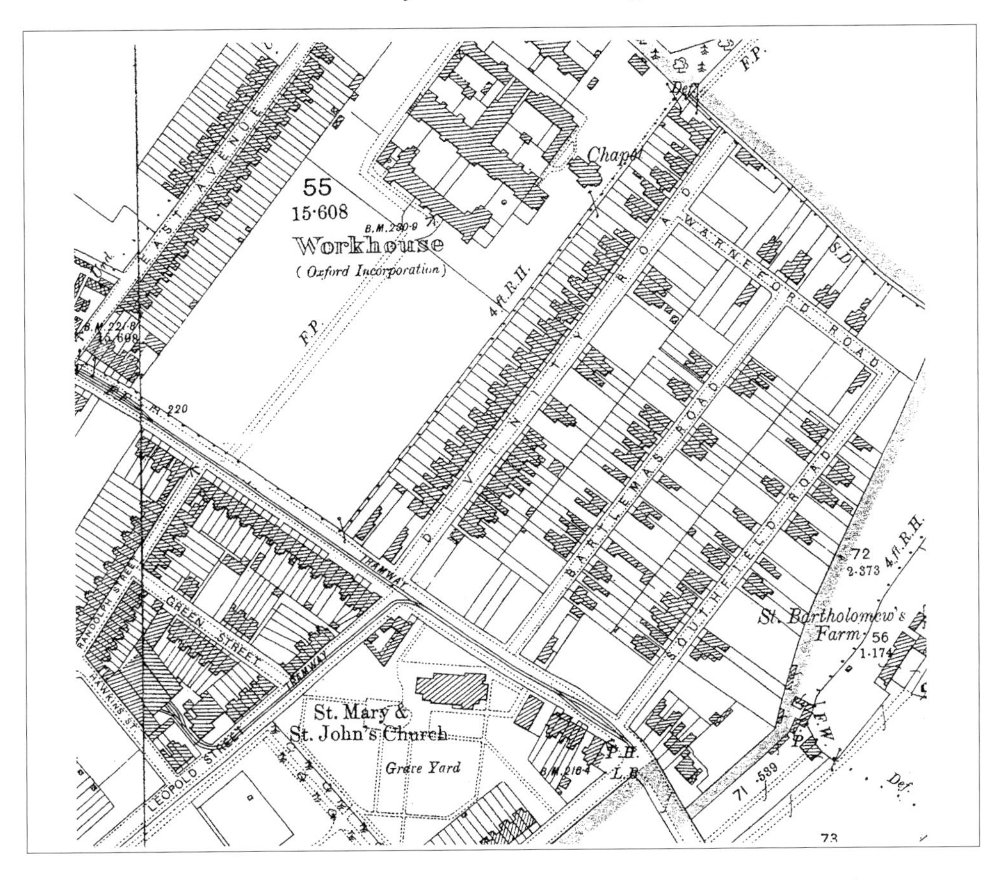

The Oxford Tramways' sole depot, by the Cowley Road terminus, on the 1899/1900 Ordnance Survey 25" to 1 mile map.

A locally-published cartoon postcard poking gentle fun at Oxford's outdated horse trams. *(Author's collection - compare with the Cambridge example on p.51)*

Postcard of the Long Causeway, Peterborough, the central terminus of the city's tramways. *(Author's collection)*

Plymouth, Stonehouse & Devonport Tramways

Authority: Plymouth, Stonehouse and Devonport Tramways Act 1870
Gauge: 4ft 8½in./3ft 6in.
Traction: Horse/overhead electric
Opened: 18 March 1872
Taken over: 1 July 1922
System: Single line
Length: 2.93 miles
Stock: 20 dd horse; 15 dd electric
Livery: Light green/emerald green & white/ivory/cream

The tramway history of Plymouth is a complicated one in relation to the size of the town. This is partly due to the fact that until 1914 it was, municipally, the 'Three Towns' of Plymouth, Stonehouse and Devonport. The trio were connected by Plymouth's first tramway – the first in Britain to open after the 1870 Tramways Act – which ran for about 2 miles from Derry's Clock in Plymouth westwards along Union Street (past the depot) and over Stonehouse bridge (where passengers had to pay a ½d toll) to terminate at Cumberland Gardens, Devonport. Owned originally by the Plymouth, Stonehouse & Devonport Tramways Co., it was taken over by PROVINCIAL TRAMWAYS within a year.

In 1874 the tramway was extended slightly in Devonport, to the junction of Marlborough Street and Fore Street (including a one-way system around Chapel Street and St Aubyn Street); the line was a single track except for a double section on the 1:11 Devonport Hill.

George Street, the hub of Plymouth's electric tramways, with Corporation No. 10 and Plymouth, Stonehouse & Devonport No. 12, both built in 1901, outside the Theatre Royal. *(Author's collection)*

Originally eight double-deck cars worked the line but these were later replaced by twelve larger versions (makers unknown). Any hope of connecting with the later PLYMOUTH, DEVONPORT & DISTRICT and the separate DEVONPORT & DISTRICT tramways was a non-starter because of the gauge difference so, when the Company decided at the beginning of the twentieth century to electrify the line, it adopted the narrower gauge of its neighbours.

After horse services ceased sometime that year, the rebuilt tramway reopened on 18 November 1901 with ERTCW open-toppers Nos 1–12 (joined by similar cars Nos 14 and 15 in 1903 and 1904); no further additions were made to the fleet until 1916 when a similar, but more modern, UEC No. 16 was acquired. Some minor alterations to the old line had been made during the reconstruction, including the building of a new depot in Market Street in Stonehouse and the doubling of the track within the Plymouth and Devonport boundaries. Those two portions of the line had already been sold to those two local authorities and leased back for twenty-one years, leaving the Company owning just 1.82 route miles of its own. The system accordingly stayed independent until 1 July 1922, when it was purchased to become an integral part of PLYMOUTH CORPORATION TRAMWAYS.

Plymouth, Devonport & District Tramways

Authority: Plymouth, Devonport and District Tramways Act 1882
Gauge: 3ft 6in.
Traction: Steam/horse
Opened: 4 November 1884
Taken over: 28 September 1892

System: Branching + single line*
Length: 2.44 miles
Stock: 4 locos, 8 sd & dd steam, 12 dd horse
Livery: Locos brown, trailers brown & white steam; red & cream horse

Plymouth's second tramway, unusually, reversed the normal pattern of events and replaced steam traction with horses. For the first year of its life Wilkinson tram locomotives were operated over a winding route from the GWR's Plymouth Milbay station near the docks, north-east along Milbay Road, Princess Square, Westwell Street, Russell Street, Richmond Street, North Road, Houndiscombe Road and Mutley Plain to the district of Mannamead. This was a distance of some 2½ miles – a far cry from the 11½-mile radial network planned by its owner, the Plymouth, Devonport & District Tramways Co. Ltd. A ½-mile branch from Princess Square ran eastwards via Notte Street and Southside Street to the Yarmouth Inn, Barbican.

Even this short, single-track system had its operating problems: the BoT would not permit trams to run through the steep and narrow Richmond Street so a two-section service had to be operated. There were also complaints about the noise and smoke of the engines, and in 1885 the Company went into liquidation after Devonport Corporation obtained an injunction on 14 November 1884 stopping it from running trams until its planned DEVONPORT LINES had been constructed – lines for which the Company had no money! (It is thought services ceased some time between 14 November and 6 December.) Accordingly, in 1889 a new concern, the Plymouth Tramways Co. Ltd, was authorised under the Plymouth & Devonport (Extension) Tramways Act to take over the existing system and construct the Devonport routes.

It is not known exactly when steam traction finished, but it seems likely that the new Company began operations with horse traction from the outset using double-deck cars Nos 1–12 and, far from extending the system as authorised, actually abandoned the Barbican branch! It was not a satisfactory solution and in 1892 Plymouth Corporation set up its own Tramways Department to run the line after paying £12,500 for it, making it the nucleus of the municipal system (see below). The depot was just off the east side of West Hoe Road in Millbay.

Details of the original company's stock are at best sketchy. It is possible that four Wilkinson tram locos were employed, these being named – according to one report – *Plymouth*, *Devonport*, *Saltash* and *Millbay* – engines which apparently found their way in 1905 (possibly via a dealer) to the Swanscombe works of Associated Portland Cement Manufacturers Ltd in Kent, where they worked for another two decades or so.

Plymouth Corporation Tramways
Authority: Plymouth Tramways Act 1892
Gauge: 3ft 6in.
Traction: Horse, overhead electric
Took over: 28 September 1892
Closed: 29 September 1945
System: Network
Length: 17.57 miles

Stock: 47? horse; 6 sd, 171 dd electric
Livery: Vermilion & white horse; red & yellow to 1922, yellow & cream to 1927, brown & white to 1930, then maroon & ivory electric*
Last Car: No. 158

As described above, Plymouth Corporation took over the two sections of the Plymouth Tramways Co.'s line in 1892, and by early the following year they had extended it in the north from Mannamead to Compton Lane End. In the south it was extended from Millbay station along West Hoe Road (past the converted PT depot) and the seafront to Pier Street, West Hoe. Corporation horse services began on Easter Monday, 3 April 1893, from Market Place to Mannamead.

In 1895 a second, more direct route to Mutley Plain was opened up with a line leaving the old route at the Guild Hall in the centre of the city and going northwards along Tavistock Road and over North Hill before rejoining the old route (thus bypassing Russell Street, Richmond Street, North Road and Houndiscombe Road). In 1896 a branch from Drake Circus just north of the Guild Hall was opened to Prince Rock to serve the hitherto neglected eastern side of the town. To work the enlarged system – now 5.15 miles in length – three open-toppers and two single-deckers (Nos 13-17) were bought from Milnes in 1894 and two more double-deckers (Nos 18 and 19) were purchased a year later. Further details of the horse car fleet are incomplete.

In the last years of the nineteenth century the Corporation decided to electrify its system, and on 22 September 1899 the first such service began, from Prince Rock to Market Avenue, with six Milnes open-toppers equipped to tow converted horse-car trailers. The service was extended very soon after as far as the Theatre Royal at the west end of George Street (shortly before Millbay Road was reached). In 1901 fourteen open-top Brush cars (Nos 7-20) were purchased to work the Compton route, which opened on 4 April that year, followed by ten more in 1902 (Nos 21-30), six in 1905 (Nos 31-36) and six single-deckers (Nos 37-42) a year later, all from Brush. In 1915 twelve more Brush open-toppers were acquired (Nos 43-54), the DEVONPORT & DISTRICT system was taken over and through services begun, with the PLYMOUTH, STONEHOUSE & DEVONPORT following suit seven years later. (The cars from these two systems were renumbered and incorporated into the Corporation's fleet as Nos 63-88 and 113-127 respectively; Nos 55-62 were Brush open-toppers acquired in 1916-7.) That year also saw, in May 1922, the opening of a new route along Alma Road to link Milehouse (where the central depot was) on the former D&D with Plymouth centre to complete the system; this utilised part of the old horse route to Mutley Plain.

In 1924 open-top EE cars 131-150 were added to the fleet, followed the next year by No. 151, a home-built bogie open-topper. In 1927 and 1928 fifteen more were constructed (Nos 152-166), the last new cars on the system. (These last sixteen cars were finished in a varnished teak livery.)

Serious bus competition began in the 1930s and the Corporation decided to join it, cutting back or closing tram routes entirely to replace them with bus services, though it did purchase another twenty-one second-hand Brush open-toppers; these came from EXETER (Nos 1-9 in 1931) and TORQUAY (Nos 10-21 in 1934), and replaced some of its ageing fleet. Only the intervention of the Second World War prolonged the tramway's existence until the Corporation's buses were able to take over completely, making it the last West Country system to close.

Poole & District Electric Tramways

Authority: Poole and District Light Railway Order 1899
Gauge: 3ft 6in.
Traction: Overhead electric
Opened: 6 April 1901
Taken over: 16 June 1905
System: Single line
Length: 3.76 miles
Stock: 17 dd
Livery: Cambridge blue & white

Whilst its counterpart in neighbouring Bournemouth was, throughout the nineteenth century, resolutely opposed to the whole idea of tramways, Poole Corporation was not. Thus, on 5 April 1899 a BET subsidiary, the Poole & District Electric Traction Co. Ltd, was registered to construct a line from Poole railway station out through the town via the district of Upper Parkstone to the Poole/Bournemouth boundary at County Gates (which also, as the name suggests, marked the Dorset/Hampshire border).

Construction began in May 1900 and the line – Dorset's only tramway – was ready less than a year later. Of its 3¾-mile length, just over 1 mile was double-tracked. On 15 June 1905 however, the Company was purchased for £112,000 by Poole Corporation who then leased the tramway to Bournemouth for thirty years. (BOURNEMOUTH CORPORATION had by this time undergone a sea-change in its opinion of the new form of public transport

A pleasing postcard view of a Poole & District tram skirting Constitution Hill, Upper Parkstone, looking towards the sea. *(Author's collection)*

and was already operating tramways of its own.) The gap of 100 yards or so between the two systems at the County Gates had been bridged that April, and on 3 July through-running was officially inaugurated by the combined dignitaries of the two municipalities. From then on the Poole line was operated as an integral part of the Bournemouth system and the taken-over cars were withdrawn slowly; these were Milnes 1-4 and ERTCW 5-11 of 1901 and Brush 12-17 of 1901-02, all open-top double-deckers shedded at Ashley Road Depot in Upper Parkstone.

Portsdown & Horndean Light Railway

Authority: Portsdown and Horndean Light Railway Order 1898
Gauge: 4ft 7¾in.
Traction: Overhead electric
Opened: 3 March 1903
Closed: 9 January 1935
System: Single line
Length: 6 miles
Stock: 1 sd, 23 dd
Livery: Emerald green & cream/ivory
Last Car: No. 6

Operated by a PROVINCIAL TRAMWAYS subsidiary, the Hampshire Light Railways (Electric) Co. Ltd (incorporated 17 May 1897), this line had its origin in the intention of PORTSMOUTH CORPORARTION in the 1890s to municipalise the PORTSMOUTH STREET TRAMWAYS, also owned by Provincial. This would have meant that the PST Co. would have been left with just a short stretch of line from the borough boundary at Hilsea north to Cosham, plus a horse bus service from there on north to Horndean; consequently it was decided to extend and electrify the line, in effect as an extension of the Corporation's system.

Formally opened on 2 March 1902, the mainly single-track line ran across the fields and beside the London Road over Portsdown Hill and through the villages of Widley, Purbrook, Waterlooville and Cowplain (the site of the depot opposite Park Lane) to Horndean.

Although the Corporation had running powers over the first mile of the tramway, the arrangement was not reciprocated until 1 August 1924 when Company cars began running into Portsmouth (first to the Town Hall and then, from 1927, all the way through to South Parade Pier). Despite the Company offering to sell the line to its neighbour on more than one occasion – the last time in 1934 – the offer was never taken up and the trams were killed off by motor and trolleybus competition.

Services began with BEC open-toppers Nos 1-9, joined later in 1903 by Nos 10-14, five similar cars; in 1905 two more of the same configuration, Nos 15 and 16, were bought from Brush. No further stock was added until 1925 when No. 17, an ex-Grimsby open toastrack, was put into service for a short while. Following the closure of the Provincial's nearby GOSPORT & FAREHAM line, seven of that tramway's open-toppers were transferred in 1930 to the P&H. Nos 8, 20 and 21 entered service with their old numbers whilst the bodies of Nos 2, 10, 14 and 22 were mounted on the trucks from withdrawn P&H cars Nos 2, 8, 10, and 14 and (re)numbered 2, 17, 10 and 14 respectively.

Car No. 16 of 1905 on Portsdown Hill, on the essentially rural Portsdown & Horndean Light Railway – one of many later tramway systems constructed under the provisions of the 1896 Light Railways Act. *(Author's collection)*

Portsmouth Street Tramways

Authority: Landport and Southsea Tramways Act 1863
Gauge: 4ft 7¾in.
Traction: Horse, steam
Opened: 15 May 1865
Taken over: 1 January 1901
System: Network
Length: 13.41 miles
Stock: *c.*70 horse; 1 dd steam
Livery: Route colour

Portsmouth had the honour of seeing Britain's first statutory street tramway when, in 1865, the Landport & Southsea Tramway Co. opened a single-track line (using step rails) from the joint LSWR and LBSCR Portsmouth station at Landport (later Portsmouth Town station) south through the town centre and on to Clarence Pier, Southsea, just a mile away. The line was intended to meet the needs of passengers travelling to and from the Isle of Wight ferries, and for that reason the gauge was chosen to permit the through-working of railway wagons. This appears never to have come about however though pairs of luggage trucks (of railway origin?) were towed behind the pair of two-horse single-deck tramcars, but the gauge had a big impact on the operation of the later tramways in the area.

The LST Co. was joined in 1873 by a second concern, the Portsmouth Street Tramways Co. (a PROVINCIAL TRAMWAYS subsidiary), who opened a much longer single-

TO THE TRADESMEN
OF
Landport & Southsea.

WHAT ARE THE
TRAMWAY
COMPANY
DOING FOR US?

1.—They are monopolizing a considerable portion of some of our most important thoroughfares, without payment of rent or compensation!

2.—They are conveying the Passengers to the Isle of Wight, direct from the Railway Station to the Southsea Pier, to the loss and injury of Tradesmen, Cab and Omnibus proprietors and drivers, and everybody else, excepting the Pier and Steam Packet Companies and themselves!

3.—They are causing a most dangerous nuisance—imperilling the safety of persons, horses, and vehicles, and seriously impeding the public traffic!

Shall we silently submit any longer? Let us all unite in getting rid of so crying an evil! No half measures! It is "NOW OR NEVER!"

A TRADESMAN.

Commercial Road, Landport,
September 16th, 1867.

Not everyone welcomed the coming of the tramways, as is shown by this 1867 notice against Portsmouth's first such line.

track north-south route from a depot at North End the following year. The route began on the London Road and continued via Kingston Crescent and Commercial Road to Landport station. There it paralleled the L&S line to Cambridge Street, which it then followed south-westwards into the High Street and along Broad Street to a second depot at Point (where a floating bridge across the mouth of Portsmouth harbour connected Portsea Island to Gosport). The line was approved by the BoT on 11 September 1874; it was presumably opened then or shortly afterwards and was better received than the LST Co.'s tramway (which was promptly relaid in 1875 with grooved rails).

A third company appeared on the scene in 1875, the General Tramways Co. of Portsmouth Ltd, though its first line did not open until 18 March 1878. This ran from the PST line at the end of the High Street, south-east along Alexandra Road to the L&S line, which it then shared along Kings Terrace and Jubilee Terrace as far as the Pier Hotel where it turned east along Southsea Terrace and Castle Road to the Queens Hotel in Osbourne Road. The GT single-deckers ran through to the Point, on what was now in effect its own line since Provincial had, in February that year, bought up both the other companies (and amalgamated them all into the PST Co. in 1883).

Many tramways operated a route to a local park, common or other beauty spot for the benefit of day-trippers. In the case of Portsmouth Corporation, one such line was to Southsea Common. *(Author's collection)*

A succession of new routes (and some abandonments) and the opening of several new depots to service the growing network now followed. By 1893 the system had reached its greatest length, extending to The Hard by the harbour to the west, East Southsea to the south-east, Fratton and Buckland to the east and as far as Cosham to the north. By now PORTSMOUTH CORPORATION was desirous of purchasing the tramways in order to electrify them, and it eventually did so under the Portsmouth Corporation Tramways Act of 1898; though the compensation agreement was complicated and slow to be reached, the Corporation eventually took possession of the company at midnight on the very last day of the century.

Details of the stock are unfortunately sparse. Both single and double-deck horse cars were used, and in 1892 fifty-eight cars were in operational use; two years later the series number 69 was reached, though whether there was any duplication of numbers is not known. The Company also operated a double-deck steamcar in regular service: constructed by an Isle of Wight firm of steam yacht builders – the Liquid Fuel Engineering Co. of East Cowes – this was a large, top-covered vehicle (but with no glazing to the upper deck) powered by an oil-fired boiler and engine. Known as 'Lifu' (after its builder's trademark), it operated from 1896 to Whit Monday 1901, always under Provincial ownership, and ended its days as an office at the Park Lane Depot of that company's PORTSDOWN & HORNDEAN LIGHT RAILWAY (see above).

Portsmouth Corporation Tramways

Authority: Portsmouth Corporation Tramways Act 1898

Gauge: 4ft 7¾in.

Traction: Horse, overhead electric

Took over: 1 January 1901

Closed: 10 November 1936
System: Network
Length: 17.7 miles
Stock: 8 horse; 1 sd, 113 dd electric
Livery: Various shades of crimson & white/cream
Last Car: No. 106 (official)

Having decided to exercise its option to purchase the PORTSMOUTH STREET TRAMWAYS (see above), the Corporation's purchase took effect at midnight on the very last day of the nineteenth century, paying the arbitrated price of £185,633 for the tramway side of the business. Reconstruction work was then put in hand, with the official inauguration of the new system taking place on 24 September 1901 with eighty DK double-deckers based at a new depot under construction in Gladys Avenue, just off the London Road in North End. In essence, the mainly double-track system was the horse tramway one with minor alterations (and the short Hilsea-Cosham section retaining horse traction until May 1903 when the Portsbridge had been strengthened).

Four more cars (Nos 81-84) were added to stock in 1903; these were the 1880 Milnes open-top horse cars already acquired (in 1896) from the NORTH METROPOLITAN TRAMWAYS, the bodies of which were mounted on new electric trucks. In 1906-7 another sixteen DK open-toppers (Nos 85-100) were bought, the last additions to the fleet until after the First World War. Their purchase was followed in 1909 by the opening of an eastwards extension from Fratton along Goldsmith Avenue to the White House, Milton;

Many tramways also ran illuminated cars to mark major national (and sometimes local) events. This is one of Portsmouth's open-toppers festooned with light bulbs on the occasion of the 1935 Silver Jubilee of King George V and Queen Mary. *(Author's collection)*

four years later this line was extended south down Eastney Road to meet the Eastney route at the Highland Chief pub. Also in July 1913, the former horse line linking South Parade Pier with Highland Road via St Helens Parade and Festing Road was reinstated, and a new extension opened from Stamshaw north, up Twyford Road and Northern Parade to Alexandra Park.

In 1919 an open toastrack (No. 104) was bought from SOUTHAMPTON CORPORATION (and later roofed), whilst in 1920 twelve EE enclosed double-deckers (Nos 105-116) were purchased, the last cars to join the fleet until 1930 when the Corporation built a new No. 1, a modern enclosed car of its own design. By this time the tramway's days were numbered, for six years later the Corporation closed the system down, replacing the trams with trolleybuses. On the tramway's final night car No. 106 led a procession of three others back to the depot on the last run. After the closure all the surviving trams were scrapped (though No. 1 escaped by virtue of having been sold to Sunderland Corporation), with the exception of No. 84, one of the converted horse cars, which was saved for official preservation and can now be seen at the Milestones Living History Museum, Basingstoke.

Provincial Tramways

The Provincial Tramways Co. Ltd, established in London in 1872, was a tramway-owning concern that began with horse lines, made the transition to electric tramways and power supply, and ended with motor bus operations. Its main focus of tramway interests was in the PORTSMOUTH AREA where it owned, through nominally independent companies, the GOSPORT & FAREHAM and PORTSDOWN & HORNDEAN lines as well as the tramways within the city. At one time or another it also owned the Grimsby system, the LONDON SOUTHERN TRAMWAYS and the PLYMOUTH, STONEHOUSE & DEVONPORT line in England, and the Cardiff system in Wales.

Ramsgate & Margate Tramways

This was an example of a tramway that almost made it to opening but fell, for financial reasons, at the very last hurdle. In 1879 the Ramsgate and Margate Tramways Act authorised the construction of 6.44 miles of 2ft 6½in. gauge horse tramway between the Kentish towns of its title, via St Peters and Broadstairs. In 1880 the Ramsgate & Margate Tramways Co. was empowered to use steam traction and, two years later, to adopt a wider (and more conventional) gauge of 3ft 6in. About a mile of track was then laid from Broadstairs station on the LCDR northwards along St Peter's Road to St Peter's church in the district of that name. By 1884 however, the Company appears to have had no reserves left to draw upon – promoting three Acts of Parliament in as many years could scarcely have helped matters – and accordingly it was wound up on 1 August 1893 by a High Court order.

The as-yet unsolved mystery is this: did the tramway ever operate a public service? It seems not, though it is believed that one double-deck car from an initial order for six (possibly from Metropolitan) was delivered to the line, probably then going the length of the country to South Shields in 1882 and five years later to Douglas Bay in the Isle of Man where it became that fleet's No. 18. However, the intrinsic value of the scheme was only proved nearly two decades after its demise with the opening of the ISLE OF THANET tramway.

Reading Tramways

Authority: Reading Tramways Order 1878
Gauge: 4ft
Traction: Horse
Opened: 5 April 1879
Taken over: 1 November 1901
System: Single line
Length: 2.37 miles
Stock: 7 sd, 6 dd?
Livery: ?

Reading's first tramway was a simple east-west line through the town centre. The western half, from the Barracks eastwards along Oxford Road to the Bull Hotel, opened first, followed on 31 May 1879 by the eastern half from the Bull out along King Street and Kings Road, then on to the London Road junction at the Cemetery Gates in the district spelled variously as Early, Earley and Erleigh. The line was single-track, except for a short central section, and was operated by the Reading Tramways Co., an IMPERIAL TRAMWAYS subsidiary; the original car fleet comprised four single-deckers with two more added for the opening of the whole line. The depot and stables were roughly midway along Oxford Road, on the south side. Later in 1879 another single-decker was added, this time from Hughes, which had a reversible body (possibly an Eades patent car). It is likely that the single-deckers were numbered 1-7 and were followed during the 1880s by double-deckers 8-10 (and later others to replace the older cars) but full details are lacking. The Company also ran horse buses.

In 1899 Reading Town Council decided to exercise its powers of compulsory purchase and a price of £11,394 was fixed, the last day of Company ownership being 31 October 1901 – by which time the Corporation had already obtained authority to extend the system as a prelude to electrification. (See below.)

Reading Corporation Tramways

Authority: Reading Tramways Order 1899
Gauge: 4ft
Traction: Horse/overhead electric
Took over: 1 November 1901
Closed: 20 May 1939
System: Radial
Length: 7.45 miles
Stock: 10 horse; 36 dd electric
Livery: ? horse; claret/dark chocolate & cream electric*
Last Car: No. 13

Reading Corporation began work on constructing and electrifying the authorised extensions to the horse tramway (see above) in April 1902. The new double-track lines were finished by mid-December (though still with horse working), after which the original tramway was converted – and doubled – with the system being completed by the following July. The new routes authorised by the 1899 Order were a 3-furlong extension west along Oxford Road from the Barracks to the Pond House, a 6-furlong extension east along Wokingham Road from the Cemetery Gates, and a 3-furlong branch north-east from the former terminus along London Road. The last horse car ran on 21 July in readiness for the electric cars' assumption of services the next day. Two of the old cars (both double-deckers) were sold to the nearby WANTAGE TRAMWAY and the others disposed of.

Before reconstruction had begun, powers for further lines had been granted under the Reading Corporation (Tramways) Act 1900; these were a northern branch along Caversham Road from the Oxford Road/Broad Street junction, a branch south from there along Bridge Street, Southampton Street and Whitley Street with a south-western branch along Castle Street and Castle Hill to the start of Bath Road, and a south-eastern branch off King Street along London Street and part of London Road, then into Erleigh Road. The new system was principally double-tracked with the new branches being in the order of a mile or so in length (the Bath Road line being half that).

The initial order of cars was for thirty ERTCW open-toppers, based on a new depot by the power station in Mill Lane off London Street; these were joined a year later by Nos 31-36, more of the same only this time mounted on bogies.

The Corporation began running motor buses in 1919, though this does not seem to have threatened the tramway, which continued to be kept in good order (with minor track adjustments made to several of the terminals in the late 1920s and early 1930s). The car fleet, somewhat surprisingly, was never added to during the rest of the tramway's life,

Broad Street, Reading, with Corporation open-toppers Nos 11 and 24 in the days when tramcars would be the only motorised vehicles visible. *(Author's collection)*

though Nos 1-9, 11-30 and 36 were all re-bodied in the 1920s at Mill Lane, with those earmarked for rebuilding painted flat grey until the work had been carried out.

The system's gradual abandonment, when it came, was brought about by a combination of increased Corporation and private bus operations, and increased private car use and its concomitant road congestion. The short Bath Road route went on 31 March 1930, the Erleigh Road route on 7 August 1932 and on 15 July 1936 the Caversham-Whitley through route was closed (to be converted to trolleybus operation). This left just the original horse tramway route (and its extensions) to survive for a further three years; after the final closure the two dozen cars still in service were sold for scrap.

Redruth *see* Camborne & Redruth

Rosherville *see* Gravesend, Rosherville & Northfleet

Rottingdean *see* Brighton & Rottingdean

Ryde Pier Tramway

Authority: Ryde Pier and Tramways Act 1865*
Gauge: 4ft 8½in.
Traction: Horse/steam/horse
Opened: 29 August 1864
Closed: March 1886
System: Single line
Length: 1.51 miles
Stock: 2 locos, 3 sd, 6 dd horse & steam
Livery: Various
Last Car: ?

The Ryde Pier Tramway was not only the Isle of Wight's sole tramway, it was the only British pier tramway that managed to progress more than a few yards inland. The original pier was opened in 1814 in response to the growing popularity of the island as a holiday resort and was gradually lengthened to 2,250ft to serve the Southampton ferries. In 1862 work began on a new pier on the eastern side of the original; also of timber construction, it eventually sported two standard gauge tracks linked by a crossover at the shore end (but apparently worked as two separate lines). The rails were laid in 1863 and were of flat-bottomed railway rather than tramway type, and in order that other vehicles might use the pier the wooden decking was asphalted to rail level. There appears to have been no legal authority for the tramway (official length 0.39 miles) other than that of the original 1812 Ryde Pier Act.

Two cars – a 1st class double-decker and a 2nd class single-decker – and a luggage van, manufacturer unknown, were delivered in September that year and the following March trials began with an MW steam locomotive named *Vectis* after the Roman name for the island. This proved to create excessive vibrations in the structure of the pier however and was returned to the makers, the tramway instead opening with horse traction and a new,

A *c.*1871 view of Ryde Pier Tramway, with the pier head turntable and car shed siding to the fore. *(Author's collection)*

A slightly later view of Ryde pier head, *c.*1875, with its separate ticket huts for the Esplanade (right) and St John's Road (left). The rear car on the left is the 'Grapes' car in double-deck form. Note the cars parked off the running lines in the middle distance. *(Author's collection)*

much lighter single-deck composite car from T.B. Ayshford, an omnibus builder of Walham Green in London. The opening was delayed by the car having to be returned to its maker for repairs after an unscheduled dip in the sea; the boat it was on, being towed to the island by a Portsmouth steamer, had been swamped in bad weather. It is presumed that this vehicle, then or later, became the tramway's No. 1; the following August Ayshford supplied a second, similar car (No. 2), and in 1867 a 1st class single-decker (No. 3) was built locally. The original two passenger carriages bought for use with the loco. were sold in 1867 to the Isle of Wight Railway (taking the numbers 25 and 26 there).

The Ryde Pier Co.'s intention was to extend the tramway southwards through the town to the IWR's Ryde terminus (renamed Ryde St John's Road in 1880), just over a mile away, and on 28 January 1870 an extension (1,180ft in length) to Ryde Castle on a widened Esplanade opened (authorised by the Ryde Pier and Tramways Act 1865). The remaining section travelled south through (literally!) Holywell House into Cornwall Street, then beside the culverted Monkton Road Brook, across Link Road and Park Road to the station. The section was opened on 7 August 1871, the whole line now being known as the Ryde Pier Railway. Two years later a parallel goods branch was laid on the Esplanade to serve the shorter Victoria Pier.

Passenger trams were horse-worked from St John's Road to the pier head (where they were turned on a turntable), with a horse-drawn luggage van following behind. More stock was added at this time (1871), including Starbuck open-toppers Nos 5-9 (one 1st class, two 2nd class and two composites) and a Company-built, 1st class ornate and luxurious open-topper, wheeled out on very special occasions, numbered 4 and known as the 'Grapes Car' on account of its carved embellishments. These later cars worked the services to St John's, while Nos 1-3 were confined to the west track shuttle service between the pier head and the Esplanade. Some through-running of railway vans and wagons occurred, but the only section of the tramway used by railway engines was that just north of St John's Road station in order for them to run round their trains. Steam traction on the tramway was again experimented with, in September 1876, using a Merryweather loco., but after trials she too was returned to her makers that December. (For details of its possible later life, see WIMBLEDON COMMON TRAMWAY.)

The double trans-shipment of ferry passengers and their luggage was not a satisfactory one, and on 5 August 1880 the railway was extended from St John's Road (via a tunnel) onto the Esplanade where a station (Ryde Esplanade) was built at the pier gates. On 12 July it was extended all the way along a new railway pier (owned jointly by the LSWR and the LBSCR but worked by the IoWR and Isle of Wight Central Railway trains) beside the tramway one. From then on the town tram service ceased, and the rails were eventually lifted about five years later.

Two steam locos were supplied by F. Bradley of Glensmore Works, Kidderminster to work the pier line from February 1881 to the end of October 1884, with horse working resuming on 1 November; they were built to run on coal gas but after unsatisfactory trials converted to burn coke. In 1885 Siemens Bros & Co. of Chorlton were contracted to electrify the line, on the third-rail system, and the tramway was fenced-off from the rest of the pier to become a single-track electric railway. This began operation on 6 March 1886, however regular services were delayed by teething troubles until 4 April. A little continuity was provided with the past by some of the horse cars (including the Grapes Car) being converted for use on the new railway, if only for a few years. The horse cars were used as trailers to the electric cars and a second track was added four years later. Electric working lasted until 1927 when the then owner, the Southern Railway, abandoned it in favour of two new Drewry petrol railcars. In 1969 BR withdrew services completely – as they did over much of the island – replacing the railcars with an ex-London Underground stock shuttle service on the adjoining railway pier. Happily the Grapes Car, which survived as a railcar trailer until an accident in 1935 led to its withdrawal (by which date it must have been the oldest working tramcar in the British Isles), is now restored and on display in the Hull Transport Museum.

Rye & Camber Tramway

This was a 3ft gauge railway that ran through open country and sand dunes by the north bank of the River Rother, from Rye in East Sussex to close to the beach at Camber Sands. The line was constructed by local businessmen on private land, thus obviating the need for Parliamentary approval. The engineer was Holman F. (later Colonel) Stephens of light railway fame, and the first 1½ miles to the Rye Golf Club opened on 13 July 1895; a further ½-mile extension to Camber Sands opened exactly thirteen years later.

Stock comprised two small Bagnall tank engines, a four-wheeled petrol locomotive (from 1925), two saloon coaches and a handful of goods wagons. The line closed in 1939 on the outbreak of the Second World War and was requisitioned by the Admiralty, never to reopen to the public.

St George & Hanham Light Railway *see* Bristol Tramways

St Leonard's *see* Rhyl Miniature Tramway (Volume 2)

Sandgate *see* Folkestone, Hythe & Sandgate

Seaton Tramway

Authority: British Railways Board (Seaton and Beer) Light Railway Order 1969
Gauge: 2ft 9in.
Traction: Battery/overhead electric
Opened: 28 August 1970
System: Single line
Length: 3.23 miles
Stock: 6 sd, 7 dd
Livery: Various*

The previous incarnations of this tramway are described under EASTBOURNE and Rhyl (see Volume 2). In the mid-1960s, with the closure of the latter line imminent, a search was made for a new site that would permit a longer run, a wider track gauge and long-term security. The site chosen was the former BR branch from Seaton Junction to Seaton, on Devon's Lyme Bay coast, which closed in 1966. Modern Electric Tramways

Seaton Tramway No. 4 of 1961, re-gauged after transfer from Eastbourne, at Colyton. *(Seaton Tramway)*

Ltd took an option on the final 3 miles from Colyton to Seaton, and set up an operating company, the Seaton & District Tramway Co., to run the new line (now known simply as the Seaton Tramway). A new gauge of 2ft 9in. was chosen as the widest that still allowed ex-BR sleepers cut in two to be used, thereby making a very considerable saving on track materials not possible with any broader a gauge.

Transfer of stock and equipment from Eastbourne began in February 1970 (the necessary Transfer Order for the new use of the trackbed having been obtained the previous June), with tracklaying commencing shortly afterwards. A limited service began later that summer over the first mile from Seaton, beside the River Axe to Bobsworth Bridge, using open-top car No. 8 and a battery trailer; on 9 April the following year the battery-powered service was extended another mile as far as Colyford.

The overhead was brought into use on 7 June 1974 and, on 17 May 1975, a short extension off the old BR trackbed at the Seaton end took the line westwards to the town centre car park. The final third of the line to Colyton opened on 3 April 1980, since when the line has operated as a genuine tramway rather than a pleasure line – though it must be the only one to run bird watchers' specials on a regular basis! The latest major alteration made to the infrastructure of the tramway was the provision of a new, more visible terminus at Seaton in 1995, officially opened on 26 August.

All stock is at least partially Company-built, and a feature is the incorporation of parts such as seats and controllers from scrapped trams from other systems. Nos 2, 4, 6–8 and 12 were transferred from Eastbourne, all being re-gauged (except No. 8, which had been constructed in 1968 to the new gauge), and all are still in service (with No. 12 rebuilt as an open-top double-decker in 1980). In addition, single-deck saloon cars Nos 14 (completed 1984) and 16 (1991) are rebuilds of METROPOLITAN LECTRIC No. 94 (LONDON

Seaton No. 8 of 1968, awaiting passengers at Colyton. Although built at Eastbourne, this car was constructed to Seaton's 2ft 9in. gauge in readiness for the move. *(Seaton Tramway)*

TRANSPORT No. 2455) of 1904 and BOURNEMOUTH No. 106 of 1921 respectively. Both were converted from bogie open-toppers to bogie enclosed single-deck cars. Car No. 17 is a 1988 covered Manx Electric Railway-type toastrack with removable seats and wheelchair access, and No. 19 is an enclosed single-decker rebuilt (completed 1998) from the remains of EXETER CORPORATION No. 19 (later No. 21), a 1906 open-topper. All the rebuilds are bogie vehicles, as are the other passenger cars, and have been finished in their former owners' liveries.

The newest arrivals are Nos 9–11, three open-top double-deckers assembled at Seaton in 2002 with bodies supplied by Bolton Trams of Wigan – the operator's first such use of an outside firm. Painted in approximations of the liveries of POOLE (No. 9), Glasgow (No. 10) and Liverpool 1st class (No. 11), they entered service over the following four years after final fitting-out and trials and have low-floor centres to facilitate wheelchair access. There is also a small fleet of fully-functional works cars, those often ignored but vital components of a working tramway.

The tramway operates daily from spring to autumn, with weekend, holiday and other special workings during the winter.

Selsey Tramway *see* Hundred Of Manhood & Selsey Tramway

Sheerness & District Tramways

Authority: Sheerness and District Light Railway Order 1903

Gauge: 3ft 6in.

Seaton No. 10 of 2002, one of the tramway's latest trio of cars, loading at Colyton in 2005. *(Seaton Tramway)*

Traction: Overhead electric
Opened: 9 April 1903
Closed: 7 July 1917
System: Radial
Length: 2.47 miles
Stock: 12 dd
Livery: Chocolate & cream
Last Car: ?

Although short in route and short-lived in years, the only tramway on Kent's Isle of Sheppey possessed a number of interesting features. Owned by the Sheerness & District Electrical Power & Traction Co. Ltd (a member of the BET group), it operated no less than three single-track routes radiating from the town's central Clock Tower. The first ran westwards along the High Street past the SECR's Sheerness Town station to terminate by that railway's Dockyard station, another went eastwards to the Marine Parade in the direction of Cheyney Roack, while the final route took passengers south-east along the High Street to Sheerness East station on the Sheppey Light Railway. At the last terminus were sited the tramway's power station and car sheds – the latter being served, most unusually for Britain, by a turntable rather than the customary track fan (or even traverser). The promoters had planned a grander system with branches out to the village of Minster and the port of Queensborough, but the SLR opposed those on account of the level crossings they would have made over its metals.

Car No. 4 of 1903 on the short-lived Sheerness & District system. The car's unusual bow current collector and the bowstring bracket arms for the overhead wire can just be made out on this postcard. *(Author's collection)*

A grand total of twelve open-top double-deckers were ordered from Brush for the opening but, hardly surprisingly, this number was found to be far too large for the needs of the system and Nos 9-12 were promptly sold to the City of Birmingham Tramways (where they became Nos 189-192). The cars were equipped with enormous Siemens bow collectors unique on British tramways (as were any bow collectors on open-top cars), whilst the overhead, installed by Siemens & Halske of Berlin, was suspended from distinctive German-style bow-shaped brackets. The line's Continental appearance was enhanced further by the practice of running the line close to the kerb (with passing loops in the centre of the road) in the narrow parts of the High Street, West Street and even in front of the Town station.

The system had the dubious honour of becoming Britain's first electric tramway to close, its demise was brought about partly by the non-availability of spare parts from Germany during the First World War, after which the eight cars were sold to Darlington. Bus competition had also appeared in 1913, and both Sheerness UDC and RDC had declined to buy the system when offered it.

Shoreham *see* Brighton & Shoreham

South Eastern Metropolitan Tramways *see* London: South Eastern Metropolitan Tramways

South Metropolitan Electric Tramways

Authority: Mitcham Light Railway Order 1901
Gauge: 4ft 8½in.

Traction: Overhead electric
Opened: 14 February 1906?
Taken over: 1 July 1933
System: Branching + branching
Length: 13.36 miles
Stock: 55 dd
Livery: Brunswick green & ivory to 1921, then Underground red & white

The South Metropolitan Electric Tramways & Lighting Co. Ltd, registered on 3 August 1904 as a BET subsidiary, operated tramways either side of the Surrey town of CROYDON (which Corporation's tramways the BET worked on lease from 1902 to 1906). Work began in 1905 on a continuation of the Corporation's line to South Norwood across the town and county boundary and into Kent, then north-west into Penge High Street (1¾ miles), as authorised by the 1902 Croydon and District Electric Tramways Act. This opened shortly after the BoT's inspection of 13 February 1906 as far as the Pawleyne Arms (1 mile) at the Croydon Road/High Street junction and was worked by the BET as a through route from Croydon until the end of May, thereafter becoming the nucleus of the South Metropolitan system. On 12 April 1906 the rest of the line along the High Street and west into Thicket Road was opened, as was a branch off Croydon Road at the Robin Hood (opposite Penge Depot on Oak Grove Road) which ran north-west along Anerley Road to the LBSC's Crystal Palace Low Level station (extended up Anerley Hill to Crystal Palace on 28 May).

UEC open-top double-deckers 1-16 of 1906 took over the working of the Penge lines after Croydon Corporation withdrew its cars. Meanwhile, work on the other half of the system was progressing and on 26 May 1906 2¾ miles of double-track line were opened, they ran from Tooting Junction south to Mitcham, then went south-east over Mitcham Common to the Croydon boundary, together with a ½-mile branch south from Mitcham to the Cricket Green. (These were the lines authorised by the 1901 Mitcham LRO.) Also opened was a continuation of the light railway along Mitcham Road past the Company's Aurelia Road Depot to Canterbury Road (authorised by the 1902 Act), extended on 14 July to Lower Church Street and on 9 October into Tamworth Road opposite West Croydon station. This was also the terminus for the Company's double-track route westwards along Epsom Road and Stafford Road (past what was to become Croydon Aerodrome) through Wallington and Carshalton to Benhill Street, Sutton, where it terminated by the Grapes pub. The Company's third depot was sited in Westmead Road, just before the terminus. This route opened in stages from August to December 1906 to complete the two-part system.

The new lines were worked by Milnes 17-26 (Nos 36-45 at Croydon), Brush Nos 27-29, 31 and 35 (Croydon's 56-60) and new Brush open-toppers Nos 36-51. Two ERTCW bogie open-toppers of 1902 built for GRAVESEND & NORTHFLEET were also acquired in 1906, which were renumbered 30 and 32 by the South Metropolitan and joined by the similar cars Nos 33 and 34 a year later.

On 13 October 1907 LONDON COUNTY COUNCIL opened a branch to Tooting Junction, which connected end-on with the Company's line. However, because the LCC used a conduit current collection supply, through-running could not take place. On 14 June 1913 ownership of the Company was transferred to the London & Suburban Traction Co. Ltd, a holding company registered on 20 November 1912 and owned jointly by the BET and the Underground Electric Railways Co. of London Ltd (the Underground group), to become part of a massive Greater London tramway, bus and railway empire.

On 4 November 1926 the LCC began through-working from Victoria to the Cricket Green, and the Company ceased its own services over this part of the system. In 1927 it purchased twelve cars from Croydon Corporation as replacements for older vehicles but put only four into service, as Nos 17, 21, 47 and 52, all Brush vehicles of 1906-07 vintage; one, Croydon No. 13, was sold to LONDON UNITED TRAMWAYS the following year for conversion to a rail grinder. Two years later the legend 'SouthmeT' began to appear on the trams, which were joined in 1931 by ten loaned LUT top-covered cars. Two years later, as at Croydon, the system was absorbed into the new LONDON TRANSPORT network.

Southall, Ealing & Shepherds Bush Tramway *see* London: West Metropolitan Tramways

Southampton Tramways

Authority: Southampton Street Tramways Act 1877
Gauge: 4ft 8½in.
Traction: Horse
Opened: 5 May 1879
Taken over: 1 July 1898
System: Branching
Length: 4.86 miles
Stock: 3sd, dd
Livery: ?

Built by the Southampton Tramways Co. (incorporated 1876) after an earlier proposal by the British & Foreign Tramway Co. had failed because of Corporation opposition, the first route opened was a simple north-south line running from Alma Road north of the town centre, down The Avenue and London Road to Above Bar Street. From here it continued south through the Bargate in the city wall and down the High Street to Holy Rood at the junction with Bridge Street. On 6 May 1879 the line was extended at both ends: east and north from Stag Gates just south of Alma Road via Lodge Road and Portswood Road to Portswood, and east along Bridge Street, Oxford Street and Canute Road to the floating bridge across the River Itchen.

A second route opened on 9 June 1879, from the end of Above Bar Street ('the Junction') west along Commercial Road and north-west down Shirley Road to Shirley High Street. Like the first route, this was a single-track line.

It is thought that services began with six single-deckers and three double-deckers (Nos 1-9) from the Bristol Wagon & Carriage Works Co. Ltd, though the double-deckers proved so heavy that many later had their upper superstructures removed (whilst the single-deckers had seats added to their roofs!). These were joined between 1879 and 1882 by Starbuck double-deckers Nos 10-20, and between 1890 and 1893 by Nos 21-27 from the NORTH METROPOLITAN works in London; the final acquisitions were Brush double-deckers Nos 28-31 in 1896. The two depots were at the Shirley and Portswood terminals. From 1887 the Company also operated horse buses, housed in a separate depot off The Avenue north of the old Alma Road terminus. (The short stretch from Alma Road back to Stag Gates was abandoned *c.*1890.)

On 30 June 1898 Southampton Corporation exercised its right to buy the tramway (the independently arbitrated figure being £51,000) in order to electrify it. (See below.)

Southampton Corporation Tramways

Authority: Southampton Corporation Tramways Act 1897
Gauge: 4ft 8½in.
Traction: Horse, overhead electric
Took over: 1 July 1898
Closed: 31 December 1949
System: Network
Length: 13.7 miles
Stock: ? horse; 142 dd electric
Livery: Variously red & white/cream/grey
Last Car: No. 9

After its purchase of the horse tramway (see above), Southampton Corporation set about electrifying it, cutting back existing services as work progressed. On 15 January 1900 the new cars began running from Shirley to the Junction with public services inaugurated on 22 June, followed on 29 May by those on the Holy Rood-Stag Gates main line. On 12 September the line from Holy Rood was reopened as far as the docks (the Canute Street section being abandoned), followed on 4 October by Stag Gates to Portswood to complete the conversion of the horse system. The routes were mainly double-track, with a short stretch of single track through the Bargate. This was not quite the end of the horse trams though, for a second north-south line was laid at this time, from the Ordnance College on London Road down Bellevue Terrace, St Mary's Street, Marsh Lane and Terminus Terrace to meet the other main line at the docks. Horse cars were used on this until 2 August 1901, when work was completed to enable the new trams to take over the service the following day.

The first electric cars were special low bridge open-toppers with knife-board seating on the upper decks (i.e. two long back-to-back seats down the centre of the car) to allow them to pass under the Bargate safely (even though the roadway had been lowered). Numbered 1-39, they were supplied by Milnes in 1899-1902 and were joined in 1903 by twelve HN cars (Nos 40-51) of a similar, but not so satisfactory design. In 1908 the Corporation began constructing its own cars at the main Portswood Depot (the old Shirley Depot was also retained), and between then and 1915 they produced twenty-one similar vehicles, Nos 52-62 and 64-73 (No. 63 was a 1911 version from UEC) with No. 74 of 1917 having conventional seating on top.

Southampton Corporation No. 40 of 1903 threading the Bargate before it was bypassed. *(Author's collection)*

Southampton No. 20 of 1900, by the Clock Tower in Above Bar Street. *(Author's collection)*

Still further north: another Southampton open-topper, this time No. 48 of 1903, in the leafy setting of The Avenue, on a postcard sent in 1910. *(Author's collection)*

After the First World War new cars were bought from ERTCW (Nos 75-80 in 1918-19) and EE (Nos 82-91 in 1919-20), while the Corporation built No. 81 in 1919 and Nos 92-109 in 1925-30 to complete the original number series. Over a similar period (1923-31) another thirty-three double-deckers were constructed and given numbers of withdrawn older cars. All cars, from No. 74 of 1917 onwards, had cross-seating on the upper deck, and all from No. 12 of 1923 had enclosed tops of a special profile, a low floor and very small wheels to enable them to negotiate the Bargate.

All this time the system had been expanding slowly, until 10 July 1930 when the last route opened from Bassett Crossroads (at the northern end of the extended Avenue route) to go eastwards along Burgess Road to Swaythling (to meet the extended Portswood Road line). The resulting system was a complicated network of routes covering the whole of the town peninsula with one route crossing the Itchen, via Cobden Bridge east of Portswood, to Bitterne. The only major alterations to the track layout before the closures began in earnest were made on 24 April 1932 and 5 June 1938 when, after decades of discussion, first the east and then the west side of the Bargate were bypassed.

The first abandonment of a line came on 4 June 1936 when the short eastern route to Northam on the Itchen was closed, after which the Second World War gave the system a respite until 1948 when the closures resumed with a vengeance, all routes going within two years. After the final closure twenty-two cars were sold to Leeds but only eleven – Nos 23, 25, 32, 50 and 104-109 – entered service there. (All were final-period Southampton-built vehicles.) Car No. 45 of 1903 was sold in 1948 to a group of enthusiasts to provide the inspiration for what became the National Tramway Museum at Crich (see Volume 2).

The all-too common fate of many of Britain's tramcars when their system closed: the breaker's yard, as here at Southampton. *(Author's collection)*

Above: The one that got away (and started a whole preservation movement): Southampton No. 45 of 1903 restored and operational at the National Tramway Museum, Crich. *(Author)*

Opposite: Southend-on-Sea Corporation No. 42 of 1914 on a Boulevards circular working. *(Author's collection)*

Southend-On-Sea Corporation Tramways

Authority: Southend-on-Sea and District Light Railways Order 1899
Gauge: 3ft 6in.
Traction: Overhead electric
Opened: 19 July 1901
Closed: 8 April 1942
System: Network
Length: 9.22 miles
Stock: 6 sd, 65 dd
Livery: Variously dark green, dark green & light green, and green & cream/ivory
Last Car: ?

Built and extended by Southend-on-Sea Corporation under a succession of Light Railway Orders, the Southend system was intended to serve residents and holiday-makers alike in this increasingly-popular Thames estuary resort. The system was centred on Victoria Circus, just south of the GER's Southend-on-Sea station, and the first two lines opened ran from here north along Victoria Avenue to Prittlewell then back in a loop via North Road and London Road. The final part took the trams east then south along Southchurch Road and Southchurch Avenue to the beach.

On 9 August (after the necessary road works had been completed) a third, longer route westwards along London Road through Chalkwell to Leigh-on-Sea was opened. The original cars were ten small open-top double-deckers, two large open-top bogie cars (Nos 11 and 12) and two small single-deckers (Nos 13 and 14), all from Brush. A further three open-top bogie cars (Nos 15-17) followed a year later. The route length was 6¼ miles of mainly single track and the depot was in London Road, about ¼ mile from Victoria Circus.

Another five open-top bogie cars (Nos 18-22) were bought in 1904, this time from Milnes, and after this some of the older cars were renumbered thus: the single-deckers became Nos 1 and 2, the old Nos 1 and 2 became 11 and 12, and the old Nos 11 and 12 became 13 and 14, thus giving consecutive numbers to the three different types of tramcar.

On 10 August 1908 an extension of the line to the beach was opened along Southchurch Beach Road (Eastern Esplanade) as far as Bryant Avenue (about ½ a mile), on 16 November another ¼ of a mile of track to the Halfway House pub was opened. The whole extension was single-track but now a track-doubling programme was begun, starting at Victoria Circus and working outwards.

The car fleet grew steadily with another twenty open-toppers being added by the end of 1912 and numbered either at the end of the sequence or given the numbers of withdrawn vehicles. These were: Nos 23-25 (UEC 1909), 26-31 (Brush 1910), 33-39 (Brush 1912) and 3, 5, 8 and 11 (Brush 1911). The former No. 1 was rebuilt at Southend in 1911 and renumbered 32, whilst in 1914 three open toastracks, Nos 40-42, were bought from Brush. The reason for their purchase was that the eastern routes had been extended further, firstly on 10 February 1912 from the Halfway House to Thorpe Bay, secondly from the High Street eastwards along Southchurch Road and Southchurch Boulevard to Bournes Green on 30 July 1913. Lastly, on 16 July 1914, a link southwards from Bournes Green to Thorpe Bay was opened along Thorpe Boulevard. This completed a large out-and-back loop from the town centre, the eastern half of which was on a reserved, tree-lined double-track section known as the Boulevards route, the whole being worked by the toastracks as a circular pleasure tour. That same year, on 1 April, Southend became a county borough. The system was now complete, the only other previous change being the closure, on 22 January 1912, of the North Road section of the loss-making Prittlewell route.

The Corporation had its own loading pier opposite the gas works where East Parade met the Eastern Esplanade, and in 1914 this was rebuilt and a tramway spur laid on to it to enable coal to be moved to the municipal power station next to the tramway depot. Early in 1915 three powered open coal cars were supplied by the firm of Grenshaw & Piers of Bolton, and numbered 1A-3A; these were used until 1931 when the coal traffic ceased with the Council's decision to stop generating electricity and take it instead from the National Grid.

After the First World War Southend's popularity soared as a cheap, accessible seaside resort close to London. To cope with this demand the tramway, with its ageing fleet, desperately needed new stock. In 1921 a Brush bogie roofed toastrack was purchased (No. 43), followed by a dozen top-covered cars from the same manufacturer (Nos 44-55); these were joined in 1924 by six similar cars (Nos 56-61) from EE. The Council however, was now considering the introduction of trolleybuses, and in 1925 they hired two for tests and driver training on the Prittlewell route. The trials were judged a success, the Council committed itself to this new mode of transport and on 18 December 1929 the last trams ran on the Prittlewell-High Street route.

During the next decade more trolleybuses were bought and their routes extended; in contrast the car fleet was slowly cut down with withdrawals and scrappings. No further stock was added until the 1934 purchase (as replacement vehicles) of Nos 62-65, four ex-Middlesbrough balcony cars and Nos 66-68, three enclosed-top ex-Accrington trams.

A Southend double-decker on a similar service. *(Author's collection)*

The next major occurence came in 1938 when, faced with the cost of renewing its deteriorating track, the Corporation closed the Boulevards section on 6 July, which meant that Southchurch and Thorpe Bay were terminals once again. (The trams were replaced by motor buses.) The Esplanade route was cut back to the end of Southchurch Avenue (the Kursaal) on 3 June 1939, to be replaced by a trolleybus service. Ageing track elsewhere on the system meant that the last routes could not survive the war years and the Southchurch line closed on 7 January 1942, just three months before the Leigh-Victoria Circus-Kursaal route.

Southend Pier Tramway

Authority: Local authority permission*
Gauge: *c.*3ft 6in.
Traction: Horse
Opened: 1875?
Closed: 1881?
System: Single line
Length: *c.*1.25 miles
Stock: 2 sd
Livery: ?
Last Car: ?

As the longest such structure in the world, Southend Pier is justly famous and, since 1890, has operated (with some interruptions) a railway of some sort along its 1¼-mile length. However, the site had been occupied since June 1830 by a wooden pier, built by the

Southend Pier Co. and which, by 1846, had grown to a comparable length and sported a luggage line, laid that year down its eastern side, worked by three hand-propelled trucks on wooden rails. (One of the trucks – or possibly a fourth – was fitted with a mast and sail for use when the wind was favourable, a method of propulsion also used on the pier at HERNE BAY.)

After passing through a succession of hands the pier was purchased in 1875 by the local authority under the Southend Local Board Act of that year. The tramway was then relaid with iron rails and three small, enclosed carriages provided for passenger transport (possibly rebuilds of the luggage trucks), which ran coupled as a train with a flat driver's truck at the seaward end; the whole rake was pulled by two horses in tandem. (Presumably the driver's truck was man-handled to the other end of the train at the pier head for the return journey.) A notable feature of the line was that it ran through the middle of the pier's entertainment tent – even during shows!

Ten years later it was decided to replace the ageing wooden structure with a new, cast iron one (opened 1889), though by then the wear and tear brought on by the weight of the train and the pounding of the horses' hooves, and the spreading of the light rails spiked directly to the decking, had resulted in the line being closed as unfit for use.

Southsea *see* Portsmouth

Stonehouse *see* Plymouth, Stonehouse & Devonport

Stony Stratford *see* Wolverton & Stony Stratford

Surrey Side Street Railway *see* London: Train's Tramways

Swindon Corporation Tramways

Authority: Swindon Corporation Tramways Order 1901
Gauge: 3ft 6in.
Traction: Overhead electric
Opened: 22 September 1904
Closed: 11 July 1929
System: Radial
Length: 3.7 miles
Stock: 13 dd
Livery: Maroon & cream
Last Car: No. 1

Corporation-owned from the outset, Swindon's tramway system had its centre – 'the Centre' – in New Town at the junction of Bridge Street and Fleet Street; from here one line travelled south-west along Faringdon Street then Faringdon Road before swinging northwards into Park Lane under the GWR main line. It then continued via Rodbourne Road to the outlying district of that name, whilst the second went north-east along Fleet Street, Milford Street, Mill Street and Manchester Road before also turning north

Swindon Corporation No. 3 of 1904 in the town's bustling Bridge Street. *(Author's collection)*

under the main railway line, this time via Drove Road and Cricklade Road to the district of Gorse Hill. The third line ran south from the Centre through the Old Town to the Market Square, via Bridge Street (over the Wiltshire & Berkshire Canal), Regent Street, Regent Circus, Victoria Road, Victoria Street, Mill Street and the High Street. A short spur from Mill Street on the Gorse Hill route, down Wellington Street to Swindon station, completed the system. All the lines were primarily single-track.

Services began with seven open-top double-deckers from ERTCW, which were joined by two more (Nos 8 and 9) the following year. In 1906 similar Brush cars Nos 10-12 were acquired, followed by a similar EE car (No. 13) in 1921 to complete the fleet. The depot was in Mill Street, almost opposite the spur to the station. The system's early demise and replacement by the inevitable bus services was hastened by the deteriorating state of the track, condemned in 1928 by the Borough Surveyor.

Apart from being Wiltshire's only tramway, the Swindon system had one thing of distinction about it: for a few yards on one of the bridge approaches the gradient is thought to have been a staggering 1:4 – by far the steepest on any British tramway.

Taunton Electric Tramways

Authority: Taunton Tramways Order 1900
Gauge: 3ft 6in.
Traction: Overhead electric
Opened: 21 August 1901
Closed: 28 May 1921
System: Single line
Length: 1.66 miles

Stock: 6 sd, 6 dd
Livery: Dark green & cream to 1903, then crimson lake & cream
Last Car: ?

The Taunton tramway – it could hardly be called a system – is generally noted for two main claims to fame: possessing the shortest route length of any British electric street tramway and one of the longest operator's titles – in this case the Taunton & West Somerset Electric Railways & Tramways Co. Ltd, a firm taken over in 1903 by the Taunton Electric Traction Co. Ltd, a BET subsidiary.

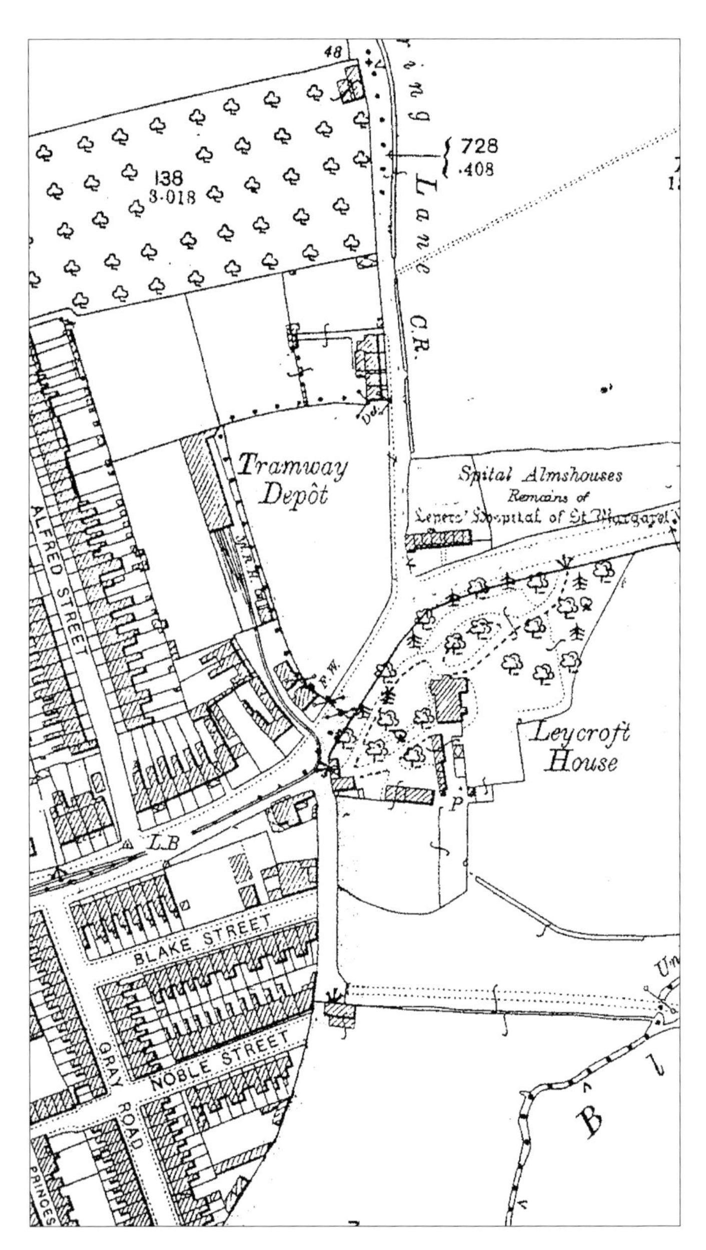

The Taunton Electric Tramways' East Reach Depot, on the 1904 Ordnance Survey 25" to 1 mile map. When former horse tramway depots were not available for conversion, many electric car sheds were built on the edge of town where land was cheap, and consequently often at the end of a route – as was the case here.

The first section of the single-track line to be opened ran from the depot in East Reach via East Street, North Street and Station Road to the GWR's Taunton station, a distance of just a mile; an extension from here down Kingston Road to terminate opposite Salisbury Street in Rowbarton was opened on 13 August 1909 to complete the undertaking.

The tramway's original car fleet comprised six Brush open-top double-deckers (with No. 6 arriving in 1902). In 1905 however, services were temporarily suspended for two months whilst the track was relaid – a move necessitated by its poor construction – and the cars were sold to the Leamington & Warwick tramway to be replaced by a similar number of Brush single-deckers (also numbered 1-6). These vehicles were more in keeping with a realistic assessment of the line's volume of traffic. Two of these latter vehicles were sold to GRAVESEND & NORTHFLEET and three to TORQUAY following closure, an event brought about by the Company's refusal to agree to new, higher charges for its electricity, which it purchased from Taunton Corporation.

Thanet *see* Isle Of Thanet

Torquay Tramways

Authority: Torquay Tramways Act 1904
Gauge: 3ft 6in.
Traction: Surface-contact/overhead electric
Opened: 4 April 1907
Closed: 31 January 1934
System: Network
Length: 9.24 miles
Stock: 3 sd, 39 dd
Livery: Maroon/brown & cream to 1929, then maroon/brown & yellow
Last Car: No. 3

The Torquay Tramways Act of 1904 empowered the Dolter Electric Traction Ltd to construct and operate the first section of this Devon town's network, using the Dolter stud system of current supply. Finance was provided by the Torquay Construction Syndicate Ltd, registered on 24 August 1905 and a subsidiary of the NEC. As built, it formed a triangle of nearly 4 miles of mainly single-track routes linking Torre station on the GWR to the west, St Marychurch (and depot) to the east and Beacon Quay on Torbay to the south. The original cars (Nos 1-18) were open-top Brush double-deckers. A fourth route of just over 2 miles from St Marychurch to Beacon Quay via Babbacombe opened on 11 November 1907, its completion delayed by road-widening work.

The system's first extension opened on 16 April 1908 with 2 miles of double-track line skirting the shore from Beacon Quay, along Torbay Road to the Grand Hotel by Torquay station on the railway line from Torre to Paignton, by which time operation was by the Torquay Tramways Co. Ltd (registered 10 December 1907), set up for that purpose in agreement with the other two concerns. The Company wanted to push the tramway on to Paignton, but with the Dolter studs increasingly prone to failure they decided that a more conventional system would have to be used – which meant that the rest of the

THE . .

DOLTER SURFACE-CONTACT SYSTEM

Obviates the use of Overhead Wires in picturesque towns, and has worked with great success in Paris from the Porte Maillot to Bois de Boulogne, Longchamps, and St Cloud Racecourses, carrying a large traffic without any accident or hitch.

One important feature of the Dolter System is that it lends itself admirably to a combination with the Overhead System. It is quite easy to use the Dolter Surface-Contact System in the middle or busy parts of a town, employing the trolley for the outskirts or for parts where it is not considered necessary to use the Surface-Contact System.

The Dolter Electric Traction Limited is prepared to put down Surface-Contact Systems on the whole or parts of any Tramway lines, and to guarantee the satisfactory working of the system for any required time.

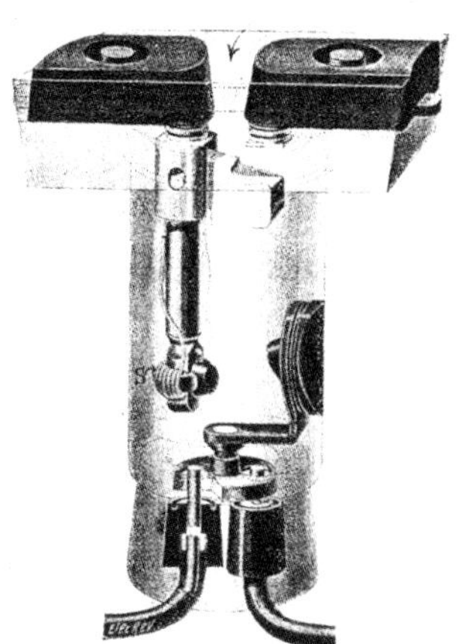

The Dolter Electric Traction Ltd.,

3 & 4 Great Winchester St., LONDON, E.C.

Telegraphic Address— "HAUVETTE, LONDON."

Telephone— "1645 LONDON WALL."

Above: Torquay Tramways Nos 13 and 14 on the opening day of the system, 4 April 1907. *(Author's collection)*

Left: Trade advertisement for the (unsuccessful) Dolter surface contact system of current supply, as used at Torquay and elsewhere.

As at Bristol, the local tramway company at Torquay also operated a cliff railway, in this case taking passengers from its Babbacombe Road route down to the bathing beach below on the northern side of the headland from the main town. *(Author's collection)*

studs in Torquay would have to go. This Torquay Council refused to countenance, on the grounds that overhead wires and standards would be unsightly in the resort; the dispute went to arbitration, which found in favour of the Company and on 6 March 1911 the conversion was completed as far as the Grand Hotel. The double-track extension from here along Torbay Road and Torquay Road to Paignton station opened on 17 July that year with the car fleet enlarged by a further fifteen Brush open-toppers (Nos 19-30 in 1911 and 31-33 in 1912). Three Brush single-deckers (Nos 34-36) for winter one-man operation were bought in 1921 from TAUNTON, and over the next seven years six open-top bogie cars (Nos 37-42) were also bought from Brush. By 1928 (when the last two cars arrived) bus competition was making the tramway's position precarious in the increasingly traffic-filled streets and the Paignton line closed on 14 January 1934, followed by the rest of the system at the end of the month.

As at BRISTOL, the tramway was also in the railway operating business, as it ran the Babbacombe Cliff Railway from that funicular's opening on 1 April 1926 until 13 March 1935 when it was sold to the Council. During the summer it is still open.

Upwell *see* Wisbech & Upwell

Walthamstow Urban District Council Light Railways

Authority: Walthamstow and District Light Railway Order 1903
Gauge: 4ft 8½in.
Traction: Overhead electric
Opened: 3 June 1905
Taken over: 1 July 1933
System: Branching
Length: 9.14 miles
Stock: 8 sd, 64 dd
Livery: Crimson lake/brown & chrome yellow/primrose

Owned and operated by Walthamstow UDC, this south-west Essex single-track system opened with Brush open-toppers Nos 1-32 working an east-west main line, with a succession of branches to the north and south. The main line began at the Napier Arms on Woodford New Road on the edge of Epping Forest, then joined Forest Road after ½ mile to run right across the borough whilst a ½-mile branch south down Woodford New Road led to the Rising Sun (the eastern terminus of LEYTON URBAN DISTRICT COUNCIL TRAMWAYS). This section, for most of its life, was worked summer weekends only (and was only connected to the Leyton system on 5 March 1931 to permit a year-round service of through-running).

After 1¾ miles along Forest Road the Bell was reached in the centre of the town, and here a branch north down Chingford Road past the depot led to Chingford Mount, and a branch south down Hoe Street led to the Baker's Arms, just across the boundary in Leyton, where it later connected with that system's Lea Bridge Road line. The main line continued for another mile to the MR's Blackhorse Road railway station, where a short northern branch led along Blackhorse Lane to Higham Hill, while a longer one south down Blackhouse Lane and Markhouse Road led to (but again stopped just short of) Lea Bridge Road. The last stretch of the Forest Road Line was terminated by the Ferry Boat Inn in Ferry Lane on the bank of the River Lea.

A track-doubling programme was commenced in 1912 with much of the system being so treated over the next thirteen years; a year later six HN top-covered cars (Nos 33-38) were purchased. As elsewhere though, the tramway was plagued by maintenance problems during the First World War and in 1919 was forced to hire six LONDON UNITED open-toppers, and in 1920 eight ERTCW bogie single-deckers (Nos 37-46) were purchased from Rotherham; the next year the hired cars were bought and numbered 47-52 (from LUT 226, 230, 232, 280, 289 and 298 variously).

Twelve new cars were bought in 1927, these being HN enclosed bogie vehicles 53-64, after which the open-top cars were fitted with top covers (except the ex-LUT cars, which were gradually withdrawn). In 1932 eight Brush enclosed bogie cars were purchased and numbered 39-46 as more cars were scrapped, the last acquisitions before the system became part of LONDON TRANSPORT.

See also *Lea Bridge, Leyton & Walthamstow Tramways*

Wantage Tramway

Authority: Wantage Tramways Order 1874
Gauge: 4ft 8½in.
Traction: Horse, steam
Opened: 11 October 1875
Closed: 31 July 1925
System: Single line
Length: 2.48 miles
Stock: 1 sd, 1 dd horse; 6 locos, 1 steamcar, 7 sd steam
Livery: Locos green, cars brown/maroon & olive green and cream
Last Train: ?

Each English roadside steam tramway had its own unique character, and the historic Wantage line was perhaps the most appealing of them all. Like many of its kind it was built to link a community with a railway that had passed it by, in this instance the north Berkshire town of Wantage with Wantage Road station on the GWR's main line to Swindon and the west through the Vale of the White Horse.

After an 1860s scheme to build a railway branch to Wantage had failed, the opportunity offered by the 1870 Tramways Act led to the promotion of a roadside tramway by the Wantage Tramway Co. Ltd (incorporated 10 November 1873). Services began with Starbuck double-deck horse car No. 1 in October 1875; this was joined in December by a single-decker (No. 2) from the same manufacturer. Even before the line had opened though, in the summer of 1875, a primitive open-top double-deck steamcar – probably allocated the number 3 in the fleet list – had been brought to the line for trials. Designed by John Grantham (and thereafter known as 'the Grantham Car'), this had been constructed in 1872 by Oldbury and was powered by a Merryweather steam engine. The intention was to use it on the tramway if the trials proved successful, and to this end the Company obtained an Act of Parliament on 27 June 1876, amending its original Order, to permit the use of mechanical traction. On 1 August 1876 regular steam passenger working began – the first such in the British Isles. Later that year the car was purchased outright for the sum of £250, the Company having calculated that it was considerably cheaper to run than horses. It lasted in service until about 1890 when it was withdrawn and broken up (after possibly running in its final years as an engineless trailer).

In 1877 a more orthodox, Hughes tramway loco. was purchased (No. 4), and from this date the use of horses gradually decreased and had probably been abandoned by 1888 when engine No. 6, a Matthews tram loco., was bought as a replacement for the Grantham Car. Two years later car No. 3, a Milnes single-deck saloon vehicle arrived and worked the passenger services with Nos 1 and 2 until 1903 when Nos 4 and 5, a pair of ex-READING single-deck horse cars were purchased. All the trailers except No. 3 lasted in service until about 1912 (with No. 1 converted to single-deck form about 1900), when two HN cars were bought. The first of these (No. 4) was a 1900 bogie double-deck electric exhibition car, cut down to single-deck form for Wantage, whilst No. 5 was a single-decker begun some ten years earlier for Bradford but never delivered.

Wantage Tramway No. 5 of 1857 (acquired 1878) and known unofficially as 'Jane' – and now preserved at the Didcot Railway Centre after many years' display on the platform at Wantage Road station – with trailers 4 and 5. *(Author's collection)*

A more conventional tramway-type locomotive on the Wantage Tramway was No. 6 of 1888, seen here with car No. 4 at Wantage Road station. *(Author's collection)*

A closer view of loco. No. 6, this time with car No. 2 in the train shed/station at Wantage. *(Author's collection)*

As was customary with such roadside lines, the tramway also operated a goods service, using conventional railway locomotives, taking all manner of wagons from Wantage Road down to the town and back again. This practice began around the end of 1878 when the Company purchased from the LNWR a George England 0-4-0 well tank engine built in 1857 for the Sandy & Potton Railway in Bedfordshire. Numbered 5 (and unofficially known as 'Jane'), she was followed by three 0-4-0 saddle tanks: No. 7, built in 1888 by MW and purchased in 1893 from the Manchester Ship Canal Co. after completion of the construction contract there; No. 1329, built in 1874 by the Avonside Engine Co. Ltd and bought from the GWR in 1910; and *The Driver*, built by MW in 1875 and bought in 1919 from the Woolwich Arsenal. Jane however, outlasted them all and can now be seen at Didcot Railway Centre. Whilst passenger services ceased in 1925, primarily because the GWR had started a competing bus service the year before, goods workings continued until 21 December 1945, the line remaining independent to the last.

The tramway was a simple, single-track affair laid with bridge rails on longitudinal wooden sleepers – a hangover from the GWR's old broad gauge practice. It ran in a south-westerly direction from beside the goods yard at Wantage Road station – a physical connection allowed the through-running of goods wagons – out along the eastern side of what is now the A338 to its terminus, depot and yard just past the gas works off Mill Street. (Plans for a short extension into the Market Place were never realised.) The only major alteration to this layout came in 1905 when a second goods yard (the Lower Yard) was opened on the west side of the gas works, close to the Wantage Arm of the Wiltshire & Berkshire Canal.

The Wantage Tramway's most successful loco was No. 7 of 1888, known unofficially as 'Mary', seen here with car No. 4 at Grove Bridge, by the (disused) Wiltshire & Berkshire Canal. *(Author's collection)*

West Ham Corporation Tramways

Authority: West Ham Corporation Act 1898
Gauge: 4ft 8½in.
Traction: Overhead electric
Opened: 27 February 1904
Taken over: 1 July 1933
System: Network
Length: 16.8 miles
Stock: 162 dd
Livery: Maroon/chocolate & cream

The first tramways in the borough of West Ham (created 1886) were horse lines operated by the NORTH METROPOLITAN TRAMWAYS Co. The first of these, running from Aldgate in London north-east along the Mile End Road and Bow Road to Bow Bridge (where it crossed into Essex) and continuing up the High Street to Stratford church, opened on 9 November 1870; it was extended later as two branches from here, north-east to Manor Park and north to Leytonstone. A parallel line to the south, linking Canning Town and Plaistow via Barking Road, opened in 1886 to make a 1¼-mile route isolated from the rest of the system.

In February 1903 West Ham Corporation agreed to buy the horse lines, in stages, in order to convert them as part of its planned electric system, paying £108,386 in all. Construction work on the new lines began that July and early the following year the first route opened. This ran south-east from Stratford Broadway down West Ham Lane, Plaistow Road, Plaistow High Street and Balaam Street to the Abbey Arms on Barking Road (thus linking the two horse routes). This was followed, on 31 March 1904, by a separate line along Barking Road from the Greengate (to the north-east of the Abbey Arms) as far as the Boleyn at the East Ham boundary.

Other routes followed, with the last section of the horse tramway being converted in February 1905. The last section of electric line to be opened, on 1 May 1912, ran south from the Greengate down Prince Regent's Road to Connaught Road by the Victoria & Albert Docks. This completed the compact, mainly double-track network of lines connected at three points in the west to the LONDON COUNTY COUNCIL system, at two points in the north to LEYTON and at three points in the east to EAST HAM (and beyond that to ILFORD and BARKING). Through-running arrangements meant that West Ham cars worked over as many miles of track outside their boundary as inside.

The first cars (Nos 1-50) were Milnes open-toppers, followed in 1905 by similar vehicles Nos 51-85 and, in 1906, by similar type Nos 86-93 from MV. (Most of these were later top-covered and some were cannibalised during the Second World War to keep the others running.) There then came a succession of top-covered cars:

Nos 94-100:	MV of 1906
Nos 101-106:	UEC of 1910
Nos 107-118:	HN bogie cars of 1911
No. 119:	Corporation of 1923, renumbered 64
Nos 60-63, 65:	Corporation of 1924
Nos 119-124:	EE bogie cars of 1925
Nos 125-137:	Corporation and Brush bogie cars of 1926
No. 138:	Corporation bogie car 1928
Nos 76-85:	Brush bogie car of 1929
Nos 69-75:	Corporation and Brush bogie cars of 1930
No. 68:	Corporation bogie enclosed car of 1931

In 1909 twenty-five of the cars were fitted with plough gear for working over the LCC's conduit tramways (commencing 1910); thereafter new cars came with this equipment as standard. The first, temporary depot was in Stratford, replaced in 1906 by a purpose-built one in Greengate Street, between the Greengate and Plaistow High Street, and connected to both the original routes.

As can be seen from the above list, the car buying/building programme continued after the First World War and, perhaps more importantly for the future of the system, all the track was relaid between 1920 and 1925 (apart from a short stretch in Beckton Road in Canning Town abandoned during the war). This meant that when, in 1933, the tramway became part of the new LONDON TRANSPORT, it did so virtually in its entirety, along with 134 tramcars which became LT Nos 211-344 (West Ham 1-26, 28-43, 45-65, 86-106, 68-85 and 107-138). As LT No. 290, West Ham No. 102 of 1910 is now preserved in the London Transport Museum, Covent Garden.

West Metropolitan Tramways *see* London: West Metropolitan Tramways

West Sussex Railway *see* Hundred Of Manhood & Selsey Tramway

Westminster Street Railway *see* London: Train's Tramways

Weston-Super-Mare & District Tramways

Authority: Weston-Super-Mare Tramways Order 1900
Gauge: 4ft 8½in.
Traction: Overhead electric
Opened: 5 May 1902
Closed: 17 April 1937
System: Branching
Length: 2.92 miles
Stock: 6 sd, 12 dd
Livery: Crimson lake & cream
Last Car: No. 8

This small system, operated by the Weston-Super-Mare & District Electric Supply Co. Ltd as part of the BET group, relied heavily on holidaymaker traffic for its revenue and was well positioned to do so since its principal route ran the length of the seafront from the Old Pier in the north to the West of England Sanatorium in the south. A branch mid-way led through the town via Oxford Street and Locking Road to the depot. Car trials began on 11 April 1902, the BoT held its inspection the following day and just over three weeks later the first services began on the Old Pier-depot section. The line's official opening ceremony was held on 13 May with the southern half of the seafront line along Beach Road opening four days later.

Despite an early setback when, on 10 September 1903, four of its double-deck cars were flooded by high seas on the promenade and had to be withdrawn from service (the

Weston-Super-Mare toastrack No. 16 of 1902 waiting to set off to the Sanitarium, with one of the Brush double-deckers behind. *(Author's collection)*

BET subsequently moved them to Swansea), the tramway survived on its largely seasonal receipts until 1 June 1936 when the Company and Weston UDC agreed – for a price – to its closure on behalf of the Bristol Tramways & Carriage Co. Ltd, who then set about replacing the trams with its own motor buses.

Tramway services began with eight open-top cars (Nos 1-8) and four roofed toastracks (Nos 13-16) from Brush; these were joined by four open-toppers in 1903 (Nos 9-12) to complete the initial order. After the four cars (numbers unrecorded) went to Swansea the other double-deckers were renumbered 1-8; the only cars added to the fleet thereafter were two more roofed toastracks (Nos 17 and 18) in 1927, again from Brush.

Weston-Super-Mare Pier Tramway

See Appendix 8.

Weston, Clevedon & Portishead Railway

Although operated as a standard gauge light railway, this north Somerset line was intended originally to include nearly ½ a mile of steam tramway through the streets of Weston-Super-Mare as authorised by the 1885 WESTON-SUPER-MARE Clevedon & Portishead Tramways Act. Progress on building the line was exceedingly slow, and it was not until 1897 that the first 8 miles from Weston to Clevedon were completed. Weston-Super-Mare UDC however, objected to the rails used on the street section (they apparently protruded above the road surface) and, indeed, to the whole notion of steam trains running through the town, and the Company was forced accordingly to lift this section. At the same time it tried, unsuccessfully, to persuade the BET to buy the line for electrification.

Public services began on 1 December 1897 though the final 6 miles to Portishead did not open for another ten years, by which time the line had become known officially as the Weston, Clevedon & Portishead Railway. Its financial problems persisted, attempts to link up with the Weston-Super-Mare electric tramway via Locking Road (see above) came to nothing – after looking promising – and from 1909 it was in receivership until the final trains ran on 18 May 1940, after which its assets – including a motley collection of second-hand locomotives – were sold to the GWR.

Westward Ho! *see* Bideford, Westward Ho! & Appledore

Weymouth Harbour Tramway

Opened on 16 October 1865, the Weymouth & Portland Railway connected the Channel port of Weymouth with the national railway network, being worked from the outset by the GWR as a mixed gauge line. Also authorised by the WPR Co.'s 1862 Act was a goods tramway from Weymouth station, running south and east down one side of the town's distinctive peninsula to the harbour. This too was of mixed broad and standard gauge, but was laid with some form of tramroad rails, and opened for horse-worked goods traffic the same day as the railway branch.

The tramway, which ran for just over a mile along the edge of the docks, was relaid with more orthodox railway rails in 1869, and then converted to standard gauge five years later. From 1880, the tramway saw the use of steam locomotives as well as horses

A postcard (sent 1930) of a train at the end of the Harbour Tramway at Weymouth, providing a connecting service with a Jersey steamer. *(Author's collection)*

(the use of the latter lasting well into the twentieth century). The principal traffic on the line was generated by the Channel Island steamers. On 4 August 1889 – after extensive reconstruction of the line – passenger traffic began with a through-boat-train from Paddington. Further modifications were made to the tramway over the years – usually to accommodate longer carriages – and new landing stages were built. A novel feature of the operating of trains over the line was the requirement that they be preceded by a man on foot carrying a red flag.

The last goods trains ran on 28 February 1972, following the cessation of freight shipments through the port. However, passenger traffic continued, if somewhat erratically, with closure threatened yearly and most of the ferry services moving to Poole, until 1989 when the boat trains ceased for good. After that, the line has seen only the occasional enthusiasts' charter working, engineers' inspection trains and token trains run for statutory reasons in 1996 and again in 1998. Although trials were carried out on the line using Parry People Mover tramcar No. 10 (see BRISTOL HARBOUR TRAMWAY), sadly plans to reopen the tramway on a regular basis – and to add a return line via the Esplanade by the beach on the western side of the peninsula to produce a circular pleasure ride – have so far come to nothing, partly because of the uncertainty resulting from on-going flood defence work and other developments. Indeed, at the time of writing the future existence of the track is threatened by a major redevelopment project known as Weymouth Pavilion.

Wimbledon Common Tramway

From 1864 to 1889 the National Rifle Association operated a seasonal tramway on Wimbledon Common to serve its summer Annual Meetings (begun in 1860). Relaid

The Wimbledon Common temporary tramway, as depicted in *The Illustrated London News* of 23 July 1864. *(Author's collection)*

every year with very light (14lb/yard) sleepered rails on the turf, it ran to the various firing points and grew over the years to about a mile in length. The initial cost of the installation, in time for the July 1864 event, was £400 and until 1876 the open, four-wheeled cars (originally four, later at least six) were towed by horses ridden by soldiers beside the single standard gauge track. In 1877 however, a Merryweather tram locomotive – believed to be the one returned from RYDE PIER – was borrowed from the manufacturers and named *Alexandra* in honour of the Princess of Wales. The line was formally opened by her husband, the future King Edward VII who – as appears to be mandatory on such royal occasions – tried his hand at driving the loco. himself.

The engine was obviously a success – it could haul six cars at once – for in 1878 it was bought and renamed *Wharncliffe*, in honour of the Chairman of the NRS, Lord Wharncliffe, and worked the line until the 1883 season when one of the cars was fitted with an electric motor. This vehicle took and returned current via two copper strips laid between the rails, and was put into service from 27 July. This experiment (in the very early days of electric traction) was not a success and *Wharncliffe* continued to work the line until 1889, its last summer of operation.

In 1890 the Annual Meeting decamped to Bisley Common in western Surrey (where it thrives to this day), and the loco. and portable line went with it, apparently being used until at least the summer of 1914, though many details are sadly lacking. The reconstruction of the tramway here as, a 1.21-mile line, was authorised by the National Rifle Association (Bisley Common Tramway) Order 1890, though it is thought that at both locations the route varied from year to year with members of the public – presumably interested spectators – as well as officials and competitors being carried from range to range.

Wisbech & Upwell Tramway

Authority: The Great Eastern Railway Act 1881
Gauge: 4ft 8½in.
Traction: Steam
Opened: 20 August 1883
Closed: 31 December 1927
System: Single line
Length: 5.9 miles
Stock: Locos*, 12 sd
Livery: Locos teak pre-1918, dark red to 1923 then brown; coaches teak pre-1918, then dark red
Last Train: ?

This roadside steam tramway was promoted, constructed and operated by the GER for the dual purpose of carrying passengers and agricultural produce from the villages south-

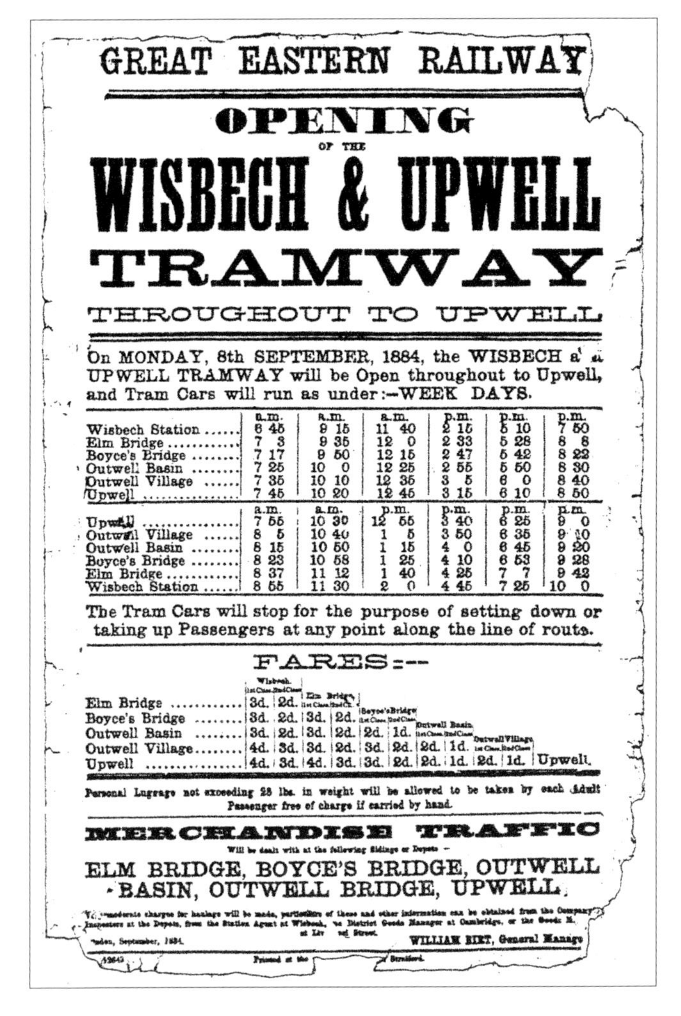

GREAT EASTERN RAILWAY

OPENING OF THE WISBECH & UPWELL TRAMWAY THROUGHOUT TO UPWELL

On MONDAY, 8th SEPTEMBER, 1884, the WISBECH & UPWELL TRAMWAY will be Open throughout to Upwell, and Tram Cars will run as under:—WEEK DAYS.

	a.m.	a.m.	a.m.	p.m.	p.m.	p.m.
Wisbech Station	6 45	9 15	11 40	2 15	5 10	7 50
Elm Bridge	7 3	9 35	12 0	2 33	5 28	8 8
Boyce's Bridge	7 17	9 50	12 15	2 47	5 42	8 22
Outwell Basin	7 25	10 0	12 25	2 55	5 50	8 30
Outwell Village	7 35	10 10	12 35	3 5	6 0	8 40
Upwell	7 45	10 20	12 45	3 15	6 10	8 50
	a.m.	a.m.	p.m.	p.m.	p.m.	p.m.
Upwell	7 55	10 30	12 55	3 40	6 25	9 0
Outwell Village	8 5	10 40	1 5	3 50	6 35	9 10
Outwell Basin	8 15	10 50	1 15	4 0	6 45	9 20
Boyce's Bridge	8 23	10 58	1 25	4 10	6 53	9 28
Elm Bridge	8 37	11 12	1 40	4 25	7 7	9 42
Wisbech Station	8 55	11 30	2 0	4 45	7 25	10 0

The Tram Cars will stop for the purpose of setting down or taking up Passengers at any point along the line of route.

FARES:—

	Wisbech 1st Class	Wisbech 2nd Class	Elm Bridge 1st Class	Elm Bridge 2nd Class	Boyce's Bridge 1st Class	Boyce's Bridge 2nd Class	Outwell Basin 1st Class	Outwell Basin 2nd Class	Outwell Village 1st Class	Outwell Village 2nd Class
Elm Bridge	3d.	2d.								
Boyce's Bridge	3d.	2d.	3d.	2d.						
Outwell Basin	3d.	2d.	3d.	2d.	2d.	1d.				
Outwell Village	4d.	3d.	3d.	2d.	3d.	2d.	2d.	1d.		
Upwell	4d.	3d.	4d.	3d.	3d.	2d.	2d.	1d.	2d.	1d.

Personal Luggage not exceeding 28 lbs. in weight will be allowed to be taken by each Adult Passenger free of charge if carried by hand.

MERCHANDISE TRAFFIC

Will be dealt with at the following Sidings or Depots —

ELM BRIDGE, BOYCE'S BRIDGE, OUTWELL BASIN, OUTWELL BRIDGE, UPWELL.

WILLIAM BIRT, General Manager

Left: The first passenger timetable for the opening of the final section of the Wisbech & Upwell Tramway.

Opposite: GER Class G15 No. 134 of 1897, and train, at the Wisbech & Upwell's Upwell terminus. *(Author's collection)*

east of the Cambridgeshire market town of Wisbech to its railway station there (Wisbech East). To avoid freight trans-shipment problems, the line was laid to standard railway gauge with bullhead rails to permit through-running of wagons.

The line was built under the provisions of the Tramways Acts in order to keep costs down, and its success helped pave the way for the 1896 Light Railway Act, which was to facilitate greatly the construction of such rural lines. For virtually all its length the tramway ran on a roadside reservation beside the moribund Wisbech Canal, until it reached the twin villages of Outwell and Upwell on the border with Norfolk. It entered Norfolk twice during the nearly 6 miles of its route – the last 1½ miles of which, from Outwell Basin to Upwell Depot, opened on 8 September 1884.

Mixed goods and passenger trains were the norm though, whilst the freight wagons travelled on from Wisbech, the passenger vehicles did not. The line's first four coaches were ex-Millwall Extension Railway carriages built by Starbuck (originally horse-drawn carriages with end balconies), Nos 1 and 2 dating from 1871 and Nos 3 and 4 from a year later. In 1884 however, the GER built four new, low coaches for the line: Nos 5 and 6 were four-wheeled vehicles and Nos 7 and 8 longer bogie vehicles, again all with ornate balconies. A purpose-built luggage van (No. 9) and an 1875 brake van (No. 16) were added to the tramway's 'own' stock at the same time. In 1890 the original Nos 1-4 were withdrawn when the GER built another four four-wheelers (which took their numbers).

To haul the trains the GER used its own distinctive steam tram locomotives drawn from a fleet of ten 0-4-0s (Class G15) and, from 1903, twelve 0-6-0s (Class C53); those used on the line were shedded at nearby March whilst the rest of the fleet was employed on the GER's freight-only quayside lines at Yarmouth, Colchester and Ipswich.

Another W&U train, this time in its characteristic roadside setting, in the care of G15 No. 131 of 1883 – one of the tramway's first three locomotives. *(Author's collection)*

Above: A rare sight in England: a goods tramway engine. This was one of the two Sentinel tramway locomotives bought by the LNER in 1930 to handle goods trains on the W&U but transferred the following year to Yarmouth to work the quayside line there. *(Author's collection)*

Opposite: In comparison, a more conventional tramway engine: one of the Wolverton & Stony Stratford Tramway's Green locomotives, with two of the line's giant trailers, in Wolverton Road, Stony Stratford. *(Author's collection)*

At the time of the 1923 Grouping the tramway passed, along with the rest of the GER, into the control of the LNER, who terminated passenger services over the line at the end of 1927 in the face of growing road competition (the tramway was subject to a 12mph speed restriction and frequent shunting stops). Goods traffic however, continued until 20 May 1966, latterly operated by BR with trains hauled by specially-adapted diesel shunters (and for a brief period from 1930 before they went to the Yarmouth Quay line the following year, a pair of 0-4-0 Sentinel locos). After the withdrawal of passenger services, carriages Nos 2-4 and 6-8 were transferred to the Kelvedon & Tollesbury Light Railway in Essex. No. 8 was set aside for preservation after that line closed in 1951 and featured prominently in the Ealing comedy 'The Titfield Thunderbolt', but it was wantonly scrapped some time afterwards. However, the body of former No. 7 was rescued after many years in a field and is currently – after several more years of museum storage around the region – restored as an exhibit on the North Norfolk Railway.

Wolverton & Stony Stratford Tramway

Authority: Wolverton and Stony Stratford Tramways Order 1883
Gauge: 3ft 6in.
Traction: Steam
Opened: 27 May 1887
Closed: 3 May 1926
System: Single line
Length: 4.72 miles
Stock: 7 locos, 1 sd, 5 dd
Livery: Variously tawny-brown/chocolate and chocolate & cream/white
Last Car: ?

This rural line was built to serve the LNWR's works in the Buckinghamshire village of Wolverton by linking it with the town of Stony Stratford, just over 2 miles to the west, where many of the railway workers lived. (Wolverton had been chosen as the site of the works because it was mid-way along the LNWR's predecessor, the London & Birmingham Railway, on what is now part of the West Coast Main Line.) The tramway had a very chequered history, despite its apparently obvious value, and it took no less than two Tramway Orders (1883 and 1884), two changes of proposed gauge (4ft 8½in. to 4ft to 3ft 6in.) and three different promoting companies before it commenced operations. It was built by a local contractor, Charles Herbert Wilkinson (then also planning the NEWPORT PAGNELL & DISTRICT tramway), who formed the grand-sounding Wolverton & Stony Stratford District Light Railways Co. Ltd (incorporated 5 October 1886) to operate it.

Laid as a single track, using grooved rails on the street sections and sleepered bullhead rails on the roadside stretches, the line as opened ran for nearly 2¾ miles from a reversing triangle on the east side of the main railway line at Wolverton, which it then crossed by means of a bridge before travelling westwards along Stratford Road through the town (for so it became) and out beside the Wolverton Road to Stony Stratford. Here, a little way past the depot, it turned north-west at the Foresters Arms to run up the High Street for ½ a mile to terminate outside the Barley Mow. The only 'branch' was a short spur at the Wolverton terminus into the railway goods yard.

The original stock comprised Krauss tram locomotives Nos 1 and 2 and four double-deck bogie cars from Midland. Three of these were enormous, 44ft-long vehicles with roofs and end glazing on the upper decks and a seating capacity of one hundred; the fourth car was similar but only seated eighty, being shorter. It soon became clear that the Krauss locos were not up to the job of pulling two of these trailers – some of the largest tramcars ever seen in Britain – and two more powerful Green engines (again numbered 1 and 2) were bought soon after the opening to replace them; these were delivered in July and October 1887 respectively.

Later in 1887, another Order authorised the construction of a 2.04-mile extension on up the High Street to Old Stratford, then south-west to the Fox & Hounds in the village of Deanshanger. The extension opened sometime in 1888, and to work it a third Krauss loco. (No. 3), similar to the first pair, was bought together with a twenty-seater four-wheeled roofed toastrack from Midland; at the same time the main route's stock was augmented by a fifty-seat trailer similar in type to the earlier four. The purpose of the extension was really to carry freight rather than passengers – several goods wagons were also bought – but the amount of traffic hoped for failed to materialise, matters not being helped by the Company (the Wolverton & Stony Stratford Tramroads Co. Ltd since 26 July 1889) going into liquidation and the line being closed by the Official Receiver on 17 December that year.

On 20 November 1891 the Barley Mow-Wolverton section reopened, backed by a private syndicate until 15 September 1893 when a new concern, the Wolverton & Stony Stratford & District New Tramway Co. Ltd took over. In 1900 a sixth loco.(No. 4) was purchased, this time from Brush, and in 1910 the Stony Stratford High Street section was abandoned, partly because of the growing traffic on what was a major trunk road (the A5), and partly because of deteriorating track. This second factor applied to the rest of the line as well, and on 17 July 1919 the Company went into liquidation.

Another WSS postcard, this time of Bagnall loco. No. 5, supplied by the LNWR, and a 100-seater trailer outside the Foresters Arms, Stony Stratford. *(Author's collection)*

In February 1920 the LNWR took control, anxious to maintain the line as a transport facility for its workers, and immediately put to work a small Bagnall saddle tank (No. 5) fitted with side-skirts and extended chimney, at the same time relaying the track. Increasing bus competition however, would almost certainly have soon killed off the tramway had the General Strike of 4 May 1926 not pre-empted any such decision by the then owner, the LMS.

Some confusion exists regarding the stock details. It is possible that the Green locos were briefly numbered 4 and 5 until the Krauss 1 and 2 were withdrawn in 1887; also, it is not known how the trailers were numbered as only one of the hundred-seaters is known to have carried a number (2), and that only in later years. This vehicle, after serving as a garden shed for many years, is currently on display (with a replacement upper deck) at the Milton Keynes Museum, Wolverton.

Woolwich & South East London Tramways *see* London: Woolwich & South East London Tramways

Wootton Tramway *see* Brill Tramway

Yarmouth & Gorleston Tramways
Authority: East Anglian Tramway Order 1871
Gauge: 4ft 8in./3ft 6in.
Traction: Horse
Opened: 25 March 1875

Taken over: 12 March 1905
System: Single line
Length: 3.25 miles
Stock: 10 dd?
Livery: ? to 1878, then red & cream and green & cream

The first passenger street tramway in East Anglia – the earliest goods tramway being one opened in 1848 on Yarmouth Quay and the earliest passenger tramway SOUTHEND PIER – was a 3-mile line from the GER's Yarmouth South Town station, just across the River Yare from the main part of Great Yarmouth, down Southtown Road to the bottom of Gorleston High Street; the depot was sited roughly mid-way along the route, just off Southtown Road in Waveney Road. It was a single-track affair originally promoted by the East Anglian Tramway Co., which concern transferred its powers in 1872 to the East Suffolk Tramway Co. who eventually built the line. It was laid to the not uncommon early 'standard' railway gauge of 4ft 8in.

In 1878 the tramway was purchased by the Yarmouth & Gorleston Tramways Co. Ltd and in 1882 extended down Lowestoft Road and Englands Lane to the quayside on the Yare; at the same time it was relaid to a gauge of 3ft 6in throughout and a new depot constructed in Baker Street to replace the Waveney Road one. In this form the line was worked by ten Midland double-deckers, though whether these were rebuilds of the original stock, or new cars, is not clear. The Company also operated seven horse buses in conjunction with the tramway, and had an interest in the Yarmouth & Gorleston Steamboat Co. Ltd.

In 1905 the concern was bought by Great Yarmouth Corporation for £13,211 with the takeover effective from 12 March that year; consequently the Corporation became a horse as well as an electric tramway operator (see below) for a brief period whilst work progressed on electrifying and extending its acquisition.

Great Yarmouth Corporation Tramways

Authority: Great Yarmouth Corporation Act 1899
Gauge: 3ft 6in.
Traction: Overhead electric, horse
Opened: 19 June 1902
Closed: 14 December 1933
System: Network + branching
Length: 9.94 miles
Stock: 35 dd electric; 3 dd horse
Livery: Maroon & cream
Last Car: No. 6 (official)

Great Yarmouth Corporation was one of a handful of operators who ran a tramway system made up of two discrete sections that were never linked. This was a result of the distinctive topography of the town: a long, thin development on a spit of land between the River Yare and the sea to the east, and the riverside suburb of Gorleston-on-Sea across

The Market Place in Great Yarmouth, with Corporation open-topper No. 4 of 1902 jostling for room amidst the horse and carts. *(Jan Dobrzynski collection)*

the Yare to the west. A road link between the two was provided high up the river by the lifting Haven Bridge, opposite Yarmouth South Town station, but this was not suitable for trams until rebuilt in 1930, by which time it was too late.

The western section of the system was the rebuilt YARMOUTH & GORLESTON horse tramway (see above), worked by the Corporation with three of the Y&G horse cars for some three months before electric services began on 4 July 1905 (horse services ceasing the same day); this ran over the same route but with a ¼-mile extension along Lowestoft Road to Springfield Road close to Gorleston-on-Sea railway station, plus a ¾-mile branch from the depot down Pier Plain to meet the (abandoned) former horse line in Englands Lane and on via Brush Quay to the beach.

The first section of the eastern two-thirds of the system was opened on 19 June 1902: this comprised two main routes, the first being from Wellington Pier northwards along Marine Parade, then along St Peters Road and King Street, through the Market Place and out along Northgate Street to the district of Newtown (with a depot here in Caister Road). The second cross-town route ran from Yarmouth Vauxhall station in the west, across the River Bure, then southwards along North Quay and Hall Quay, up Regent Street to the Market Place (where it joined and left the first route), thence via Regent Road to the northern end of Marine Parade on the seafront, then south to Wellington Pier.

The first services were worked by open-top Brush cars 1-14, which were joined in 1905 by twelve more (Nos 15-26), the Gorleston-allocated cars working out of a new depot built by the old horse car sheds. Lines were a mixture of single and double tracks.

The quayside at Great Yarmouth, looking south down the River Yare, with a Corporation tram on the left beyond the quayside tramway (in effect a long goods branch from Vauxhall station). The opening Haven Bridge (right) over the Yare prevented connection to the Gorleston portion of the passenger system. *(Author's collection)*

On 14 October 1904 a short branch from St Peters Road along Blackfriars Road to Camden Road was opened as an extension of the Kings Street line; shortly after this the short section in St Peters Road down to the Marine Parade was abandoned. On 19 August 1905 the Camden Road branch was extended to the Fish Wharf on the Yare and on 16 May 1907 the Newtown route was extended northwards beyond the town boundary as a single-track line along the main road for some 1½ miles, past the racecourse, to Caister-on-Sea. To work the new routes – which completed the system – another nine Brush open-toppers (Nos 27-35) were bought during 1906 and 1907, completing the car fleet. (In 1928 Gorleston's allocation of cars was increased from twelve to fourteen when Nos 17-28 were joined there by Nos 15 and 16.)

In the years immediately following the First World War poor financial returns from the tramways led the Corporation to take remedial action. In 1920 it started its own motor bus services and the cost of the track renewal led, on 14 May 1924, to the closure of the Fish Wharf route. The remainder of the system was then refurbished – but only as a temporary expedient whilst the bus fleet was built up – with the next closure coming at the end of the summer season in September 1928 when the Vauxhall station branch closed for the last time – though some reports give a date a year later. (Several sections of the Yarmouth system, as in other seaside resorts, were always or often worked summers only.)

The last Gorleston tram, No. 17, ran on 25 September 1930 and the last service car over the surviving Wellington Pier-Caister route ran on Thursday 14 December 1933, both services replaced by motor buses. The next day car No. 6 was brought out for a ceremonial 'last trip'. The trams were then all scrapped, with more than twenty of the bodies becoming chalets at Caister Holiday Camp just up the coast.

Great Yarmouth Corporation No. 16 of 1905 on the rural Caister Road route before, as elsewhere, suburban sprawl began. *(Author's collection)*

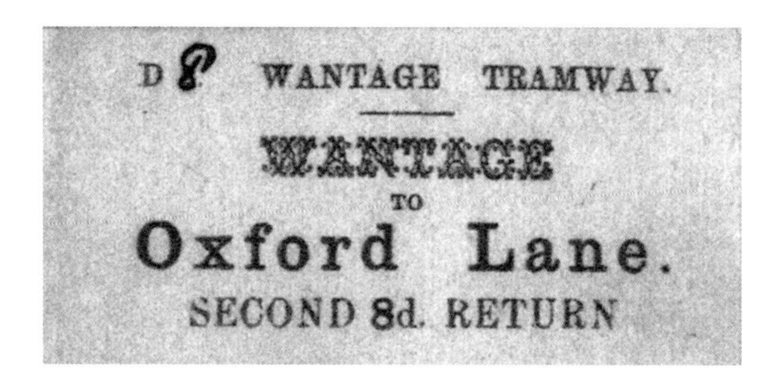

Above, left, and next four pictures: A selection of English tramway tickets, from six different systems, showing the two basic types used: flat fare or priced by number of fare stages to be travelled (with the destination marked by the conductor, when issued, with a punch hole).

Hb 1288
1d
21 20 19 18 17 16 15 14 13 12 11
1 2 3 4 5 6 7 8 9 10
Walthamstow Council Light Railways.
Issued subject to Bye-laws. Available only on car on which issued and to station at punch hole. To be shown on demand.
Punch & Ticket Co. London, N.

Am 0412
1d
22 21 20 19 18 17 16 15 14 13 12
1 2 3 4 5 6 7 8 9 10 11
WEST HAM CORPORATION TRAMWAYS.
Issued subject to the Bye-laws. This ticket must be shown on demand.
This ticket is punched at the stage number where fare stage terminates, and is available on day of issue only.
Punch & Ticket Co. London, N.

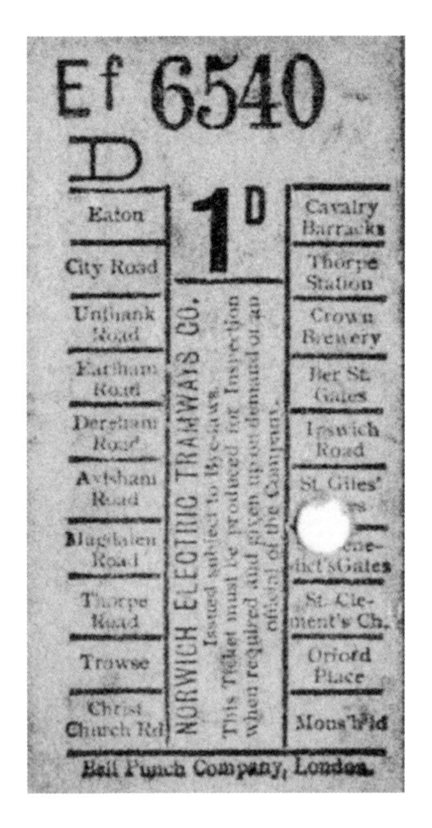

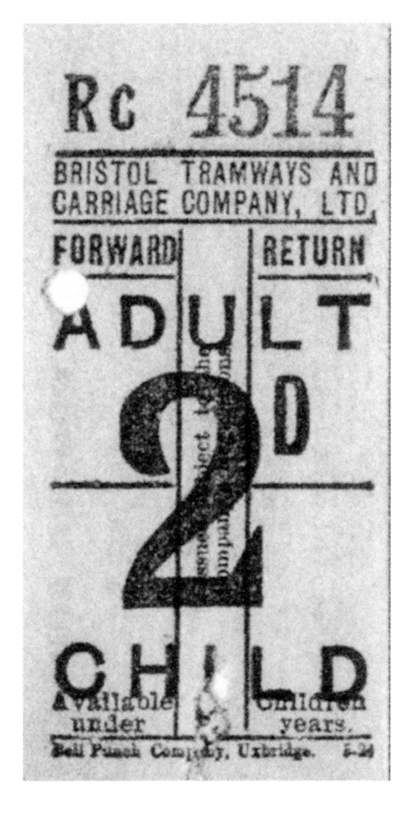

Part 2

Tramways of the Channel Islands

Despite their comparatively small size, the Channel Islands have been, over the years, rich in rail transport systems. At one time or another the four largest islands of Jersey, Guernsey, Alderney and Herm could boast standard and narrow gauge public railways, standard and narrow gauge freight-only lines, a network of military railways laid during the German occupation of the Second World War – but only ever one passenger tramway.

Elsewhere in the British Isles, proposals for tramways far outnumbered those actually constructed and in this respect the Channel Islands were no different. The main focus for these schemes was Jersey, a fact reflected in the title of the Jersey Railways & Tramways Co. Ltd which, notwithstanding its name, never succeeded in bringing tramways to that island, only a railway.

Whether railway or tramway, public rail transport did not survive on the islands beyond the 1930s. The reasons for this early demise are not hard to find: the short length of the lines, no centres of population large enough to support an urban system, the increase in car ownership and, above all, the development after the First World War of competing bus services. In this last respect too the Channel Islands were no different from any other of the British Isles and, for their solitary tramway, the outcome was sadly much the same.

Guernsey Railway
Authority: Order in Council 1877
Gauge: 4ft 8½in.
Traction: Steam, overhead electric
Opened: 6 June 1879
Closed: 9 June 1934
System: Single line
Length: 2.81 miles
Stock: 8 locos, 7 sd, 2 dd steam; 6 sd, 14 dd electric*
Livery: Chocolate/maroon & stone/cream
Last Car: No. 6

Running from the harbour in the capital St Peter Port, to the harbour at St Sampson's, this short line was operated originally by the Guernsey Steam Tramway Co. Ltd (registered

The Guernsey Railway's St Sampson's terminus, with electric car No. 1 of 1905 to the fore. *(Author's collection)*

in London on 29 May 1878) to replace an existing horse bus service between these two major centres of population on the island's east coast. The scheme, the concession for which was granted by the States of Guernsey on 2 May 1877 and confirmed by an Order in Council later that year, was fine on paper – and initially successful in practice – but the locomotives proved prone to breakdowns and the bus owners refused to accept defeat; in 1888 the Company went into liquidation and on 22 January of the following year services were suspended, not to be resumed until 2 December, this time operated by the reformed and renamed Guernsey Railway Co. Ltd.

The single-track tramway hugged the shore for almost all of its length, running north-eastwards from St Peter Port via various esplanades, Bas Courtils Road and Bulwer Avenue to St Sampson's. The track was a mixture of flat-bottomed and grooved rails, ballasted or paved depending on its roadside or roadway location.

Ten years or so later the Company decided to electrify the line, the work being completed enough for trials by October 1891; public running of the new cars began on 20 February 1892 but teething troubles necessitated the retention of the steam trams for another four years. Steam workings finally ceased in November 1896 after a fire in the sheds on Bulwer Avenue – on 5 November – destroyed one of the last three locos, three cars and the sheds themselves. The other two locos were sold later for scrap and a new depot built at Hougue-à-la-Pierre, roughly halfway along the route and close to the line's power station.

Following trials in 1877-78 with a Merryweather tram loco, two had been ordered for the start of services in 1879; these were numbered 1 and 2 (and in 1890 named *Shooting Star* and *Sampson* respectively). Later in 1879 they were joined by No. 3 from Stephen

Lewin of Poole, then by four Hughes engines (Nos 4-7) in 1882-83; the last arrival, in 1890, was No. 8 *Haro* from Hawthornes. Only the three named locos survived until the end of steam working, the one destroyed in the fire being *Sampson*.

Information regarding the passenger trailers is patchy, especially as to makers; what seems likely is that services began with single-deck saloons Nos 1 and 2 and roofed toastracks 3-5, though in December 1879 the last two of these were rebuilt as saloon cars. These were joined at an unknown date by a curious open passenger car (No. 6) that looked as much like a coke wagon as No. 7, the official coke wagon, did! In 1881 a roofed, double-deck bogie car (No. 8) was purchased, followed in 1884 by a single-deck bogie saloon (No. 9) from Starbuck. The last arrival, in 1890, was replacement No. 4, another roofed, double-deck bogie car. Trains of up to three trailers were run behind a single loco.

As with the steam stock, details of the electric cars are still not complete and the following account may not be correct. Electric services were worked by a combination of new vehicles and rebuilt steam trailers and, as in steam days, trailer workings were the norm. The first powered cars were Nos 7, 10 and 11, built by Falcon in 1891 as open-top double-deckers, and these were joined by bogie cars 5 and 6, also from Falcon, in 1893 (with No. 5 possibly a rebuild of a steam trailer) whilst former steam trailers 9 of 1884 and 4 of 1890 were electrified in 1891 as powered cars. Another bogie car, No. 8, arrived from Milnes in 1896, and in 1903 and 1905 another two open-toppers, Nos 2 and 1, were bought from Brush. Original trailers were Nos 12-14, roofed Falcon toastracks, joined in 1897 by two more (Nos 14 and 15) from Milnes following the depot fire, together with an open-top double-decker (No. 3) which was converted in 1901 to a powered car. The last trailers to be bought were Nos 16-19 in 1903, four ex-Cardiff double-deck horse cars.

In 1895 the Company bought out its bus rival, the Guernsey Omnibus Co., and

197 GUERNSEY. — St Sampson. — South Side. — Saint-Samson. — Les Quais du Sud. — LL.

Another postcard view of GR No. 1 again, this time by the harbour at St Sampson's. *(Author's collection)*

operated its horse buses; in 1909 three motor buses were acquired, the horse buses being withdrawn two years later. By the 1930s though, bus competition from other operators was being felt by the tramway and in 1934 it closed for good. The Company however remained very much in existence, as it does today, as a bus operator – never, despite its name, having owned a railway.

Converted trailer No. 3 was rescued in the 1970s from its new life as a summerhouse, restored and motorised as a steerable road vehicle by the Guernsey Old Car Club. Since donated to the States of Guernsey, it keeps hopes alive of it perhaps operating on rails once again, possibly behind a replica tram engine.

Jersey Railways & Tramways

The Jersey Railways & Tramways Co. Ltd was incorporated in 1896 to take over the assets of a 3ft 6in gauge steam railway some 6 miles in length running from the capital St Helier, in the south of the island, to Corbiere on the west coast. Despite its title the Company never built or operated any tramways (or indeed any other railways) although electrification of the line was considered at one time.

The first section of the railway (from St Helier to St Aubin) had opened as a standard gauge line in 1870; the whole railway closed in 1936 after a fire destroyed much of its passenger stock.

Chronology

Major Landmarks in British Passenger Tramway History

1807 World's first railed passenger service inaugurated on the Oystermouth Tramroad in Wales

1859 William Curtis runs his patent omnibuses on a line in Liverpool Docks

1860 George Train opens the first genuine street railway in the British Isles (Birkenhead)

Tramways Act (Ireland)

1863 First Act of Parliament for a street tramway (Portsmouth)

1864 First trials of steam traction (Ryde Pier)

1870 Tramways Act

1876 First regular use of steam traction on a British tramway (Wantage)

1877 First regular use of steam traction on a British street tramway (Vale of Clyde)

1879 Use of Mechanical Power on Tramways Act

1883 Giant's Causeway, Portrush & Bush Valley Tramway pioneers the use of electricity (third rail)

Huddersfield becomes the first municipal operator

Tramways and Public Companies (Ireland) Act

1884 Highgate Hill Cable Tramway pioneers the use of cable traction (London)

1885 First (conduit) electric tramway opens (Blackpool)

1889 Light Railways (Ireland) Act

1891 First overhead electric tramway opens (Leeds)

1896 Light Railways Act

1909 Last regular use of steam traction on a street tramway (Rossendale Valley)

1917 First abandonment of an electric system (Sheerness)

1924 Last new system for forty-six years opens (Dearne District)

1927 Last steam passenger service in England ceases (Wisbech & Upwell)

1928 Last use of horse traction outside the Isle of Man (Pwllheli & Llanbedrog)

1933 Last steam passenger service outside Ireland ceases (Glyn Valley)

1934 Channel Islands' only tramway closes (Guernsey)

1952 Largest system closes (London)

1959 Last steam passenger service (Arigna)

Ireland's last tramway closes (Hill of Howth)

1960 Swansea & Mumbles Railway closes leaving the Great Orme as Wales' sole surviving tramway

1961 Grimsby & Immingham Electric Railway closes leaving Blackpool as England's sole surviving tramway

1962 Scotland's last tramway closes (Glasgow)

1963 National Tramway Museum opens at Crich in England

1970 First tramway to be built since 1924 opens (Seaton)

1992 Manchester Metrolink ushers in a new era of urban tramways

Appendix 1

English Passenger Tramway Locations by Former County

Bedfordshire
Luton

Berkshire
Reading; Wantage

Buckinghamshire
Wolverton & Stony Stratford

Cambridgeshire
Cambridge; Wisbech & Upwell (part)

Cheshire
Birkenhead; Chester; Manchester and district (part); Stalybridge and district (part); Stockport (part); Wallasey; Warrington (part)

Cornwall
Camborne & Redruth

Cumberland
Carlisle

Derbyshire
Burton & Ashby (part); Chesterfield; Derby; Glossop; Ilkeston; Matlock; Nottinghamshire & Derbyshire (part)

Devon
Exeter; Plymouth; Seaton; Torquay and district

Dorset
Poole

Durham
Darlington; Gateshead; The Hartlepools; Jarrow; South Shields; Stockton & Thornaby (part); Sunderland and district

Essex
Barking; Canvey Island; Colchester; East Ham; Ilford; Leyton; London (part); Southend-on-Sea; Walthamstow; West Ham

Gloucestershire
Bristol (part); Cheltenham; Gloucester

Hampshire & Isle Of Wight
Aldershot & Farnborough; Bournemouth; Gosport & Farnham; Portsmouth and district; Ryde; Southampton

Hertfordshire
London (part)

Huntingdonshire
Peterborough

Kent
Bexley (part); Chatham; Dartford; Dover; Erith; Folkestone, Hythe & Sandgate; Gravesend & Northfleet; Herne Bay; Isle of Thanet; Maidstone; Sheerness; South Metropolitan (part)

Lancashire
Accrington & District; Ashton-under-Lyne; Barrow-in-Furness; Blackburn; Blackpool and district; Bolton; Burnley; Bury; Colne & Trawden; Darwen; Farnworth; Heywood; Lancaster and district; Liverpool and district; Lytham St Annes and district; Manchester; Middleton; Morecambe; Nelson; Oldham; Preston; Rawtenstall and district; Rochdale; St Helens; Salford; South Lancashire; Southport; Stalybridge and district (part); Stockport (part); Warrington (part); Waterloo & Great Crosby; Wigan

Leicestershire
Burton & Ashby (part); Leicester

Lincolnshire
Alford & Sutton; Grimsby and district; Lincoln; Skegness

London
Bexley(part); London (part)

Middlesex
London (part)

Norfolk
Norwich; Wisbech & Upwell (part); Great Yarmouth

Northamptonshire
Northampton

Northumberland
Newcastle; Tynemouth; Tyneside

Nottinghamshire
Mansfield; Nottingham; Nottinghamshire & Derbyshire (part)

Oxfordshire
Oxford

Somerset
Bath; Bristol (part); Taunton; Weston-Super-Mare

Staffordshire
Birmingham (part); Black Country (part); Burton and district (part); Kinver (part); Potteries; Walsall; Wolverhampton

Suffolk
Ipswich; Lowestoft

Surrey
Croydon; South Metropolitan (part)

Sussex
Brighton and district; Hastings; Shoreham and district

Warwickshire
Birmingham (part); Coventry; Leamington & Warwick; Stratford & Moreton

Wiltshire
Swindon

Worcestershire
Black Country (part); Kidderminster & Stourport; Worcester

Yorkshire
Barnsley; Batley; Bradford; Dearne District; Doncaster; Halifax; Huddersfield; Hull and district; Keighley; Leeds; Mexborough & Swinton; Middlesbrough; Rotherham; Scarborough; Sheffield; Shipley; Stockton & Thornaby (part); Wakefield and district; York; Yorkshire (West Riding); Yorkshire (Woollen District)

Herefordshire, Rutland, Shropshire and Westmoreland have had no regular passenger tramways.

Appendix 2

Welsh Passenger Tramway Locations by Former County

(Including Monmouthshire)

Caernarvonshire
Llandudno and district (part); Pwllheli and district

Carmarthenshire
Llanelli

Denbighshire
Colwyn Bay and district (part); Glyn Valley; Wrexham

Glamorgan
Aberdare; Cardiff; Merthyr Tydfil; Neath; Pontypridd; Rhondda; Swansea and district

Merionethshire
Barmouth Junction & Arthog; Fairbourne; Harlech

Monmouthshire
Newport

Anglesey, Brecknockshire, Cardiganshire, Flintshire, Montgomeryshire, Pembrokeshire and Radnorshire have had no regular passenger tramways.

Appendix 3

Scottish Passenger Tramway Locations by Former County

Aberdeenshire
Aberdeen; Cruden Bay

Angus
Dundee & District

Ayrshire
Ayr; Kilmarnock

Buteshire
Rothesay

Dunbartonshire
Dumbarton

Fife
Dunfermline; Kirkcaldy; Wemyss

Lanarkshire
Airdrie & Coatbridge; Glasgow and district; Lanarkshire

Midlothian
Edinburgh; Leith; Musselburgh

Perthshire
Perth

Renfrewshire
Greenock & Port Glasgow; Paisley

Stirlingshire
Falkirk; Stirling & Bridge of Allan

Argyllshire, Banffshire, Berwickshire, Caithness, Clackmannanshire, Dumfries-shire, East Lothian, Inverness-shire, Kincardineshire, Kinross-shire, Kircudbrightshire, Morayshire, Nairn, Orkney, Peebleshire, Ross & Cromarty, Roxburghshire, Selkirkshire, Sutherland, West Lothian, Wigtownshire and Zetland have had no regular passenger tramways.

Appendix 4

Irish Passenger Tramway Locations by County

Antrim
Belfast (part)

Armagh
Glenanne & Loughgilly

Cork
Cork

Down
Belfast (part); Warrenpoint & Rostrevor

Dublin
Dublin and district (part); Hill of Howth

Fermanagh
Clogher Valley (part)

Galway
Galway & Salthill

Leitrim
Arigna (part)

Londonderry
Derry; Portstewart

Roscommon
Arigna (part)

Tyrone
Clogher Valley (part); Castlederg & Victoria Bridge

Wicklow
Dublin and district (part)

Carlow, Cavan, Clare, Donegal, Kerry, Kildare, Kilkenny, Laois, Limerick, Longford, Louth, Mayo, Meath, Monaghan, Offaly, Sligo, Tipperary, Waterford, Westmeath and Wexford have had no regular passenger tramways.

Appendix 5

Horse-only Tramways

Although the normal course of events for early British tramways was to start with horse traction and then modernise with electrificiation around the end of the nineteenth century (sometimes experimenting with steam traction along the way), a significant number of lines remained faithful to horse traction until the end without it being replaced (or the tramway being rebuilt in some other form). The reason was usually financial, with low traffic receipts not justifying the cost of conversion. These horse-only systems are listed below, with their dates of operation and location.

BARMOUTH JUNCTION & ARTHOG	1899-1903	Wales
CAMBRIDGE	1880-1914	England
DERRY	1897-1919	Ireland
DOUGLAS BAY	1876-	Isle of Man
FAIRBOURNE	*c.*1896-*c.*1915	Wales
FOLKESTONE, HYTHE & SANDGATE	1891-1921	England
GALWAY & SALTHILL	1879-1918	Ireland
GLENANNE & LOUGHGILLY	1897-1918?	Ireland
HARLECH	1878-1880s	Wales
LANCASTER & DISTRICT	1890-1921	England
MORECAMBE CORPORATION	1898-1926	England
OXFORD	1881-1914	England
PWLLHELI CORPORATION	1899-1919	Wales
PWLLHELI & LLANBEDROG	1894-1928	Wales
SKEGNESS	*c.*1880-*c.*1882	England
WARRENPOINT & ROSTREVOR	1877-1915	Ireland

Appendix 6

Steam-only Tramways

Tramways that employed steam traction were of two broad types: urban street systems and isolated rural roadside lines. The type of locomotives used corresponded generally with the type of line: box-like, purpose-built tramway engines for the street systems and adapted railway engines for the others. In the towns, steam traction lasted little more than twenty years, from *c.*1880 to *c.*1900; in rural areas its use survived well into the twentieth century – and sometimes right up to a line's closure (though often with internal-combustion traction as well). The following list is of those tramways which used steam traction exclusively, with their dates of operation and location.

ALFORD & SUTTON	1884-1889	England
ARIGNA	1887-1959	Ireland
BRIGHTON & SHOREHAM	1884-1913	England
HULL: Drypool & Marfleet	1889-1901	England
PORTSTEWART	1882-1926	Ireland
WISBECH & UPWELL	1883-1927*	England
WOLVERTON & STONY STRATFORD	1887-1926	England

* retained steam (later diesel) traction for goods trains

Appendix 7

Cable Tramways

Cable traction on tramways, because of the complicated mechanical arrangements needed if more than one route was involved, was almost exclusively limited to short, single-line systems where steep gradients had to be conquered. (The one exception was Edinburgh.) Listed below are all British cable lines with their dates of cable operation and location where their main entries can be found.

BIRMINGHAM: Hockley Hill	1888-1911*	England
DOUGLAS: Upper Douglas	1896-1929	Isle of Man
EDINBURGH	1888-1922*	Scotland
LONDON: Brixton Hill	1892-1904*	England
LONDON: Highgate Hill	1884-1909*	England
LLANDUDNO: Great Orme	1902-	Wales
MATLOCK	1893-1927	England
SWANSEA: Constitution Hill	1898-1902?	Wales

* converted to electric traction

Appendix 8

Pier Tramways

Many of Britain's piers, quays and jetties have had, at one time or another, rails laid on them. In many cases these were simple extensions of the national railway system and used for the loading and unloading of passengers and goods from ferry boats and pleasure steamers; occasionally railway vehicles themselves would be transhipped. A few piers though possessed their own self-contained lines to carry passengers and their luggage between pier head and shore and, when there were no boats to service, to give rides to holidaymakers. Most of these lines were railways, fenced-off from the rest of the pier – a necessary precaution as many were electrified on the third-rail system – but a handful were true tramways laid flush with the decking. Those lines that carried passengers are listed below, with their dates of operation and location.

BLACKPOOL: North Pier	1991 -	England
HERNE BAY (1)	1833?-1864	England
HERNE BAY (2)	1899-1939	England
RAMSEY	1899-1981	Isle of Man
RYDE	1864-1886	England
SOUTHEND-ON-SEA	1875?-1881?	England
SOUTHPORT	1863-1863?	England

A number of other piers are known to have had simple 'luggage lines' with hand-propelled trucks; that on the Old or Birnbeck Pier at Weston-Super-Mare is known to have also carried passengers at some time, though further details are lacking.

Appendix 9

Railway-owned Tramways

A small number of British tramways were owned and/or operated by railway companies, for reasons almost as numerous as the lines themselves. The following list includes all such lines, with their original operating railway and location.

ARIGNA	Cavan & Leitrim	Ireland
BURTON & ASHBY	Midland	England
CRUDEN BAY	Great North of Scotland	Scotland
FOLKESTONE, HYTHE & SANDGATE	South Eastern	England
GRIMSBY & IMMINGHAM	Great Central	England
HILL OF HOWTH	Great Northern (I)	Ireland
HOYLAKE & BIRKENHEAD	Hoylake	England
PORTSTEWART	Belfast & Northern Counties	Ireland
WATERLOO & GREAT CROSBY	Liverpool Overhead	England
WISBECH & UPWELL	Great Eastern	England
WOLVERTON & STONY STRATFORD	London & North Western	England

Appendix 10

Tramway-owned Railways

Three British railways were owned an/or operated by tramway concerns, for at least part of their lives. The following list gives the owner and location of each.

BABBACOMBE CLIFF RAILWAY	Torquay Tramways Co. Ltd	England
CLIFTON ROCKS RAILWAY	Bristol Tramways & Carriage Co. Ltd	England
CORRIS RAILWAY	Bristol Tramways & Carriage Co. Ltd	Wales

The two cliff railways were acquired as they were seen as useful adjuncts to the tramway system; the narrow-gauge Corris Railway was an investment asset to the Imperial Tramways Co. Ltd, owned by its Bristol Tramways subsidiary.

Bibliography

The Tramways of Bournemouth and Poole, R.C. Anderson (The Light Railway Transport League, 1964)
The Tramways of East Anglia, R.C. Anderson (The Light Railway Transport League, 1969) 0 900433 00 0
Cheltenham's Trams and Buses Remembered, J.B. Appleby & F. Lloyd (The Transport Publishing Co., Glossop, 2nd ed. 1973) 0 903839 00 8
Peterborough Tramways (Peterborough Papers No. 1), G.D. Austin (Greater Peterborough Arts Council, 1975)
The Tramways of Croydon, G.E. Baddeley (The Light Rail Transit Association, rev. ed. 1983) 0 900433 90 6
Tramways in Great Yarmouth Volume 1: Electric Tramways 1902-1918, T. Baker (Author, Chipping Sodbury, 1980) 0 950688 90 8
Tramways in Great Yarmouth Volume 2: 1919-1933 Electric Tramways & Petrol Omnibuses, T. Baker (Chipping Sodbury, 1983) 0 950688 91 6
Cornwall's Electric Tramcars, L. Barham, (Glasney Press, Penryn, 1972)
Torbay Transport, F. Barham, (Glasney Press, Falmouth, 1979) 0 950282 54 5
The Selsey Tram, D. Bathurst, (Phillimore, 1992) 0 850338 39 5
The Guernsey Railway (The Railways of the Channel Islands Volume 3, The Oakwood Library of Railway History 58B), N.R.P. Bonsor, (The Oakwood Press, 1987 reprint of 1967 ed.) 0 85361 329 X
The Jersey Railway (J.R. & T.) (The Railways of the Channel Islands Volume 1, The Oakwood Library of Railway History No. 58), N.R.P. Bonsor, (The Oakwood Press, 1962)
Luton Trams: The Story of a Small System 1908-1932, C. Brown, (Irwell Press, Clophill, 1999) 1 871608 91 0
The Tramways of Southend-on-Sea, V.E. Burrows (The Advertiser Press Ltd, Huddersfield, 1965)
Tramways in Metropolitan Essex Volume 1, V.E. Burrows (The Advertiser Press Ltd, Huddersfield, 1967)
Tramways in Metropolitan Essex Volume 2, V.E. Burrows, (Arthur Upminster, 1976)
The Rye & Camber Tramway: A Centenary History, L.A. Cooksey (Plateway Press, Brighton, 1995) 1 871980 26 7
The Selsey Tramway Volume 1, L.A. Cooksey (Wild Swan Publications, 2006) 1 978 1 905184 15 6
The Selsey Tramway Volume 2, L.A. Cooksey (Wild Swan Publications, 2006) 1 978 1 904184 16 4
The Swindon Tramways and Electricity Undertaking, (Locomotion Papers No. 65) L.J. Dalby (The Oakwood Press, new ed. 1985) 0 85361 320 6
Portsmouth Corporation Tramways 1896-1936, (The Portsmouth Papers No. 45) E. Course (City of Portsmouth, September 1986) 0 901559 66 0
The Wantage Tramway 1875-1945, N. de Courtais (Wild Swan Publications, 1981) 0 906867 06 1

Tramways of the West Country, P.W. Gentry, (The Light Railway Transport League, 2nd ed. 1960)
Herne Bay's Piers, H. Gough, (Pierhead Publications, Herne Bay, 2002) 0 9538977 6 1
The Hellingly Hospital Railway, P.A. Harding (Author, Woking, 1989) 0 9509414 5 X
The Tramways of Portsmouth, S.E. Harrison (The Light Railway Transport League, 1963)
The Hythe & Sandgate Railway, B. Hart (Wild Swan Publications, 1987) 0 906867 53 3
The Wisbech & Upwell Tramway, C. Hawkins & G. Reeve (Wild Swan Publications, 1982) 0 906867 09 6
100 Years of Southampton Transport, J.B. Horne (Southampton City Transport and Southampton City Museums, 1979)
The Tramways of Kent Volume 1: West Kent, 'INVICTA' (The Light Railway Transport League, 1971) 1 900433 38 8
The Tramways of Kent Volume 2: East Kent, 'INVICTA' (The Light Railway Transport League, 1975) 0 900433 45 0
Volk's Railways, Brighton: An Illustrated History, A.A. Jackson (Plateway Press, Brighton, 1993) 1 971980 18 6
Next Stop Seaton! 50 Years of Modern Electric Tramways Limited, D. Jay & D. Voice (Adam Gordon, Brora, 2003) 1 874422 43 5
Bideford, Westwood Ho! and Appledore Railway (Oakwood Library of Railway History No. 89) S.C. Jenkins (The Oakwood Press, 1993) 0 85361 452 0
The Tramways of Reading, H.E. Jordan (Adam Gordon, Chetwode, 2nd ed. 1990) 1 874422 00 1
The Trams of Plymouth - a 73 Years Story, M. Langley & E. Small (Ex Libris Press, Bradford on Avon, 1990) 0 948578 25 4
The Weymouth Harbour Tramway J.H. Lucking (Oxford Publishing Co., 1986) 0 86093 304 0
Bath Tramways, (Locomotion Papers No. 52), C.G. Maggs (The Oakwood Press, 2nd rev. ed. 1992) 0 85361 392 3
Weston-super-Mare Tramways (Locomotion Papers No. 78) C.G. Maggs (The Oakwood Press, 1974)
The Weston, Clevedon & Portishead Light Railway, C.G. Maggs, (Locomotion Papers No. 25) (The Oakwood Press, 2nd rev. ed. 1990) 0 853613 88 5
The Piers, Tramways and Railways at Ryde (Oakwood Library of Railway History OL136) R.J. Maycock & R. Silsbury (The Oakwood Press, 2005) 0 85361 636 1
The London County Council Tramways Volume 1: South London, E.R. Oakley (The London Tramways History Group, 1989) 0 951300 10 5
The London County Council Tramways Volume 2: North London, E.R. Oakley (The London Tramways History Group, 1991) 0 951300 11 3
London Transport Tramways: 1933-1952, E.R. Oakley & C.E. Holland (The London Tramways History Group, 1998) 0 9513001 2 1
Joyce Green and the River Hospitals, F. Payne, (Author, DWS Print Services Ltd, Sevenoaks, 2001)
The Wantage Tramway, S.H. Pearce-Higgins, (Adam Gordon, Brora, 2002 reprint of 1958 1st ed.) 1 874422 36 2
The Weston, Clevedon and Portishead Railway, C. Redwood, (Sequoia Publishing, 1981) 0 905466 42 X
Trams and Buses of Poole (Series X72), C.G. Roberts & B.L. Jackson, (The Oakwood Press, 2001) 0 85361 572 1
The Tramways of East London, 'Rodinglea', (The Tramway & Light Railway Society/The Light Railway Transport League, 1967)
Exeter, A Century of Public Transport, R.C. Sambourne (Glasney Press, Falmouth, 1976) 0 9050282 53 7
The Brill Tramway, B Simpson, (Oxford Publishing Co., 1985) 0 86093 218 4
The Wolverton & Stony Stratford Steam Trams, F.D. Simpson, (The Omnibus Society, 1981) 0 901307 42 4
London United Tramways Volume 1: Origins to 1912, C.S. Smeeton (The Light Rail Transit Association/The Tramway & Light Railway Society, 1995) 0 948106 13 1
London United Tramways Volume 2: 1913 to 1933, (The Light Rail Transit Association/The Tramway & Light Railway Society, 2000) 0 948106 24 7
The Metropolitan Electric Tramways Volume 1: Origins to 1920, C.S. Smeeton (The Light Rail Transit

Association/The Tramway and Light Railway Society, 1984) 0 900433 94 9
The Metropolitan Electric Tramways Volume 2: 1921 to 1933, C.S. Smeeton, (The Light Rail Transit Association/The Tramway and Light Railway Society, 1986) 0 948106 00 X
The Tramways of Woolwich and South East London, 'Southeastern', (The Light Railway Transport League, 1963)
Tramlink Official Handbook, M. Stewart, J. Gent & C. Stannard (Capital Transport, Harrow Weald, 2000) 185414 222 4
Cambridge Street Tramways (Locomotion Papers No. 61), S.L. Swingle, (The Oakwood Press, 1972)
Cliff Railways of the British Isles (Locomotion Papers No. 223), K. Turner (The Oakwood Press, 2002) 0 85361 594 2
Pier Railways & Tramways of the British Isles, (Locomotion Papers No. 60) K. Turner (The Oakwood Press, 2nd rev. ed. 1999) 0 85361 541 1
Hospital Tramways and Railways, D. Voice (Adam Gordon, Brora, 2nd ed. 2006) 978 1 874422 63 1
Fares Please - The History of Passenger Transport in Portsmouth, E. Watts, (Milestone Publications, Portsmouth, 1987) 0 903852 98 5
Lowestoft Corporation Transport, M.R. White, (Coastal Publications, Lowestoft, 2003) 09532485 9 3

Index

This index to Parts 1 and 2 of the Directory covers tramway promoters and operators not referenced or cross-referenced in the main alphabetical listings, other bus operators, and tramways outside the geographical scope of this volume.